Playing with Languages

Playing with Languages

Children and Change in a Caribbean Village

Amy L. Paugh

Berghahn Books
New York • Oxford

First published in 2012 by
Berghahn Books
www.berghahnbooks.com

©2012 Amy L. Paugh

Library of Congress Cataloging-in-Publication Data

Paugh, Amy L.
  Playing with languages : children and change in a Caribbean village /
Amy L. Paugh.
    p. cm.
  Includes bibliographical references and index.
  ISBN 978-0-85745-760-8 (hardback : alk. paper) 1. Language awareness
in children--Dominica. 2. Communicative competence in children--
Dominica. 3. Language acquisition--Dominica. 4. Language shift--
Dominica. 5. Linguistic change--Dominica. 6. Language and culture--
Dominica. 7. Dominica--Social life and customs. I. Title.
  P118.4.P38 2012
  306.44'609729841--dc23

                                                            2012013689

British Library Cataloguing in Publication Data
A catalogue record for this book is available from the British Library
Printed in the United States on acid-free paper.

ISBN 978-0-85745-760-8 (hardback)
ISBN 978-0-85745-761-5 (ebook)

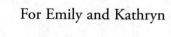
For Emily and Kathryn

Contents

List of Maps, Figures, and Tables   viii

Acknowledgments   x

Note on Transcription   xiii

Introduction   1

1. Discourses of Differentiation, Unity, and Identity   28

2. Childhood in a Village "Behind God's Back"   57

3. Learning English: Language Ideologies and Practices in the Classroom and Home   86

4. Becoming "Good for Oneself": Patwa and Autonomy in Language Socialization   115

5. Negotiating Play: Children's Code-Switching as Symbolic Resource   143

6. Acting Adult: Children's Language Use in Imaginary Play   171

Conclusion   199

Bibliography   222

Index   241

List of Maps, Figures, and Tables

Maps

0.1	The Caribbean	5
0.2	Dominica	6
2.3	Penville Village	59

Figures

1.1	A coastal village surrounded by mountains	34
1.2	The Penville Cultural Group performs in Roseau	45
1.3	The Penville Children's Cultural Group dances at a Cultural Gala	49
2.1	Farmers cut and carry bananas to pack for export	59
2.2	Villager carries a basket of produce harvested from her garden	60
2.3	Wooden house with a neatly maintained yard	68
2.4	Residents build concrete block homes if they can afford them	68
2.5	Parishioners congregate after Sunday services at the Catholic Church	81
3.1	Villagers watch a cricket match on the playing field below the Penville Government Primary School	88
3.2	The teacher removes Patwa from "picture study" in the first grade class	96
3.3	Female caregivers, like Tamika's (left) and Kenrick's (right) mothers, monitor children's speech and actions	102
4.1	The road is an important site of community interaction	119
4.2	People socialize outside a village shop	126
5.1	Jonah plays with his sister and fostered cousin while his eldest brother does chores	146
5.2	Natalie cares for her younger siblings Alisia (in her arms) and Tedison	147
5.3	Kenrick and Tamika's large peer group of siblings and cousins	160

6.1 Marissa (front left) and her siblings sing and clap to songs from the Pentecostal Church, while their mother helps baby Oscar dance behind them 178

6.2 Marcel stands over the members of his peer group with his hands on Alex's (left) and Junior's (right) heads and Reiston (left) and Sherona (right) crouching below 186

Tables

2.1 The focal children and their families and playmates 65

4.1 Examples of Patwa and English baby talk lexicon 121

Acknowledgments

Numerous individuals helped to make this book possible. My deepest gratitude goes to the six Dominican families who participated in my project. I was moved by their unending patience, generosity, and friendship during the months I spent with them. They welcomed me into their homes and shared their understandings about language, children, and life. I treasure the relationships that we built during the initial fieldwork and consider them lifelong friends. I am particularly indebted to the six focal children and their peer groups for giving me a glimpse into their social worlds. I cannot mention them by name to keep the confidentiality I promised them.

I thank all the villagers of Penville for their warm welcomes and willingness to chat each time I return. Conversations with Jennifer and Giet during preliminary fieldwork drew me back to Penville. Their families welcomed my husband and me into their homes, offering guidance, companionship, and a sense of belonging. Lucy and Steve and their children have acted like family as much as neighbors. I am thankful to many people in public roles who offered much appreciated assistance: Anthony George and the Penville Village Council, former principal Cynthia Joseph and the teachers at the Penville Primary School and Preschool, Maria Seamen and the Penville Cultural Group, and Nurse Royer for use of her village statistics. I also thank the numerous contacts I made during my preliminary research in Vieille Case, including Vernice Bellony, the Parliamentary Representative of the North at the time.

I am grateful to Gregory Rabess, the late Marcel Fontaine, and other members of the Konmité Pou Etid Kwéyòl for their support of my project and lengthy discussions. The Ministry of Education and Sports, headed by Rupert Sorhaindo and then Ronald Green, also offered its support. Many education officials graciously took the time to speak with me. Raymond Lawrence and the Cultural Division were similarly supportive. Lennox Honychurch and Beryl Harris were very helpful in understanding Penville's history. Comparative discussions with anthropologists Gary Smith and Deidre Rose were informative. A special thanks goes to "Ma" Watty for opening her home to us during trips to Roseau. Clive Sorhaindo and Arun, Liz, and Dylan Madisetti also provided occasional accommodations as well as good friendship. I am appreciative of Harry Sealey and others at the Frontline Bookstore and the Dominica Writer's Guild who were always willing to speak with me. Many other Dominicans have taken time to share their perspectives during my visits to different areas of the island.

At New York University my doctoral dissertation committee provided support and invaluable comments and suggestions. I thank Bambi Schieffelin, Constance Sutton, John Singler, Fred Myers, and Don Kulick. All were inspiring throughout my graduate career, and the depth and broadness of their perspectives significantly shaped my research, writing, and teaching. A very special thanks goes to Bambi, my advisor, mentor, and role model. She unwaveringly continues to offer direction and support whenever needed. After receiving my Ph.D. at NYU, I traveled from the east coast to the west coast for a postdoctoral fellowship with Elinor Ochs at the UCLA Sloan Center on Everyday Lives of Families. Ellie generously shared her research skills, analytic insights, and friendship. As a scholar of language socialization I feel most privileged to have had the opportunity to work with and learn from both Bambi and Ellie. I thank them for their constructive comments on various versions of the material presented in this book.

James Madison University and my colleagues in the Department of Sociology and Anthropology have been very supportive of my research and my writing sabbaticals. I am grateful to JMU's Alternative Spring Break and Community Service Learning Program, and in particular Rich Harris and Karen Ford, for the opportunity to return to Dominica as a learning partner and course instructor for brief periods in 2005, 2006, 2008, and 2010. These trips facilitated my return to Penville, allowed me to renew and extend contacts in Roseau, and helped me develop new relationships in another village. I thank the residents of Paix Bouche for their hospitality and discussions with me, which have expanded my understandings of Dominican social life and language use. Experiencing Dominica with JMU students during all four trips was invigorating and I am thankful to each one of them for their enthusiasm, fresh ideas, and questions (and there were many!).

In addition to the individuals mentioned above I have been greatly influenced by other colleagues at NYU, UCLA, and JMU. Many people at these institutions and elsewhere have read and commented on various permutations of the book, including presentations and grant applications. At the risk of leaving someone out, I thank Ayala Fader, Paul Garrett, Candy Goodwin, Chuck Goodwin, Daniel Hieber, Kathryn Howard, Carolina Izquierdo, Amy Kyratzis, Tamar Kremer-Sadlik, Laura Lewis, Heather Levi, Kristen McCleary, Barbra Meek, Amanda Minks, Kate Riley, David Valentine, Ana Celia Zentella, and members of my dissertation writer's group. Three reviewers for Berghahn Books asked probing questions and gave very useful suggestions. Carole Nash and Peter J. Hof at JMU prepared the maps included in the book. I thank Marion Berghahn, Ann Przyzycki DeVita, Mark Stanton, and Lauren Weiss, at Berghahn Books, and Kate Pedlar, the copyeditor, for their careful attention and commitment to my book project. I alone take full responsibility for all shortcomings here.

A number of institutions have generously funded my research. NYU supported preliminary fieldwork with a CLACS Summer Research Grant and a GSAS Dean's Summer Fellowship. My dissertation research was funded by a Fulbright-Hays Doctoral Dissertation Research Fellowship, a National Science Foundation Grant, and a Wenner-Gren Foundation Predoctoral Grant, with an extension. Sustained periods of writing were made possible by the Spencer Foundation, the National Endowment for the Humanities, and the JMU Program of Grants for Faculty Educational Leaves. A postdoctoral fellowship with the UCLA Center on Everyday Lives of Families, funded by the Alfred P. Sloan Foundation and directed by Elinor Ochs, also made writing possible even as I developed new research interests on American families. I am very grateful to these organizations for their assistance. Any views, findings, conclusions, or recommendations expressed in this book do not necessarily represent those of any of the granting institutions.

I am grateful to my family for their enduring support and anticipation of this book. Thanks to my parents, Donna and Richard, and my sister, Beth, for their encouragement over the years and insightful comments when they visited us in Dominica. John Paugh offered photography advice and asked many questions about the research; I wish he were here to see the book in print. My profound appreciation goes to my husband, Thomas Leary, for taking part in it all. He helped in collecting and understanding the research data and has been a constant source of support throughout the many stages of this project and my academic career. My daughters, Kathryn and Emily, have experienced the writing of this book at its various stages. Their curiosity, playfulness, humor, and love have sustained me throughout the process. My experiences in Dominica influenced my parenting style; my experience as a mother, playmate, and observer of my own daughters has in turn helped me to develop new perspectives on the research material. I dedicate this book to my girls.

Some materials have appeared in different forms in two earlier publications: "Multilingual Play: Children's Code-switching, Role Play, and Agency in Dominica, West Indies," *Language in Society* 34(2): 63–86, 2005. Copyright © 2005, Cambridge University Press, reprinted with permission; "Acting Adult: Language Socialization, Shift, and Ideologies in Dominica," in *ISB4: Proceedings of the 4th International Symposium on Bilingualism,* eds. J. Cohen, K. McAlister, K. Rolstad, and J. MacSwan, 1807–1820, Somerville, MA: Cascadilla Press, 2005.

Note on Transcription

Patwa is an Afro-French creole language. I transcribed Patwa speech using the orthography developed by the Konmité Pou Etid Kwéyòl (Committee for Creole Studies, or KEK) in *Dominica's English-Creole Dictionary* (Fontaine and Roberts 1992; Fontaine 2003). My spelling of the name of the language as "Patwa" rather than *Patois* follows their orthography. Despite KEK's preference for the name *Kwéyòl* for the language, I have chosen to refer to it as Patwa because that is how it is known where I do research and in rural areas generally.

The following conventions were used to transcribe examples of recorded social interaction:

italics	Patwa speech
<u>underline</u>	English glosses of Patwa speech, provided in parentheses underneath or beside the Patwa usage
CAPITALS	Emphasis
:	Elongated speech
(1)	Pause between utterances in seconds
((action))	Non-verbal action
(xxx)	Unintelligible speech
*	Ungrammatical utterance as judged by speakers
?	Rising intonation, question
!	Exclamation
?!	Rhetorical question
[	Overlapping speech
=	Adjacent turns with no interval between them, with the second turn "latched" onto but not overlapping the first turn
-	Cut-off or self-interrupted speech

Introduction

In Dominica, children are at the center of a linguistic paradox. Two languages are in tension on their post-colonial island nation: English is the official language of government and schools, while an Afro-French creole commonly called Patwa (also Kwéyòl) has been the oral language of the rural population for centuries. In the past education officials and urbanites denigrated Patwa as the impoverished language of poor rural peoples and did not allow their children to speak it. Since independence from Britain in 1978, however, the state and an urban intellectual elite claim that Patwa is integral to the nation's development and cultural identity. They have undertaken preservation efforts and plan to introduce Patwa in schools. Meanwhile rural parents are concerned that Patwa hinders children's acquisition of English and thus restricts social mobility; they have instituted their own family and community-level policies prohibiting children from speaking Patwa in most settings. This is contributing to a rapid language shift from Patwa to varieties of English. In the rural community where I have conducted anthropological fieldwork since 1995, children are now learning English as their primary language, performing better in school, and even earning financial aid to attend secondary school in another town. Why then, despite children's increasingly successful mastery of English, do parents continue to forbid them from speaking Patwa in the home? Why are village teachers and parents adamantly against teaching Patwa at school when they say they are neutral toward or supportive of language revitalization efforts? Why do adults speak Patwa directly to children for particular functions and sometimes encourage children to use it as well? And, critically, what role do children play in the transformation of ideology and practice?

In this complex yet little-studied Caribbean society, local and national agendas concerning language use often conflict. It presents a case study of a much broader phenomenon, in that researchers predict roughly half of the world's 6,000 to 7,000 languages will disappear within the century. This grim forecast is accompanied by rising academic and public concern over the loss of linguistic and biocultural diversity, and disrupted transmission of unique cultural knowledge.[1] Efforts to reverse language loss have intensified worldwide; however, the majority meet with limited success. In those efforts language preservation and revitalization are often perceived as resting in the hands of community elders, educators, and policy makers. Yet another set of key actors has been consistently overlooked and underestimated in the process of language shift and attempts to reverse it—children. As language shift is centrally about transmission, or lack thereof, it is essential to examine how children contribute to these processes, engaging with rather than simply "absorbing" cultural and linguistic knowledge. This book addresses this omission by investigating children's agency in dynamic processes of linguistic and cultural change on this post-colonial island nation.

Caribbean societies have been described as an "open frontier" for anthropological and sociolinguistic study (Trouillot 1992). The social worlds of Caribbean children, and children generally, are even more of an open frontier. As Green (1999: 1) states of Latin America and the Caribbean, "although children are ever-present, their lives largely remain invisible. They are seen, but not heard and almost never listened to." Researchers have likened this lacuna in research on the region to the absence of women in scholarly research several decades ago (Green 1999; Hecht 2002). When Caribbean children are discussed it tends to be in terms of violence, crime, school failure, "unstable" family structure, and poor health. However, as Bluebond-Langner and Korbin (2007: 242) advise:

> Studies of children and childhoods are the next logical steps in a more inclusive view of culture and society. In this more inclusive view, rather than privileging children's voices above all others, it is more productive to integrate children into a more multivocal, multiperspective view of culture and society.

This study aims to do just that. It documents children's daily lives, voices, and the spontaneous social interactions that shape their childhoods. Children are not considered apart from the social world they share with adults nor viewed simply as passive receptacles of adult culture. With a focus on everyday social interaction, this book offers much needed insights into Caribbean children's agency and their roles in large-scale processes of cultural and linguistic change, contributing to the burgeoning interdisciplinary study of children's cultures.[2] This study stands out in its investigation of language socialization and language shift from birth through early adolescence with attention to caregiver–child, teacher–student, and children's peer interactions.

Playing with Language

Language shift occurs when an individual or group stops using a language(s) in favor of the language of another, usually dominant, group. This is not a neutral process. It may occur by choice or coercion, but tends to be a response to or consequence of conditions of acute social inequality and symbolic domination. At a community level the process of language shift can result in varying degrees of obsolescence or "death" of a language over a few generations of speakers. A language is considered endangered when it is losing fluent speakers and is no longer passed on to children. Despite growing attention to language endangerment, only a few studies examine the mundane interactions between children and adults that lay the groundwork for such processes, within their broader socioeconomic and political contexts. Even fewer investigate the impact of children's peer and sibling interactions, which provide critical spaces for children to try out linguistic varieties not otherwise available to them, or, conversely, to pass on dominant languages and ideologies that contribute to the demise of vernacular languages.[3]

Like adults, children constitute their social worlds and identities through talk (M. Goodwin 1990, 2006). I employ an interpretive approach to children and caregivers' talk-in-interaction, drawing on a growing body of research that analyzes children's naturally occurring talk in naturalistic family, peer, and school settings. This analysis of micro-level speech practices and attitudes in one Caribbean community is contextualized within macro-level processes of change at the national level. I illustrate how children contribute not only to the language shift through accommodating their caregivers and teachers by speaking English, but also to Patwa maintenance by utilizing this forbidden language during unmonitored peer and sibling play. This age-graded dynamic is critical to linguistic and cultural revitalization efforts, but is not well understood. I integrate approaches to language ideologies, multilingualism and emotion, and language endangerment and revitalization to provide a model for investigating language shift through multiple facets of social life.

It is critical to bear in mind that it is the speakers, rather than languages themselves, who are the agents of language shift (Jaffe 2007a; Kuipers 1998). Here, I probe the multiple ways in which various social actors have "played" with Dominica's languages over time and with competing goals. These actors include colonial officials, policy makers, language activists, education officers, teachers, caregivers, and, significantly, children. I use the verb "play" because of its polyvalent and agentive nuances, including the active manipulation of a situation so as to achieve a desired result; movement as in a move in a game or match, or the freedom of movement in a mechanism; and the more common notion of recreation and taking part in an enjoyable activity primarily for amusement. The trope of play, however, is not meant to imply equality amongst actors or playmates. Indeed, social stratification and inequality loom large across these groups, from the colonial encounter to the parent–child relationship to the negotiation of roles in a children's play scene. Within each of the groups Patwa is imagined and played with in different ways.

Under British colonial rule, language was manipulated as a tool of domination: English speakers were empowered by government legislation while Patwa speakers—first predominantly slaves, later a freed black population—were disparaged and excluded from official settings. English has been the sole language of compulsory schooling since 1890 and remains a criterion for political participation according to the Constitution. Since independence, government officials have played with languages by advocating competing messages and policies whereby English is the only official language, yet Patwa is promoted during cultural events, heritage tourism, and the marketing of Dominican culture abroad. Language activists play with language through Patwa literacy activities and attempts to teach Patwa in schools. In their discourses, they frame the language as "dying" and in need of "rescue." Village teachers and caregivers also play with language. They consciously choose to speak English to children, hoping to make their first and primary tongue the language perceived as the tool of financial success. Meanwhile, children play with both English and Patwa in their peer groups to structure their relationships and construct vivid imaginary play scenarios. Further, in everyday social encounters both children and adults play with language in creative ways, seeking to control interactions, compete over symbolic and material resources, demonstrate verbal proficiency, and engage in verbal play for its own sake, as in jokes, storytelling, and sound play. By framing formal and informal language use, performance, and policy as play, I highlight how people actively construct cultural and linguistic practices and ideologies in real yet socially constrained ways. I explore how these forms of language play contribute to the shift away from Patwa and to its potential maintenance.

"Tall is Her Body": A Mountainous Caribbean Island Nation

Dominica is located between the French overseas departments of Martinique and Guadeloupe in the Eastern Caribbean (Map 0.1). The island's pre-Columbian name is *Wai'toucoubouli*, meaning "tall is her body." Now officially called the Commonwealth of Dominica, it is also known as *Donmnik* in Patwa or *Dominique* in French. Although often confused with the Spanish-speaking Dominican Republic in the Greater Antilles, it is an independent nation that had very little Spanish influence. Its complex linguistic ecology was shaped by indigenous Kalinago (Carib),[4] enslaved West Africans, and a dual French-British colonial history. "Discovered" by Columbus in 1493, the island was unclaimed by European colonizers until it became a French colony in 1635. The French began the importation of West Africans as a source of estate slave labor, and it was in this context that Patwa had arisen by the early eighteenth century. Due to Dominica's strategic location between two French islands, however, Britain repeatedly challenged France's claims. Dominica exchanged hands at least seven times. In 1763 the French ceded Dominica to the British, who replaced French with English as the official language. When independence was granted over two centuries later in 1978, the government retained English as the sole official language.

The island is only 29 miles long and 16 miles wide, however, those who have tried to develop it have for centuries struggled with the difficulties of accessing its approximately 290 square miles of land area (Map 0.2). It is the most mountainous island in the Lesser Antilles with peaks over 4,500 feet high; for that reason, it was one of the last in the Caribbean to be colonized.[5] Dominican historian Lennox Honychurch (1995[1975]: ix) describes it vividly:

> This rugged landscape of blue-green slopes, rushing streams and cloud drenched mountain peaks has given the island a legendary beauty, a fatal gift some call it, which has created both major problems and great advantages for those who have lived here. More than most islands, the environment has guided the course of Dominica's history.

The mountainous interior provided refuge for the Kalinago and later for escaped slaves. The capital, Roseau, and second major town, Portsmouth, grew up on the calm Caribbean Sea on the western coast; the rougher Atlantic

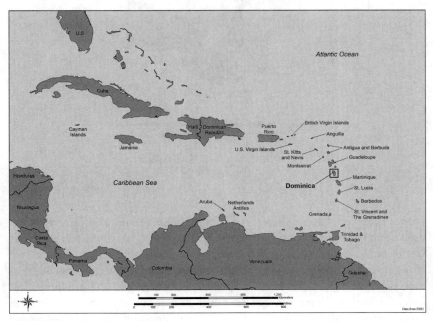

Map 0.1 The Caribbean

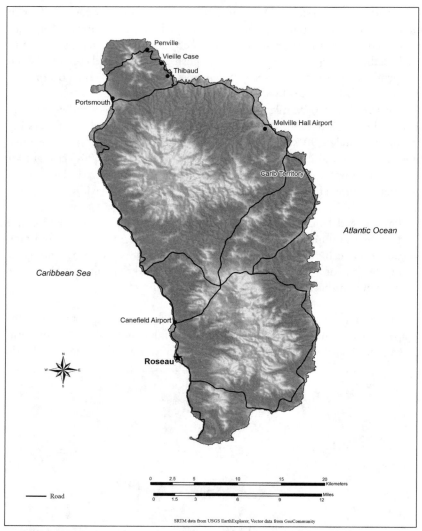

Map 0.2 Dominica

Ocean meets its eastern shore. The mountainous terrain also prevented the development of the large-scale sugar plantations that characterized other Caribbean colonies. Small estate settlements concentrating on one or two crops emerged around the rugged coast and remained relatively isolated from each other and from the towns for centuries (Baker 1994; Trouillot 1988). Today agriculture remains a mainstay of the economy, with bananas the chief export crop, followed by citrus and coconut products. The economy historically has relied on a successive monocrop strategy. However, shifting markets and fluctuating prices in the global economy, compounded by natural disasters like hurricanes, have increased calls to diversify, including efforts to expand tourism (Payne 2008).[6]

Dominica's contemporary demographic situation reflects its early settlement patterns. The census records a population of 69,625 (Commonwealth of Dominica 2001),[7] with the rural majority clustered in villages that arose from the early estates. Nearly 20,000 people reside in Roseau and its environs, exemplifying a drift to the urban center. The majority of the population (87 percent) identifies as being of African descent, with an additional 9 percent "mixed," 3 percent Amerindian/Carib, and 1 percent white, Syrian, Lebanese, East Indian, and "other." Although in the minority, Syrian, Lebanese, and Chinese merchants have influenced the economy since the beginning of the twentieth century, establishing the largest shops, automobile dealerships, and other businesses. There was never a significant white European population, nor an indentured East Indian workforce as in other colonies like Trinidad, Guyana, and Jamaica. An estimated 3,400 descendants of indigenous Kalinago reside on 3,700 acres of land on the rugged northeast coast, known as the "Carib Reserve" or "Carib Territory."[8]

Linguistic Ecology of the Island

Dominica's complex colonial past is reflected in its languages. With increased contact, the Kalinago shifted from their language to varieties of Patwa and English, with the last fluent Kalinago speaker dying in the 1920s (Taylor 1977). Kalinago lexical influence remains evident in both Patwa and English varieties, including names of places, plants, and animals. Some Kalinago have begun efforts to revive the language. A distinct English-based creole called Kokoy is spoken in two villages (Wesley and Marigot) settled by Methodist missionaries, estate owners, and slave laborers from Antigua and other Leeward Islands in the eighteenth century (Christie 1990, 1994). Patwa and varieties of English are spoken there now as well.

Patwa is an Atlantic creole classified with the French-based creole languages of the New World group, including those spoken in the Caribbean (the Lesser Antilles and Haiti), on the bordering mainland of South America (French Guiana), and in North America (Louisiana) (Holm 1989b: 353). The term "creole" refers to a distinct language that was created from the blending of two or more languages during cultural contact, as in the context of plantation slavery and exploitation during European colonial expansion and importation of enslaved West Africans to the Caribbean.[9] Linguists have theorized that African-descendant slaves brought by settlers from the French islands transported Patwa to Dominica and other Windward Islands in the seventeenth and eighteenth centuries.[10] Some early sources indicate that the French already communicated with the Kalinago using a restricted pidgin trade language based on French, Carib, and Spanish in the early 1600s, and this may have influenced communication with West Africans. In a study of the genesis of Dominican Patwa, Wylie (1995: 79–80) describes the linguistic heterogeneity of European expansion from 1635 to 1700:

> Patois [Patwa] arose from an immensely complex linguistic situation: a veritable Babel of French (in many dialects), of other European tongues, of various South American Indian languages, and of Carib (including not only mainland Carib but also both Karina or True Carib "men's speech" and an Arawakan "women's speech")—not to mention the African languages spoken by imported slaves, or the nautical vocabularies salted with borrowings from even more exotic tongues used by the traders, freebooters, adventurers, refugees, and what-not who swarmed these seas in the 17th century.

Patwa gained much of its lexicon from French, and the West African languages of the slaves "filled in the blanks" grammatically, including a preverbal tense-mood-aspect (TMA) system rather than inflecting verbs for tense. This created "the immediate precursor of modern Patois" by 1700 (Wylie 1995: 89). By the early eighteenth century, Patwa became the first language of new generations of the slave population.[11]

What is striking in Dominica, as in nearby St. Lucia, is that for over two centuries Patwa has been spoken without the continual presence of French and instead has co-existed with English. Patwa is not mutually intelligible with either standard French or English. This contrasts with Caribbean societies where a creole language exists with the standard or lexifier language, such as creole and standard French in Haiti, Martinique, and Guadeloupe, and creole and standard English in Jamaica and Barbados. The persistence of Patwa was aided by the historical isolation of communities and influence of French Catholic missionaries, who helped establish strong links between the rural masses and the creole language (versus British Protestants who adhered to English). With the absence of French as a resource, however, Patwa has incorporated English lexemes when no Patwa equivalent existed, or when an English word became interchangeable with the Patwa word.[12] In recent decades, contact with English has intensified as new roads, schools, cable television, and a telecommunications network have increased intra-island communication. Regional variations in Patwa phonology, lexicon, and degree of influence from English are very salient according to speakers, who say they can recognize a person's geographic origins or place of residence by the variety of Patwa they speak (Fontaine 2003).

Once the primary oral language of rural peoples, Patwa use appears to be declining among younger generations. Language proficiency varies across geographic, generational, and socioeconomic lines, with the most Patwa spoken by village elders and the least by urban youths. Stuart (1993) describes it as a "fragmented language situation": monolingual Patwa speakers are primarily over age sixty and live in rural areas. Middle-aged villagers speak English more fluently than their parents, but with restricted vocabulary and in restricted contexts. Rural youth are usually bilingual in Patwa and at least one variety of English, but tend to view Patwa as a liability for socioeconomic mobility. Middle-aged (35–60) urbanites speak little or no Patwa but may understand it, while a small group of young middle-class urban adults are beginning to value Patwa and are learning to speak it (Stuart 1993: 61–62; also Christie 1994). My research suggests that rural children are increasingly acquiring varieties of English as their first language, and may acquire more or less Patwa later depending on their verbal environments. The rural youth that Stuart described as bilingual in 1993 seem to be the same demographic as the parents of the children in my study. Further, there appears to be at least one more group: urban children and teens who neither speak nor understand Patwa and have mixed feelings toward the language (Fontaine and Leather 1992). Other key factors that influence language competence and preference are explored in the chapters that follow.

Concerned about the generational shift toward English, the government created the Konmité Pou Etid Kwéyòl (Committee for Creole Studies, or KEK) in 1981 to preserve Patwa. KEK became the main language-planning organization and has undertaken many documentation and revitalization projects to legitimize Patwa, including establishing an orthography, publishing literacy materials, and promoting Patwa use in mass media. However, literacy in Patwa is a recent development restricted to urban intellectuals, particularly KEK members, and the language remains for most an exclusively oral medium. Activist and government entities like KEK, as well as the National Development Corporation that focuses on tourism promotion, may have vested political and economic interests in declaring a language endangered, including promoting a distinct local identity on the world stage. However, when I searched for young participants for my language socialization study in one village I found that no child under the age of five was actively speaking Patwa as their first language. The language is losing fluent speakers and is no longer spoken as a first language by the majority of Dominican children; by most measures, then, Patwa would be considered an endangered language. Yet contact languages like creoles are often neglected in discourses of language endangerment in favor of more "exotic" or "heritage" languages; further, the focus has been more on the "birth" of such languages than their potential "death" (Garrett 2006). However, creole languages remain central to the complex identities and histories of their speakers, thus it is important to attend to the processes that lead to their obsolescence and to potential resources for their revitalization if a community so desires it.

English is the only official language of the state and schools, in both written and spoken forms. Literacy in English has been estimated at 88–94 percent, but this is likely restricted to basic functions for many adults. Far from being homogenous, however, Dominican English ranges from "standard" to "non-standard" varieties of Caribbean English, with variation in Roseau as well as the countryside.[13] Christie (1990, 1994) suggests that there is an emergent English creole, which she calls "Dominican English Creole" or DEC, that shares many grammatical features with Patwa, largely through calquing (word for word translation) of Patwa syntax and phrases. The sociohistorical origins of this variety are more recent than that of Patwa and other Caribbean creoles, however, being more rooted in educational institutions than the colonial encounter (see Garrett 2003 for a discussion of vernacular English in St. Lucia). For the purposes of this study, I refer to the "Englishes" spoken by rural and urban residents as "varieties of English." Locally there are no specific terms for these varieties other than Kokoy, which is considered a separate language. However, many teachers, urban activists, and educated professionals comment on the "non-standard," "vernacular," or "creole" English spoken by Dominicans. Most villagers distinguish only between "good" and "bad" (or "broken") English.

In everyday speech practices, there is much code-switching, or alternating, between English and Patwa both within the same sentence and between sentences. There are also many borrowings in both languages, such as the use of Patwa *wi* (yes) and *non* (no) as sentence-final tags in English, and various English discourse markers such as "so," "because," and "then" in Patwa. However, speakers clearly differentiate between what is "Patwa" and what is "English," which relates to the pervasive strategy of speaking "only English" to children so they will succeed in school. The variety of English does not necessarily matter, as long as children speak "English" rather than "Patwa." Christie (1990: 64, emphasis added) points this out as well:

> Parents not only actively encourage their children to speak it, but they make a special point of addressing the younger ones *in their version of English*, even if they customarily use Patois to each other and to other adults.

Despite this variation, Dominica is characterized locally as a "bilingual" nation with two distinct languages: Patwa and English. In multilingual settings, the boundaries between languages may be fuzzy to researchers, yet "the contrast between language systems is psychologically real and ideologically meaningful to speakers, and remains a resource they can mobilize in action"

(Woolard 2004: 83).[14] I examine how the linguistic varieties are identified and talked about by speakers, especially to and in the presence of children. As children acquire the languages of their communities, they also acquire and may transform the ideologies about those languages.

Learning Language and Culture: The Language Socialization Approach

Language use is a critical means of cultural reproduction and transformation across generations. It is also a form of social action. Through everyday interactions with family members, peers, and others around them, all normally developing children learn language in conjunction with cultural practices that enable them to live in a social group.[15] In Dominica this includes learning to negotiate multiple varieties of language and the complex ideologies concerning them. I investigate this process of learning and exploration through the ethnographic study of language socialization, an approach that examines how children and other novices are socialized through language as they learn to use language (Ochs 1988; Ochs and Schieffelin 1984, 2008; Schieffelin 1990; also Duranti et al. 2012; Duff and Hornberger 2008; Garrett and Baquedano-López 2002). Linguistic and sociocultural learning are viewed as jointly occurring processes achieved over developmental time and across the life span. Taking a longitudinal and ethnographic approach, language socialization research seeks to provide "a processual account of how individuals come to be particular kinds of culturally intelligible subjects" (Kulick and Schieffelin 2004: 351). To that end, I document and analyze everyday talk and micro-level socializing events during which novices, like children, and experts, like adults and older children, jointly negotiate activities and meanings.

It is through such mundane social interactions with more knowledgeable members that children learn and are socialized to learn the cultural and linguistic knowledge needed for participation in everyday life. This knowledge includes speech practices but also cultural practices, values, and ideologies concerning class, status, ethnicity, gender, social relationships, morality, and language itself. In other words, novices acquire a culturally specific *habitus,* learned dispositions to act in particular ways, including verbal and embodied practices as well as taken-for-granted cultural assumptions about the world (Bourdieu 1977, 1985; Kulick and Schieffelin 2004).[16] During early socialization activities, caregivers often make explicit for children's benefit cultural rules and knowledge that are usually tacit. This is accomplished through repetition and paraphrasing of their speech and the speech of others, correcting children's errors, expanding children's utterances to be grammatical and socially appropriate, and modeling linguistic behavior for children. Cross-cultural studies have detailed diverse examples of caregivers prompting children to speak or act in certain ways through "say" ("tell," "ask," etc.) routines. Children are socialized to understand and linguistically encode social relationships and to learn relevant problem-solving strategies through conversational turn-taking procedures, person reference, routines, and the management of miscommunication unfolding moment by moment in their verbal environments. The study of such socializing activities allows exploration of local theories of child rearing and expectations of children (de León 2005; Paugh 2012a) and can reveal much about cultural notions of the self and society.

Critically, a focus on interactions involving caregivers and children allows detailed study of how cultural and linguistic practices and ideologies are transformed or not transmitted, including ways of being, acting, and thinking that are discouraged or rendered invisible (Fader 2009; Kulick and Schieffelin 2004; Zentella 1997). Micro-level socializing interactions are linked both to local social structures and institutions, and to macro-level sociopolitical and economic processes like globalization and modernization. It is critical to explore speakers' interpretations of these large-scale processes, however, as it is their interpretations rather than the processes themselves that affect use or non-use of language(s), whether consciously or not (Kulick 1992; also Gal 1984[1978]). How speakers socialize new cultural members—and what those members do in turn—is crucial. The first wave of language socialization research, exemplified in Ochs (1988) and Schieffelin (1990), examined such processes in monolingual societies. A second wave of research has extended this approach to the study of multilingual speech practices and language contact phenomena like language shift and maintenance (see Friedman 2012; Garrett 2012; Howard 2008; and Nonaka 2012 for useful reviews). My study also attends to micro- and macro-level processes. However, it extends language socialization research further into children's social worlds, including not only adult–child interaction but also peer interaction across a range of ages in child-controlled settings.

Theorists of language revitalization highlight the critical importance of intergenerational transmission for the maintenance of a language (Grenoble and Whaley 2006). However, only a few studies detail the ways in which language socialization practices contribute to language shift, sometimes in unexpected ways that might contrast with or even undermine official language revitalization efforts (e.g., Meek 2007, 2010). Even less explored aspects of language socialization are ways in which a threatened language might be maintained or transformed, as in the retention of particular speech genres (categories of discourse like stories, gossip, and joking) despite a shift to a new language (Kulick 1992), or in the emergence of new blended varieties or stylistic innovations (Fader 2009; Field 2001; Garrett 2007; Makihara 2005;

Snow 2004). It is thus necessary to examine what is maintained as well as lost in situations of sociolinguistic contact and change.

While this approach attends to novice–expert interaction, it does not view children as passive objects of socialization or language loss. Language use is a critical site to examine the enactment of agency, the capacity or ability to act in a way that affects other beings or objects in the world (Duranti 2004; also Ahearn 2001). The process of becoming a competent communicator entails being able to use language meaningfully, appropriately, and effectively to accomplish particular goals (Ochs 1996); in other words, to use language as a social tool (Vygotsky 1978). Language socialization research highlights that children are active agents in their socialization and are able to choose between, alter, and resist cultural and linguistic practices. Yet, agency is mediated by specific social structures and historical conditions. Through their engagement with the structures around them, children reproduce but also can subtly change those very same power structures, ideologies, and practices (James et al. 1998: 90). In Dominica, children are subordinate to adults in home and institutional settings, but their unmonitored peer interactions allow for exploration of roles, positions of power, language varieties, and alternative experiences as they negotiate their own alliances, hierarchies, and moral standards. Children's attitudes and patterns of language use are as relevant as those of adults in the process of language shift and efforts to halt it.

Drawing on the work of post-structural theorists like Althusser, Foucault, and Lacan, Kulick and Schieffelin (2004) make a compelling argument for a shift to "subject" and "subjectivities" from "person" and "personhood," which characterized earlier language socialization analysis. The notion of subjectivity posits the individual as an agentive social actor who also is constrained by their subject position in the social order. This shift in focus opens up new questions in language socialization research, particularly in attending to relations of power, as Kulick and Schieffelin (2004: 357) point out in a set of provocative questions:

> How do individuals come to perceive the subject positions that are available or possible in any given context? How is the taking up of particular positions enabled or blocked by relations of power? How do particular positions come to be known as intelligible and desirable, while others are inconceivable and undesirable?

Garrett (2007: 234, emphasis added) extends this to multilingual contexts by asking, "How do *bilingual subjectivities* emerge?" These questions guide my analysis of language socialization practices and children's agency in Dominica. I show that while a Patwa-speaking child has become an undesirable subject position in adult-controlled settings, rural children are nevertheless expected to gain competence in Patwa and related expressive stances over developmental time. Thus while trying to produce more educated English-speaking Dominican citizens, rural caregivers simultaneously encourage at least some Patwa speaking in an age-graded manner, helping to maintain the language in subtle ways that contrast with the national Patwa revitalization movement.

Code Choice: Language Ideologies and Indexicality

As in many societies, children in Dominica grow up in complex multilingual environments where several linguistic varieties are used. Code choice is rarely neutral or unproblematic, whether in formal situations like school or informal ones like home. Multilingualism is accompanied by multiple language ideologies concerning language choice. Language ideologies refer to shared bodies of cultural conceptions and commonsense notions about the nature, structure, uses, values, and purposes of language.[17] It is essential to give direct attention to the linguistic ideologies that make it possible or desirable for a community to abandon a language (Ochs and Schieffelin 1995). My approach examines how language ideologies are mobilized in language socialization, with attention to ambivalences or contradictions within them and related consequences. Importantly, children's own language ideologies and ways in which they might transform the language ideologies of their communities remain largely unexplored (though see Meek 2007, 2010). In Dominica multiple ideologies about the languages, including when, where, and with whom to use them, influence their manipulation in everyday interactions in both town and village, and are reproduced and contested in socializing activities. These practices are contributing to widespread language shift, but also to potential language maintenance through the development of age appropriate language use and bilingual subjectivities.

Central to understanding how language socialization and language ideologies function in social life is the concept of indexicality (Hanks 2001; Ochs 1992, 1996; Ochs and Schieffelin 2008; Peirce 1960; Silverstein 1976). Indexicality refers to the capacity of linguistic forms, including grammar and discourse features like language choice, to point to or index sociocultural information, such as gender, class, ethnicity, religion, rank, status, and geographic origins, as well as culturally recognizable activities, social relationships, and affective stances. In other words, linguistic structures convey more than content; they come to be indirectly associated with, and thus index, social meaning according to context. Learning to interpret and convey these social meanings is critical to the development of communicative competence, which encompasses knowing grammatical rules and how to use language appropriately in social interaction. Children learn through regular interaction to recognize and produce indexical meanings, becoming "increasingly adept at constituting and interpreting sociocultural contexts from linguistic cues" (Ochs and Schieffelin 2008: 8–9). A central focus in this study is how multilingual practices index sociocultural information and how children come to understand and utilize such information through language socialization activities with adults and peers. Patwa and English have long indexed sociological variables like geographic residence and level of education, but in the course of the language shift have come to index differences related to age/generation, status and authority, gender, religion, and emotional intensity. Children explore these indexical meanings in their play when apart from adults, demonstrating an acute awareness of how the languages differentially index certain kinds of people, practices, places, and stances.[18]

Indexing Affect: Emotion and Code-switching in Language Shift

The display and recognition of emotion, or affect, plays a central role in interaction and it is a critical component of language socialization research.[19] It may also play a key role in processes of language maintenance and shift (Kuipers 1998; also Pavlenko 2005, 2006 for recent studies of multilingualism and emotion). In all social interaction, participants communicate a particular affective stance to others, which can be understood as "a mood, attitude, feeling, and disposition, as well as degrees of emotional intensity vis-à-vis some focus of concern" (Ochs 1996: 410). Lexical, grammatical, and discourse features act as "affect specifiers" and "affect intensifiers," which refer to the nature (particular affective orientation) and intensity of the affect being conveyed, respectively. Affective devices are multifunctional and embedded in social context; but rather than a problem, their multifunctionality and ambiguity make them communicative resources for language users (Besnier 1990: 429).

Affect encoded in language serves many functions, including setting a tone for an interaction, indexing social relationships and statuses, and influencing a person's actions to bring about a more desirable effect, such as caregivers trying to control children's behavior and affective displays. Affect may be "keyed" (Goffman 1974) through a range of linguistic features, including lexicon, pronouns, determiners, mood, tense/aspect, reduplication, phonological variation, intonation, sound symbolism, and word order, as well as discourse structures, like speech acts and activities (see Ochs and Schieffelin 1989: 12–14; Pavlenko 2005: 116–124). For example, many speech acts with children are affect-loaded in positive or negative ways, such as teasing, shaming, appeals, refusals, accusations, cursing, apologizing, compliments, assessments, and complaints, as well as expressions of pleasure, sympathy, fear, disappointment, and respect. Through such speech acts, and through participation in and observation of social interaction generally, children learn to produce language- and culture-specific affective displays and to recognize those of others. From the earliest stages of language development, young children have been shown to use affective lexicon and grammatical constructions to express their feelings, moods, and attitudes.

Code-switching is a potent resource for expressing affective stance, though there has been little focused attention on it as a means of performing affect (Pavlenko 2005: 131).[20] Yet multiple functions have been attributed to code-switching across diverse populations, many of which entail affective stance taking. It can act as a rhetorical device (creating dramatic contrasts in narrative; emphatically denying an accusation) and a way to change topics or enable a participant to gain the floor, express social solidarity or exclusion, and distinguish between reported and direct speech. Code-switching is an important means of negotiating one's way as a social actor in multilingual settings. It can establish or mark one's social identity(s) and signal attitudes toward languages, individuals, or entire social groups. Code-switching into a minority language in a domain characterized by the dominant language can evoke the intimacy and solidarity of the home or community (the "we-code"), whereas use of the dominant language marks formality, sophistication, expertise, authority, distance, and status (the "they-code").[21] Code-switching can be employed playfully as a sociolinguistic resource, as in using a dominant language to create "mock distance" (Jaffe 1999: 110), or drawing on other differences, like ethnicity, to create humor (Siegel 1995; Pavlenko 2006; Woolard 1988). Code-switching also functions as a means of emphasis or intensification, such as aggravating or mitigating the force of requests (Hill and Hill 1986; Zentella 1997).

I assert that analyzing the ways in which different codes index affect in multilingual settings is crucial to understanding local language ideologies and processes of language maintenance, innovation, and shift. As Kuipers notes, while studies of language shift often acknowledge speakers' sentiments *about* the loss of a language, "discussions about the role of emotion *in* the creation of the conditions of shift themselves are not so easily found" (1998: 42, emphasis in original). Rather than a unidirectional or wholesale shift from one language to another, different codes may become associated with particular affective stances and functions, thus contributing to language maintenance, or, conversely, further advancing the shift. For example, Kulick (1992) found that in Gapun, Papua New Guinea, where Tok Pisin (a creole lingua franca) is replacing Taiap (an indigenous language), adults often speak to children in Taiap, but then switch to Tok Pisin for attention getting when they particularly want a child to attend to what they are saying. While this situation contrasts with the case of Dominica in that Gapun caregivers blame their children for the shift and not their own language socialization practices with children, Kulick mentions that Taiap is increasingly linked to the reprimand and scolding of children (1992: 217), as Patwa is in Dominica. Similarly, Garrett (2005) suggests that some genres might be "code-specific" relative to how they index particular affective stances. In St. Lucia, as in Dominica, there is an ongoing shift from a French-based creole (Kwéyòl, which is mutually intelligible with Dominican Patwa) to varieties of English, the official language. Despite fears that Kwéyòl might impair children's English acquisition, there are times when adults actively encourage children to use Kwéyòl, namely, to curse or *jiwé* (Garrett 2005). Kwéyòl is the preferred code for this genre and a means of socializing verbal assertiveness and related affective stances. Thus while the "ideal" St. Lucian child speaks to an adult only when spoken to, is respectful, and speaks English, self-assertion, autonomy, and related affective stances indexed by Kwéyòl are also necessary and are modeled for children through socialization to curse. In situations of language shift, then, it may not solely be the act of code-switching that indexes intensified or mitigated affective stance, but the switch into one language in particular.

Playing with "Voices": Register Variation and Language Choice

When considered in conjunction with the linguistic encoding of affect, the study of register variation can offer insights into processes of linguistic and social change (Silverstein 1998). A register is a language variety associated with a situation, context of use, or set of social practices and the persons who engage in such practices (Halliday 1964). A register is distinguished from a dialect, which is a language variety related to the regional or social background of the user. Register studies have focused on specialized varieties like baby talk and professional languages (such as law, medicine, military strategy, prayer, and sportscasting), as well as social factors that affect ways of speaking, such as participants' relationships, social ranks, and differences in age or gender, observance of respect and etiquette, and formality versus informality. A language variety becomes "enregistered" when a group of speakers begin to link its forms and values to characteristic social personae or practices (Agha 2004: 37).[22] The study of patterns of register variation must be situated within the sociocultural systems and linguistic ideologies that render them socially meaningful. For example, Fader (2009) illustrates how Hasidic Jews in New York are able both to participate in and reject mainstream American culture, thus contributing to cultural continuity, by employing new blended and gendered registers: "Hasidic Yiddish" associated with Hasidic males and "Jewish English" associated with Hasidic females.

The term "register," like "code," "variety," and even "language" itself, is not unproblematic in terms of definitions or boundaries. Recent work has turned to Bakhtin's (1981) concept of heteroglossia to make sense of the stratified linguistic diversity within any society, even monolingual ones, as multiple varieties or styles can be encompassed in one linguistic code (Bailey 2007; Woolard 2004). Examining registers as alternate yet socially stratified varieties associated with particular uses and practices offers a perspective for understanding code choice in multilingual settings, particularly if one thinks of registers as a central part of performing social identities or "voices" in Bakhtin's sense. Irvine (1990: 130) clarifies this:

> Thus our verbal performances do not simply represent our own social identity, our own feelings, and the social occasion here and now. They are full of allusions to the behavior of others and to other times and places. To put this another way: One of the many methods people have for differentiating situations and marking their moods is to draw on (or carefully avoid) the "voices" of others, or what they assume those "voices" to be.

In multilingual settings, the use of one code may convey a different type of rhetorical force or social meaning than the other, acting as an affect intensifier and potentially serving as a register to mark particular kinds of affective stances and "voices" vis-à-vis other codes (Biber and Finegan 1994; Errington 1988; Irvine 1990; Ochs 1988; Patrick 1997).

Of course, not all registers or other linguistic varieties are available or appropriate to all speakers at a given time, contributing to and creating asymmetries of power and prestige, but also a space for creativity and resistance. I link this understanding of register variation to Bourdieu's (1977, 1991) notions of symbolic capital, linguistic markets, and symbolic domination. This allows us to envision multilingual language use, like other linguistic practices and resources available to both monolingual and multilingual speakers, as embedded in power relations. Different codes have value (positive or negative) within local speech economies, thus code-switching can be an important resource in the exercise of or resistance to power, and is inherently political, like language use generally (Gal 1988, 1989; Grillo 1989; Heller 2003, 2007, 2010; Irvine 1989; Woolard 1989). This applies to children as well as adults, although one rarely hears about children's speech economies. Yet a growing body of literature on peer interactions in multilingual settings illustrates that adolescents and school-age children alternate codes for negotiating power, such as when structuring games and other activities, disputing meanings and rights, and asserting their shifting identities and allegiances.

Understanding how children are socialized and socialize others into code and register choice, including how language varieties index sociocultural information, is central for making sense of processes of cultural and linguistic reproduction and change (Ochs and Schieffelin 2008: 10). What is unusual in the case of Dominica as compared to other studies of affect in language socialization is that caregivers employ contrasting languages—Patwa and English—in affect-laden socializing activities and acts that transmit to children competing ideologies about the languages. As the following chapters demonstrate, Patwa has become enregistered as an adult language associated with adult status, roles, and activities. Children learn to use this otherwise prohibited register to intensify their speech and control others during peer interaction, while they usually speak English. This begs the question: will children's heteroglossic language practices lead to continued language maintenance instead of loss? This question is explored through attention to language socialization practices, official and unofficial language policies, local language ideologies, the affective power of language, and the role of indexicality in the negotiation of codes in everyday life.

Investigating Language in the Home, Village, and Nation

My analysis draws on over twenty months of ethnographic and linguistic fieldwork in Dominica between 1995 and 2010. The primary ethnographic research and language socialization study took place between October 1996 and March 1998 in one northern village called Penville (population approximately 750). Prior to this I conducted two months of preliminary research in Roseau and a village neighboring Penville in the summer of 1995. I returned to Dominica for brief visits in 2005, 2006, 2008, and 2010. I chose Penville for the primary research site because it had a reputation, along with Grand Bay in southern Dominica, for being a Patwa-speaking community. I obtained permission and letters of support from KEK and the Ministry of Education, both of which expressed interested in the research. My first contacts in Penville were teachers, who introduced me to other residents. At first, villagers were surprised that I wanted to study Patwa, but most were eager to help me. My husband accompanied me when I returned for the longer fieldwork period. We rented a small concrete block house centrally located near the village school and health center. The house is surrounded by five homes occupied by members of one large family.

Being accompanied by my husband contributed to my research in numerous ways. It facilitated entry into the community, both by being a couple, which makes more cultural sense than a single female with no partner or family, and by offering villagers a glimpse into my own personal life. After we settled in, my husband was able to take part in activities that I did not have the time for or easy access to, such as working with men on banana harvesting day or farming vegetables and fruits. He accompanied them on trips to Portsmouth and other villages to sell produce, and spent leisure time with them at the rum shop (which, as a woman, I was warned against doing). His experiences provided me with insights into other dimensions of village life.

The research consisted of participant observation in and video recording of daily family, school, and community life. At its core was a longitudinal language socialization study in six families with a child between the ages of two and four years. These six children comprise the focal group; however it is through examination of social interactions among their social networks of kin and family friends that it is possible to get at more general attitudes and practices regarding language use and identity.[23] In Dominica as in other Caribbean societies, children are not isolated from these larger networks but experience them throughout their everyday lives. Children frequently reside in households with siblings, cousins, aunts, uncles, and grandparents, or with child fosterers, such as an aunt or grandparent, when left in the home society by their transnational parent(s). Moreover, children spend much of their time engaging in extensive play and social interactions with their peers, siblings, and cousins as they are often left in the care of older children for much of the day. Through socialization activities involving members of these networks, children learn wider community patterns of communication, as well as language ideologies and social expectations. To aid in understanding salient kin and social ties, I sketched basic genealogies of the families. During recordings, every effort was made to record children engaging with as many members of these networks as possible. This facilitated the observation of children with a range of interlocutors across at least three generations, providing data on the language development of older children, the effects of school-age siblings on the socialization of younger siblings, and intergenerational variation.

The focal children formed a gender-balanced sample of three girls and three boys (see Chapter 2, Table 2.1 for more information). At regular one-month intervals I systematically video-audio recorded each child during diverse daily activities with family and community members. Video-audio recording allows direct investigation of speech practices, as parental ideology often does not match actual multilingual language use with children. Five of the children were recorded for at least twelve consecutive months, while one was recorded for six months. The recording sessions lasted as long as the activity or situation permitted, often ending when a child became cranky or needed a nap, and sometimes continuing at a later time. The use of a tripod was virtually impossible; I typically carried my video camera in hand as I chased the focal children, particularly during play with siblings and peers. I also used a tape recorder as a back up and to ensure quality audio. I would position it in a convenient location or carry it strapped over my shoulder, with the microphone clipped to it or placed nearby. I carried a small notebook in my pocket and often filled in contextual notes during breaks. At least two hours of speech were obtained per child each month. These recordings resulted in approximately 130 hours of videotaped naturalistic social interaction among the six families. While a main goal was to gather data on the focal children's language development and interactions with caregivers, the recordings of children's older siblings, cousins, and friends provided rich and unexpected insights into children's social worlds and peer socialization of both English and Patwa.

Sample recording was employed before the actual recordings began so that families would become accustomed to the research methods and equipment. I would not assume that my presence had no effect, but the participants became very comfortable with me and rarely paid attention to the recording equipment once they were involved in the day's activities.[24] Many enjoyed watching themselves on the LCD screen of my video camera, so I often played segments at the end of the day. I tried to assume the role of observer rather than participant during recordings and did not elicit speech from the children. Nevertheless, children and adults alike frequently pulled me into ongoing conversations as a participant. Sometimes I was recruited as a babysitter and had to wait patiently until a caregiver returned or other children came to play. This offered interesting insights as well, as children often used the opportunity to show and tell me about me things and places that they considered important.

Establishing rapport with the children was just as important as building relationships with the adults who allowed me access to them. I was able to achieve this in part by doing whatever children did—following them wherever they went, being attentive to their activities and speech, and not scolding or evaluating their actions, unless someone's safety seemed compromised. The attitudes of their primary caregivers toward me helped significantly as well. All the families welcomed me into their homes and treated me like a close friend or family member. Many introduced me as the focal child's "friend," thus positioning me in a less authoritative role than other adult roles like "aunt" or "teacher." The children that I spent the most time with tended to treat me like another child rather than an adult, to the point that during transcription, their caregivers sometimes disapprovingly noted when they called me "girl" or led me through the bush. I always reassured them that this was how I wanted the children to perceive me. My rather in-between status as a married woman with no children made this more acceptable than if I had my own offspring. However, it is impossible to eschew the power differentials involved between researcher and researched, and ultimately the voices and descriptions provided here are my representations (Clifford 1988; Geertz 1988). Further, I recognize that these stories and voices cannot represent all Dominican children or their individual differences (James 2007). Nevertheless, they offer a glimpse into children's social worlds, which are generally not paid attention to by adults.

As soon as possible after each session, I transcribed and annotated the recordings with the help of the children's caregivers, often including family members other than the parents, such as older siblings who were in the recordings.[25] This helped to verify my accuracy in transcribing and to elicit analysis and metacommunicative reflections by culturally competent members. Transcribing data with native speakers provides ongoing interpretation and evaluation of social and linguistic practices. It was during the transcribing sessions that the video proved immensely valuable, as consultants often pointed out things they did not notice during the interactions. The resulting transcripts form the main corpus of data for the study.

This home and community component was complemented by the study of classroom language use, shedding light on the multiple spheres of children's social lives. I made periodic observations and recordings of language use at the preschool and grades one and two at the primary school. Schools act as central forces in the production and reproduction of social structure, including relations of power and dominance (Bourdieu 1977; Bourdieu and Passeron 1990[1970]). In Dominica schools are prime sites for the transmission of institutional norms privileging English over Patwa. Points of contention between the language(s) learned at home and the language required in school become visible as children are assessed by teachers when they express their ideas, feelings, and notions of self and other. In the classroom recordings students (including siblings of the focal children) attempted to respond to questions, construct personal narratives, and relate to peers during "news telling" and language, math, and social studies lessons. Their responses often provoked explicit commentaries by teachers on their language choice and the quality of their speech (e.g., "good" or "bad" English). Yet teachers themselves occasionally used Patwa in the classroom, and their own speech frequently differed from the "standard" English children were expected to learn. I was able to explore this in interviews with teachers and other Ministry of Education personnel. The school-based data yield insights into the language ideologies that inform pedagogical policy and practice.

Accompanying the corpus of home and school recordings are extensive ethnographic notes taken on community and family life, social interactions, and village meetings and events. Investigating the planned performance of culture in the national arena provided a point of contrast to these quotidian practices. Particularly during Independence celebrations, state-sponsored regional competitions draw cultural groups from the countryside to perform and keep "alive" particular genres of dance, music, song, and storytelling. These practices, labeled "traditional," are associated with rural peoples as opposed to "modern" urbanites who no longer or perhaps never engaged in them. I observed and recorded practices and performances of Penville's "cultural group" as they entered these competitions. This gives insights into which forms of creative expression are considered part of "traditional Dominican culture" and must be preserved, and how this is being discussed and organized at local and national levels. I also followed the literacy and Patwa-promoting efforts of

KEK, including its role in the development of the first World Creole Music Festival in 1997. Public events that focus on language and culture, such as national celebrations, KEK workshops, and Parent–Teacher Association meetings, provide opportunities for the explicit discussion of language ideologies, such as those concerning literacy and official policy.

The observation of these intersecting spheres provides a critical perspective on how Patwa is actively used, discussed, portrayed, and documented in private and public arenas. In Dominica as elsewhere in the West Indies, linguistic skills are a highly valued resource. The ability to command more than one code and to move freely between them as each situation demands carries with it considerable social value and may help one acquire social or political legitimacy and authority. Each code choice signals an "act of identity" that positions both speakers and hearers in particular, though not always intended or even conscious, ways (Le Page and Tabouret-Keller 1985). Children growing up in multilingual societies must learn to negotiate this linguistic terrain and manipulate it in their own identity construction. Parents thus have a vested interest in ensuring that their children learn the relevant language varieties and how to use them appropriately.

Outline of the Book

The following chapters integrate the approaches described above to provide a multifaceted analysis of language ideologies and linguistic practices with and among children. The book has several overarching goals. One is to theorize how patterns of use contribute to language shift in rural communities, despite attitudes valorizing Patwa among educated urban elites fluent in "good English." Another primary goal is to explore how children actively play a role in language shift, such as through accommodation to adults by speaking English in adult-controlled settings, but also in language maintenance, such as through their active exploration of both languages during unmonitored peer play. A third objective is to examine the paradox posed by Patwa activism and language revitalization efforts in light of widespread socioeconomic and educational inequalities within the rural population. In their attempts to create a unified national community and express a pan-Afro-Caribbean identity, the state and urban elite highlight Patwa not as an official, modern language of the state but as an expression of traditional creole culture carried down through time that must be preserved and performed. It is set apart from everyday life as something to be performed once annually on "Creole Day," offering little socioeconomic incentive for rural peoples to maintain it. These urban goals are contrasted with pedagogical practices of rural teachers, who claim that the Patwa-influenced varieties of English children learn at home differ from the "standard" required at school and create language-related educational challenges. These historically rooted ideologies continue to impact villagers' views and linguistic practices as they take part in the formal education system.

While my study focuses on one rural village, I aim to situate the local within the national and regional contexts, and to provide a historical backdrop for understanding recent developments. Chapter 1 therefore situates Dominica's complex sociolinguistic ecology within its equally complex history. I utilize archival materials and my research on language revitalization efforts to analyze official ideologies and policies on language from the colonial period to the present—in other words, how various actors and agencies have "played" with Dominica's languages while promoting various colonial and post-colonial agendas. The chapter draws on academic research, colonial records and education reports, interviews with education officials and KEK members, and observations of public performances and discourses. I explore the perpetuation of a rural/urban dichotomy in discourses on the transmission and loss of culture, language, and "traditional" values.

Chapters 2, 3, and 4 work together to describe the primary field site and contextualize children's interactions and language use in the flow of everyday life. Chapter 2 introduces Penville, a historically Patwa-monolingual community undergoing economic, ideological, and linguistic change. I provide portraits of the six focal families as representing a range of family types. These case studies allow me to explore discourses and perceptions of "tradition" and "change" that permeate community life. Chapters 3 and 4 analyze rural language ideologies in conjunction with patterns of language use by caregivers, teachers, and other adults. A central insight of language socialization is that children learn both as active participants and observers. I thus provide detailed discourse analysis of adult–adult interaction in the presence of children, as well as teacher–student interaction at school. In Chapter 3, I illustrate how educational institutions were at the forefront of encouraging the shift to English, and played a key role in reconfiguring intergenerational communicative activities into place- and age-graded ones. Chapter 4 then investigates links between language socialization practices and age-graded language ideologies. I analyze code-switching, discourse structures, and patterned ways of speaking to children as they develop bilingual subjectivities. I examine the "division of labor" between Patwa and English, whereby adults primarily use English with children but employ Patwa to direct and evaluate children's actions and speech.

Chapters 5 and 6 explore children's peer interactions and code-switching practices during child-directed activities. Chapter 5 details the social and linguistic organization of children's peer groups. I illustrate how peer play provides a "safe" space for children to explore otherwise restricted roles, positions of authority, and languages. I analyze children's linguistic practices to show how they use code-switching as a potent tool to enact agency and socialize one another through and to use Patwa. Chapter 6 draws systematic attention to children's use of multiple languages to construct adult roles during pretend play. Children tend to use more Patwa in role-playing than in other activities, employing verbal resources and physically embodied social action to create imaginary play spaces organized by and appropriate for Patwa. Their code-switching practices sustain play frames and demonstrate their sensitivities to how languages index social identities, places, and activities. The chapters illustrate that despite the dominance of English in children's lives, those aspects of Patwa with particular affective saliency in their verbal environments become part of their growing linguistic repertoires. Adults' reactions to these linguistic "transgressions" illustrate how age-graded language ideologies link differential language use to local notions of respect, authority, adult–child status differences, and place, and in turn help to naturalize the language shift.

The book's conclusion provides an assessment of how conflicting rural and urban agendas for language use may impact efforts to preserve and revitalize Patwa. It explores how children are agents of transformation by being active participants in the shift to English and by using Patwa in new ways, but also agents of language maintenance. I situate this in a comparative discussion of studies of language revitalization cross-culturally, many of which under-theorize how languages are transmitted and which strategies may be more effective for intervening in language shift. Children's peer interactions play a critical role in the transmission and transformation of linguistic practices. Ultimately, they may determine the fate of a language.

Notes

1. Significant works on language endangerment include Crystal (2000), Evans (2010), Fishman (1991, 2001), Grenoble and Whaley (2006), Hinton and Hale (2001), Krauss (1992), Maffi (2005), and Nettle and Romaine (2000). For more critical discussions of academic approaches, see Duchêne and Heller (2007), Garrett (2006), Ladefoged (1992), and Mufwene (2004, 2008).
2. Reviews of this growing literature include M. Goodwin and Kyratzis (2012), Hirschfeld (2002), James et al. (1998), Kyratzis (2004), LeVine (2007), and Schwartzman (2001).
3. Exceptions are language socialization studies by Fader (2009), Garrett (2005, 2007, 2012), Kulick (1992), Meek (2010), Paugh (2005a, 2005b), and Zentella (1997). Friedman (2012), Howard (2008), and Nonaka (2012) provide useful reviews of language socialization research on language shift and revitalization.
4. I have chosen to call this group Kalinago, the name they use to refer to themselves, rather than Carib, a name rooted in the Spanish colonial encounter (see Honychurch 1995[1975]: 20–21).

5. Tropical rainforest covers two-thirds of its surface, and annual rainfall ranges from 50 inches on the coast to 300 inches in the mountains.

6. Agricultural products, handicrafts, and manufactured goods (coconut soaps, bay leaf oils, juice concentrates, rum, cigarettes, paint, plastic sandals) are produced for sale. There is a small commercial fishing industry, and some commerce in timber and pumice. Tourism, billed as ecotourism, is developing, but is hindered by the lack of an international airport and sufficient accommodations.

7. This population figure represents a decrease of 1,558 from the 1991 census (population 71,183), suggesting an implied net migration of 8,968 between 1992 and 2001. This is less than the previous decade, which had an implied net migration of 15,325 between 1982 and 1991. The 1981 census registered 73,795 persons.

8. The Kalinago have been a focus of anthropological research (Honychurch 1997; Hulme 2000). Other research has focused on colonialism and economic development (Baker 1994; Trouillot 1988). Like elsewhere in the Caribbean, gender roles have been studied (Blank 2005; Krumeich 1994), including the contributions of female hucksters to the local "market chain" (Mantz 2007a). Flinn and colleagues have conducted extensive longitudinal biocultural anthropological studies of childhood stress, family relationships, and health in one community (e.g., Flinn 2008; Quinlan and Quinlan 2007).

9. Creole linguistics is permeated by debates over the sociohistorical origins of creole languages, and if and how they differ from non-creole languages. See Kouwenberg and Singler (2008) and Mufwene (2008) for useful discussions.

10. This explanation may account for typological similarities between Lesser Antillean Creole French varieties (Holm 1989b: 372; also Christie 1990: 62; Wylie 1995).

11. The grammar, phonology, and genesis of Patwa have been extensively studied (Amastae 1979a, 1979b, 1983; Christie 1969, 1982; Holm 1989b; Wylie 1995). Linguist Douglas Taylor devoted his life to the study of Patwa and the Kalinago language, and readers are referred to the bibliography in Taylor (1977) for his publications. Sociolinguistic work describes contexts of and general attitudes toward Patwa and English usage (Christie 1990, 1994; Stuart 1993). The verbal genre *kont* (folktale) has been analyzed for its forms and social meanings (G. Smith 1991).

12. See Garrett (2004: 55–56) for a description of similar English influences on St. Lucian Kwéyòl.

13. For more on this variation, see Amastae (1979c), Christie (1983, 1990, 1994), and Holm (1989b).

14. As Bailey (2007: 258) points out, "languages or codes can only be understood as distinct objects to the extent to which they are treated as such by social actors." The underlying assumption of the coherence and separability of codes in most traditional models of language cannot adequately address the fluidity of language use and highly mixed or varied input children receive in creole settings (Carrington 1996; Youssef 1996).

15. See Paugh (2012b) for an annotated bibliography reviewing key studies of child language learning across disciplines.

16. Similar to Giddens's (1979) "discursive consciousness" (Ochs 1988; Schieffelin 1990).

17. See Irvine and Gal (2000), Jaffe (1999), Kroskrity (2000a, 2004), Schieffelin et al. (1998), and Woolard and Schieffelin (1994). Riley (2012) reviews research linking the study of language socialization to the study of language ideologies.

18. It is largely through manipulation of the indexical links between stance or act and social meanings, that social identities, or the "boundaries" between one group and another, are constructed (Bailey 2007; Bucholtz and Hall 2004; Ochs 1996).

19. Kulick and Schieffelin (2004: 352) highlight this: "Affect is a central dimension of any theory of becoming, regardless of whether the theory is a scholarly one or a local one" (also Ochs and Schieffelin 1989). It is important to note that all uses of language carry affective meaning, including those interpreted by speakers or analysts as "neutral" or "low-affect" (Besnier 1990). The study of the discursive construction of emotions, in contrast to other approaches (like psychology), does not aim to judge speakers' "actual" feelings or sincerity, but rather to examine how affect is displayed, interpreted, and socialized through language use.

20. Pavlenko (2005: 124) finds that, "To date, there are no studies known to this researcher that examine bi- and multilinguals' spontaneous emotion talk and allow us to see how repertoires are selected and interpretations negotiated in interaction."

21. This distinction was introduced into code-switching literature by Gumperz (1982: 66): "The tendency is for the ethnically specific, minority language to be regarded as the 'we-code' and become associated with in-group and informal activities, and for the majority language to serve as the 'they-code' associated with the more formal, stiffer and less personal out-group relations." See Blom and Gumperz (1972) on "metaphorical code-switching."

22. It is speakers' perceptions of a variety and their metapragmatic activity marking it as a special type of language (e.g., "slang") that identifies a register for analytic study (Agha 2004: 26–27).

23. The names of all participants have been changed to protect their anonymity. Some details in my descriptions of their households and in transcript examples that might compromise it have been altered or omitted. The names of teachers are not provided. The real names of officials, activists, and politicians acting in the public arena are provided since this is part of public record.

24. See M. Goodwin (2006: 25–27) on the use of video as a method.

25. The caregivers were given the choice of who would help me transcribe. All were astonishingly patient during the time-consuming transcription process.

Chapter 1

Discourses of Differentiation, Unity, and Identity

> With a mixed triple heritage of Europeans, Africans, and Amerindians, its history as an eighteenth century Anglo-French pawn, protestant, British rule of a largely Catholic, French Creole-speaking population, and a name altogether too similar to a much larger Caribbean nation, it is little surprise that Dominica has long been an island with an uncertain identity. (Myers 1987: xxii–xxiii)

Those who have tried to govern Dominica have for centuries struggled with issues of differentiation and unity, exclusion and inclusion, at multiple levels. The island experienced a complex colonial history of French and British rule with an associated "spatial dismemberment" (Trouillot 1988) and linguistic divide isolating villages from each other and from the towns. Its history, geography, and particular configuration of cultural and linguistic contact mark its uniqueness from other Caribbean nations, expect perhaps for St. Lucia with its similar French–British colonial past. Since colonization, the multiple ideologies surrounding Dominica's languages have been complex and often oppositional. They have taken shape differently across geographic, socioeconomic, and ethnic lines. Today Patwa is viewed among many urban intellectuals and nationalists as Dominica's "authentic" language, a symbol of national identity, and a link to French creole-speaking regions worldwide. Contemporary nationalist discourses highlight an inclusive "shared' linguistic heritage through Patwa and concerns about the "decline" of Dominican culture. These discourses, however, minimize the existence of deeply felt historical, social, and economic divisions between rural/urban groups and the exclusion experienced by rural Patwa speakers. Meanwhile, there is an emerging discourse about culture and language as commodities in the newly developing heritage and ecotourism industry; this often intersects with the other discourses. In this chapter I examine how social and linguistic boundaries have been historically shaped and discursively constructed by colonial officials, political leaders, and cultural activists who have struggled to define Dominican identity. As I sketch out this history I ask, how have various authorities played with and framed Dominica's language varieties over time?

Language and Post-colonialism

Language is often a significant and highly contested issue in nationalist movements and nation building generally (Anderson 1991[1983]; Blommaert and Verschueren 1992; Grillo 1989; Heller 2010), particularly in multilingual post-colonial settings where language and identity issues are overtly linked. A large and growing literature focuses on language issues in nation building, the politics of development, sentiments of belonging, and the defining of borders, boundaries, and ethnic groups.[1] As Anderson states, "the most important thing about language is its capacity for generating imagined communities, building in effect *particular solidarities*" (1991[1983]: 133, emphasis in original). For Anderson, the development of print capitalism and shared literacy activities such as newspapers and novels in national languages is central in creating national communities. This, however, has been critiqued as a naturalization of the standardization process and replication of a nationalist ideological position itself (Kroskrity 2000b; Silverstein 2000).

Languages also divide. An approach that problematizes a focus on unity is exemplified by Bourdieu's work (1977, 1984, 1991), which considers how the differential distribution of linguistic practices relates to the structure of social hierarchy. Certain linguistic practices and varieties, such as state-legitimated standards or "ethnic" or "indigenous" languages, are viewed as valuable resources that are ultimately convertible into social and economic capital, which may uphold dominant power structures and support symbolic domination (Duchêne and Heller 2007; Gal 1989; Heller 2010; Jaffe 1999, 2007b; Kroskrity 2000b). In many Caribbean nations, a major state project since independence has been developing cultural policies that promote distinct post-colonial national identities. Such policies raise questions about "authenticity" and "ownership" of (often racialized) cultural and linguistic practices.[2] For example, the creation of an Haitian Kreyòl orthography has generated profound questions about inequality, representations of the nation, and what it means to be Haitian (Schieffelin and Doucet 1994). The analysis of standardization processes, authoritative discourses like language purism, and the promotion of some practices over others reveals broader social meanings and power relations (Hill and Hill 1986; Woolard and Schieffelin 1994).

Until recently, attitudes toward creole languages such as Patwa have been mixed at best and typically derogatory. Historians, linguists, colonial officials, and speakers themselves have denigrated them as "broken" or "bastardized" versions of the European standards upon which they are lexically based.[3] In the context of national identity movements in post-colonial settings since World War II, impacted by the women's and civil rights movements in the United States, this began to change. Creole languages are being reevaluated and revalued as unique dimensions of island and pan-Caribbean identity. Creole languages have been introduced to varying degrees into politics, mass media, education, and other formal contexts, including English creole in Jamaica, French creoles in Haiti, Guadeloupe, Martinique, and St. Lucia, and Papiamento in the formerly Dutch islands of Aruba, Bonaire, and Curaçao (see Migge et al. 2010). The elevation of creole languages at the national level has generated controversy, most often among native creole language speakers themselves (Appel and Verhoeven 1994; Craig 2008; Devonish 1986; Garrett 2000; Migge et al. 2010; Nwenmely 1996; Schnepel 2004). This is due partly to the fact that while revitalization movements often have the altruistic goal of helping communities and raising national consciousness, they also obscure differences in wealth, access, and resources. Revitalization efforts that elevate a language without elevating the status of its speakers often clash with the daily experiences of those they claim to help—paradoxically strengthening existing power structures in new ways. Further, they can even undermine local strategies that allow speakers to adopt a more powerful "global" language like English while continuing to maintain the creole language as an important identity marker and affectively salient linguistic resource in particular contexts.

A look into Dominica's complex colonial past, history of sociolinguistic variation, and contemporary discourses about cultural and linguistic heritage and loss shed light on the paradoxes posed by Patwa revitalization efforts. Despite efforts to eliminate it, especially by British colonizers, Patwa has persisted for well over three and a half centuries, often serving as a form of opposition to ruling powers (cf. Burton 1997). As previously discussed, Dominica differs from other Caribbean societies in that its French-Afro creole language exists alongside varieties of English, not standard French, due to its specific history of cultural and linguistic contact. This chapter illuminates contemporary ideologies and their continual articulation with the colonial past, as Caribbean societies are "inescapably historical" (Trouillot 1992: 21). The chapter probes the ideological aspects of linguistic differentiation, "the ideas with which participants and observers frame their understanding of linguistic varieties and map those understandings onto people, events, and activities that are significant to them" (Irvine and Gal 2000: 35).

Cultural and Linguistic Contact in the Colonial Period

When Columbus sighted Dominica in 1493, Kalinago from the Orinoco delta occupied it and the islands to either side of it. There had been an

Amerindian presence for potentially thousands of years (Honychurch 1995[1975]), but despite this, Columbus named the island Dominica for the day: *dies Dominica*, "the Lord's Day" or "Sunday" in Latin. Spain had little interest in the mountainous terrain, however, preferring to settle the flatter Greater Antillean islands (Hispaniola, Cuba, and Puerto Rico) and the Latin American mainland, and principally stopped there to replenish wood and water supplies. Dominica was left to the Kalinago until France and Britain began competing for its strategic position between the French-controlled islands in the seventeenth century. While the French made no formal claims, they had established the earliest European settlements by 1635. French settlers arrived from Martinique and Guadeloupe, bringing island-born slaves (descendants of earlier West African groups)[4] and developing small prosperous coffee estates. By the eighteenth century Patwa had emerged in the context of the unequal contact between these groups and was spoken on French estates around the coast. Accompanying the early settlers were French Roman Catholic missionaries who spread the use of Patwa and established the predominance of Catholicism that persists today. Few slaves would have learned French; instead most would have acquired Patwa as their first language as it was passed on to new generations.

Threatened by French hegemony in the Lesser Antilles, the British vied for control. The Kalinago often sided with one European power, usually the French. In the mid-seventeenth century, Afro-Caribbean slaves from other islands began escaping to Dominica, many inter-mixing with the Kalinago. In 1660 a French treaty gave the Kalinago rights to Dominica and St. Vincent in exchange for them abandoning claims to other islands. However, the French refused to leave and the British fought for control. In 1686 France and Britain signed another treaty making Dominica a neutral island belonging to the Kalinago. Both nations violated it and the Kalinago, like other indigenous peoples of the Americas, were decimated as they were pushed to the rugged windward coast. They had numbered 5,000 in 1647, but by the turn of the century there remained only about 2,000. By 1730 there were only 400, which offered little threat to European colonizing efforts.[5] French settlers and buccaneers, poor whites, and freed slaves from other islands continued to arrive. The rest of the population grew from 776 in 1730 to 7,890 in 1763 (Baker 1994: 47).

The island exchanged hands at least seven times before becoming British in the 1763 Treaty of Paris, with the French gaining one last brief period of control from 1778 to 1783. But the French had established the earliest and most significant European settlements, making an indelible cultural, linguistic, and economic impact. This influence continued as French residents were allowed to remain on their profitable coffee estates, albeit for rent and under British law, and other French settlers arrived from Guadeloupe and Martinique to further settle the countryside.[6] A major difference between these colonizers was that the French were more interested in permanently settling than the British, who ruled from the capital town. Unlike British absentee owners, French owners typically lived on and managed their small-scale operations. They also permitted their slaves to cultivate marginal land for their own consumption and to inherit property upon the owner's death. No such arrangements were made by British attorneys overseeing their absentee owner's estates or by the few title-holders who actually lived there. Slavery was based on extreme exploitation and dehumanization of African populations; however, there reportedly emerged a more cooperative relationship between the French and their slaves, offering slaves more independence and giving rise to a proto-peasantry long before emancipation (Baker 1994; Trouillot 1988). Not insignificantly French slaves overwhelmingly adopted Catholicism, which remains the religion of 61.5 percent of the population with no other denomination exceeding 6 percent (Commonwealth of Dominica 2001).[7] As in religion French influence is discernable in Dominica's linguistic ecology.

The Persistence of French Creole Culture and Language

When the British seized control in 1763, they replaced French with English as the official language. This effectively separated the British-controlled towns of Roseau and Portsmouth from the rest of the French and Patwa-speaking population. The British further attempted to erase linguistic evidence of over a century of French influence by replacing French places names with British ones. Many took hold, like Portsmouth, but a number of French names persisted, like Roseau. In addition, the British were threatened by subversive political and military activity among French inhabitants, free mulattos, and maroons (escaped slaves), and were unprepared to work the mountainous land. Due to the paucity of the sugar industry, British officials focused on the free ports of Roseau and Portsmouth for trade. Little money was invested in developing roads, amenities, or large plantations like on the richer sugar islands of Jamaica and Barbados. Meanwhile, a steady flow of white and mulatto smallholders from the French islands bought up estates from disillusioned British settlers. French culture and the creole language became firmly entrenched in the rural population, with the spread of English outside the towns limited by the difficulties of traveling and "a language barrier created by Patois" (Christie 1990: 63).

Ruled by England but populated by French planters and slaves, colonial Dominica was torn by the conflicting desires and influences of two opposing powers:

> [T]he island's position between two of the most important and valuable colonies of the French Empire created a constant imbalance between

British occupation and French influence. The majority of the European population on Dominica was French and by cultural transfusion, so were their slaves. ... The culture of the French families on their scattered estates triumphed over that of the British officials huddled in Roseau, or of the attorneys on the dwindling number of British estates. (Honychurch 1995[1975]: 100)

The language barriers came to represent the opposition between the British and French, and increasingly between the ruling class and the rest of the population. In 1825 one visitor noted:

[T]he community is first divided by language [English versus Patwa and French], then by religion [Protestantism versus Catholicism], and the inconsiderable residue, which is supposed to represent the whole, is so torn to pieces by squabbles as bitter as contemptible, that the mere routine of government was at a dead stand while I was on the island. (Henry Nelson Coleridge, in Honychurch 1995[1975]: 120)

Official erasure of Dominica's linguistic complexities only made Patwa more subversive, as French slaves transmitted Patwa to British slaves who could use it to communicate without their English-speaking masters understanding them (Baker 1994; Christie 1983). For French slaves, who often remained loyal to their estates, Patwa symbolized their "Frenchness" (Christie 1990: 63). For the British, Patwa increasingly represented the obstacles posed by the French and the failure of their own colonial project. English, as the only written medium and the language of British colonial administration, came to index the ruling white elite, their culture, and the two towns, especially Roseau.

Emancipation: The Rise of a Peasant-based Society and Mulatto Elite

When slavery was abolished in 1834, two new social classes emerged: a growing population of Patwa-speaking peasant farmers eager to work their own land, and a smaller English-speaking mulatto ascendancy with political power concentrated in Roseau. Central to understanding the contemporary national speech economy is an examination of how these two very separate groups fit into the patterns established during the conflict between the two colonial powers, and how this mapped onto language ideologies and usage. But rather than two foreign nations, this was a struggle between two groups that considered Dominica their home.

Prior to emancipation there were over 14,000 slaves, 4,077 free colored, and only 791 "whites" (Baker 1994). Once freed, most former slaves were far from eager to work for the estates and rapidly left to form new settlements.[8] In the years that followed, older villages grew and new ones sprang up. Unlike other Caribbean islands where large plantations occupied most available land, there was abundant land in Dominica where freed slaves could establish smallholdings. Maroons from Guadeloupe and Martinique, where slavery was not abolished until 1848, joined the freed slaves. "Black" ex-slave villages emerged between the British estates and older French creole villages. These were the beginnings of a peasant-based agricultural society with most of the population dominant in Patwa, not French or English.[9]

The settlement patterns of the post-emancipation period had important economic and social consequences. Lacking road and communication networks, the new communities were largely self-sufficient. Residents grew their own food and only occasionally labored for cash on neighboring estates. The existing isolation increased as small communities emerged around the coastal periphery, separating them from each other and Roseau (Figure 1.1). The available means of transportation included footpaths or boats. The northern and southernmost villages retained more regular contact with communities in Guadeloupe and Martinique than with other Dominican villages, while the eastern villages had little outside contact at all. This contact with residents of the creole-speaking French islands only strengthened use of Patwa. Tight-knit communities developed where the "influence of a French co-operative ethic was pervasive" (Baker 1994: 104). The custom of *koudmen* was practiced, whereby a large job requiring lots of hands, such as building a house, was accomplished through cooperative labor that would be reciprocated in turn. From this emerged isolated and inward-looking communities since cooperation between them was rarely necessary or possible. Strong stereotypes

Figure 1.1 A coastal village surrounded by mountains

developed, often based on family name and skin color related to the degree of intermixing between estate owners and slaves in each area.

With greater access to land than the populace of other Caribbean societies, Dominican peasants were less reliant on the metropolitan-dominated market system for their survival. Gradually, however, they became incorporated into that system through a monocrop cash economy and increasing reliance on imported manufactured goods. The isolation and independence of villages tended to inhibit the creation of a strong collective class-identity among the peasantry. In addition, the freed slaves regarded the ruling colonial government with suspicion and mistrust (Baker 1994: 123). When officials went into the countryside to take a population census in 1844, rumors spread that the abolishment of slavery had been repealed and people were going to be re-enslaved. Many refused to give their names, others abandoned their houses and hid, and some took up arms (Honychurch 1995[1975]: 135–136). The isolation of communities and rifts between the rural peasantry and town-dwelling officials persist to some degree in the present day. What also persists is a spirit of independence among rural villagers that may have helped to preserve Patwa as a counter to colonial and even contemporary government policy.

Alongside the peasant social class, there emerged a mulatto elite who struggled to gain more control of the administration, while a small number of white representatives from Britain tried to preserve colonial rule. Like other Caribbean plantation societies, Dominica was rigidly divided by color according to degrees of intermixture of African and European "blood" and its associations with social class. With physical attributes more like the ruling class, a "white ancestry," and claims to greater economic resources, the mulattoes produced from unions between estate owners/managers and slaves were typically accorded different social status than ex-slaves with darker skin. Even before emancipation many owned estates and businesses, but were excluded from government. By 1838 there was a colored majority in the Dominican Assembly.[10] As this "mulatto ascendancy" pressed for legislation to promote local concerns, such as the welfare of emancipated slaves, they continually opposed the white planters, merchants, and attorneys. The latter group frequently criticized the former in the newspaper *The Colonist*, targeting their language abilities as a means of marking difference: "Very few of them articulate English decently, and a still smaller number are able to write it with any degree of accuracy or propriety" (July 1, 1854, in Boromé 1969: 27). Despite or perhaps because of the criticisms of their speech and writing, "standard" English became the goal of this rising mulatto elite.

Although more invested in local interests than the transient British officials preoccupied with metropolitan concerns, this group nevertheless adopted many colonial values stressing all things English, including language and education. They became an influential class lasting well into the twentieth century and sought to distinguish themselves from the masses by speaking English, the language of power. Patwa activist Felix Henderson (1988: 4) describes it thus: "To protect their social status, the upper and middle classes would not speak creole, at least not in public and forbade their children from learning or even speaking it." Associated with slavery, backwardness, and illiteracy, Patwa became indexically linked to a dark-skinned rural peasantry and their perceived identity. The first schools in English opened in Roseau in 1838, followed by the Compulsory Education Act in 1890, but most of the population was without physical access to formal education until the mid-1900s. This further established a pattern whereby English was the language of educated middle/upper-class urbanites and Patwa was "a distinguishing mark of the lower class" (Henderson 1988: 4). Patwa was viewed as "broken," impoverished, and not a "real" language, and this was used to exclude rural peoples from island politics. With little if any access to English, the majority spoke Patwa as their first and only language until roads began to open up the countryside in the mid- to late- twentieth century.

Moving toward Independence: Patwa as Cultural Heritage

By the turn of the twentieth century the British lamented their lack of influence. One visitor wrote in 1887: "England has done nothing, absolutely nothing, to introduce her own civilisation; and thus Dominica is English only in name" (J.A. Froude, in Honychurch 1995[1975]: 145). He later called English rule in Dominica "a comedy" (Froude 1888: 151). A member of the Legislative Assembly reported in 1893 that:

> The natural connexion [sic] is with the French Islands. People understand good French, though they do not speak it, and French priests are more acceptable to the people than the Irish whom they have sometimes had. If the Island is to be English, Anglicise it, if not, give it to France. The Island would be more contented under French rule, if not more prosperous. (A.R. Lockhart, in Goodridge 1972: 151)

Others attributed the island's "backwardness" to Patwa, which was not a written language. Visits from two royal commissions in 1893 and 1896 resulted in a grant for colonial relief, partly to build roads. But despite a brief prosperous time as Dominica began cultivating limes,[11] most British families had left the island by the 1920s in apparent frustration.

Despite a dwindling British presence, Patwa continued to signify lack of education, social mobility, and prestige. Middle/upper class Dominicans distanced themselves from the rural masses in part by debasing Patwa. These included descendants of the mulatto elite, who were no longer as "light skinned" but retained prominent family names, held political and professional positions, and owned most large businesses in town (along with Lebanese and Syrian immigrants).[12] In the early twentieth century, there was even a "League for the Suppression of French-Patois" attended by Roseau elite, including the father of prominent island politician Phyllis Shand Allfrey (Paravisini-Gebert 1996: 22). Allfrey claimed to have learned Patwa from her family's servants as a child, although her father forbade its use. Taylor (1954: 31) similarly noted socioeconomic differences in language use: the upper classes sometimes used Patwa in private, while poorer classes struggled "to address their children in what they believe to be English." There are few statistics on language use in Dominica's history, although the 1946 census included a language category: out of 47,581 people, 32,543 were bilingual, 11,801 were monolingual in Patwa, and 3,237 were monolingual in English. Assuming this was accurate, about 25 percent of the population did not speak any English (Christie 1969: 8, 1990: 64).

In this British colony populated by Afro-French creole speakers, colonial education reports claimed well into the twentieth century that English was "a foreign tongue" among the rural population (Maurice 1949/1950). An education officer in 1945 summed up official attitudes as he called for the eradication of Patwa:

> The position of Dominica is exceptional in that in many of the districts patois [Patwa] is the language of the population even where English is known. *This patois is of no cultural value* and there is no question of preserving a racial language as in Wales or Quebec. The aim should not be to make the children bi-lingual but ultimately to make English the mother tongue. (Hammond 1945, emphasis added)

Those children who were able to attend school were subjected to a policy of subtractive bilingualism. Teachers required English only and corporal punishment was used for a child caught speaking Patwa on school grounds. However, many rural teachers enforced a policy of transitional bilingualism in practice, as they had to use Patwa in early education "only to the extent that is necessary for allowing the official language to become the medium of instruction" (Craig 2008: 600). The school remains a powerful context for ideological and practical erasure of Patwa in both town and village (see chapter 3).

A Changing Society

In the 1950s and 1960s rural areas experienced rapid social and economic changes as the banana industry boomed and new roads facilitated transportation of crops.[13] By 1965 roads connected most coastal settlements to Roseau and Portsmouth. This had a major impact on local socioeconomic dynamics, increasing the flow of produce and people out of the villages, and importing goods and ideologies, such as English, into them. Honychurch (1982: 8) highlights the dramatic transformation: "When the roads came, changes swept through the closely-knit villages shattering certain patterns of life within months, bringing tinned foods, new building materials, new ideas, banana production and taking away much of the younger generation to Roseau." There was large-scale migration to Britain between 1959 and 1962 and a flow of rural peoples to Roseau that continues today. The government began building more schools and established the first national radio station in 1971, bringing English to Patwa-speaking villages.

With these changes, the geographic and sociolinguistic separation of village from town began to break down and the rural population had to be accounted for in island politics.[14] This was facilitated by the election of Edward Leblanc to Chief Minister and then Prime Minister from 1961 to 1974. He had village origins himself (from Vieille Case) and frequently peppered his political speeches with Patwa to identify with the farming population. LeBlanc distinguished himself from the Roseau elite and addressed long-ignored rural concerns. He is recognized as having started a "cultural nationalism" with his promotion of National Day celebrations when Dominica gained Associated Statehood in 1967.[15] It became an annual cultural festival that "brought the island together in a burst of spirited patriotism" (Honychurch 1995[1975]: 205), and was chosen as the official Independence Day over a decade later.[16] This new cultural consciousness was embraced by younger generations of upper-class urbanites, many of whom had studied abroad and returned during the liberal political climate of the 1960s.

Dominica became independent in 1978. Social and political unrest, including attempted coups, economic instability, and devastating Hurricane David, complicated the transition to independence. A new government headed by Eugenia Charles of the Freedom Party, the first female prime minister in the Caribbean (see Higbie 1993), came into power in 1980 and remained until 1995. As a newly independent post-colonial nation state lacking resources, its leaders attempted to reassure the population and generate a spirit of community identity, and an identity to project to the world. The national identity seized upon was the creole culture highlighting French, African, and Kalinago influences. Native-born urban intellectuals and government leaders began to proclaim Patwa as their "cultural heritage," something to unite the young nation across rural/urban and class divisions. It represented a nostalgic vision of a more independent French past and a link to other creole societies such as Haiti, Guadeloupe, Martinique, and St. Lucia, where similar creole recognition movements were underway. Further, it symbolized other identities represented by the rural population in opposition to those traditionally in power: "African," "creole," and "authentic" ones, rather than "British," "English," and "colonial" ones. For many, Patwa represented affect-laden ties to their rural roots.

As Dominica moved toward independence, the discourses about its languages began to change. Patwa had gained recognition in the National Day celebrations, and in 1977 it entered the English domain of radio through short five-minute Patwa news programs each day for farmers. At first the use of Patwa on the radio generated complaints, particularly from English-speaking Roseau residents. The show garnered such success, however, that it was expanded to a longer daily program known as *Èspéwéyans Kwéyòl*, which remains popular today (broadcast ninety minutes per day, five days a week).[17] Government officials began to recognize that Patwa could serve as a tool for instilling developmental messages among the rural masses and bridging the rural/urban divide. A 1988 independence publication entitled *Palé Kwéyòl Donmnik* (*Speak Dominican Creole*) describes the ideological shift:

> But it was with the deepening awareness of our cultural identity during the years of the West Indies Federation that we truly began to grow conscious of those aspects of our cultural life that made us a distinct people within the Caribbean Nation. Creole came to the forefront as one of the most outstanding contributors in pinpointing a distinct Dominican identity. (Henderson 1988)

To highlight this uniquely Dominican identity, the government adopted a national motto on the coat of arms in Patwa using an adapted French orthography: *Apres Bondie C'est La Ter* (After God, it is the land). This symbolizes Dominica's French-African creole heritage, strong religious orientation, and dependence on the soil, without reference to British influences.

Paradoxically, however, English was retained as the sole official language of the nation, hence maintaining its pragmatic and symbolic power. Dominica's Constitution, for example, specifies that to hold a government position as Representative or Senator, a person must "be able to speak and, unless incapacitated by blindness or other physical cause, to read the English language with a degree of proficiency sufficient to enable him to take an active part in the proceedings of the House." English is the language associated with the political entity of the modern nation-state and with the international community, while growing discourses designate Patwa as a symbol of the "cultural heritage" of the imagined national community.

From Practice to Performance: Language and Culture since Independence

Since independence, efforts to promote creole cultural and linguistic practices have surged through the expansion of cultural festivals and preservation endeavors. In 1978 the new government established a Cultural Division to document and promote "traditional" Dominican cultural forms. "Culture" in this context refers primarily to the performing arts, folklore, Patwa storytelling and song, and creole foods and dress. Accompanying these efforts have emerged two prominent discourses about tradition and change. One is that Dominican culture is "dying" and "under attack" from outside influences, thus contributing to a declining village ethos of cooperation, sharing, and goodwill. Rural villagers are portrayed as the keepers of traditional culture, but are perceived as shifting toward Americanized entertainment, manufactured foods, and use of English. The second is a discourse of modernization and development encouraging a more diversified market economy through cultural heritage tourism (for more on cultural tourism in the Caribbean, see Gmelch 2003; Sheller 2003; Strachan 2002; also Baud and Ypeij 2009 on Latin America). Both discourses emerge frequently among a range of actors including government representatives, cultural activists, language planners, development personnel, tourism officials, and villagers. Each group constructs language and its relevance in different ways, often conflating differences between rural/urban populations and their goals. These sometimes competing, sometimes complementary discourses were pervasive during the late 1990s and continue to circulate today.

Language Planning and Revitalization: The Konmité Pou Etid Kwéyòl (KEK)

Soon after independence, cultural activists became concerned that urban youths appeared neither to speak nor even understand Patwa, thus threatening the loss of Dominica's rediscovered "heritage." In 1981 the Cultural Division founded KEK, a language revitalization organization with the fundamental mission of preserving and promoting Patwa.[18] Gregory Rabess, President of KEK in the late 1990s, explained the goals to me: "To preserve the Creole language and to ensure its continued growth and development for the future generations." Though affiliated with the government, KEK seeks external funding for projects from organizations like UNESCO and the University of the West Indies, or through independent fundraising. KEK members are mostly volunteers. They include government staff, NGO employees (particularly from SPAT, the Small Projects Assistance Team), and performers (such as singer/song-writer Ophelia Marie and radio personality Felix Henderson). Most are middle-class urbanites and foreign-educated intellectuals who learned English and not Patwa as their first language. Rabess, for example, described himself as "a head teacher's son" and claimed that, "head teacher's children are not supposed to speak Creole." He explained that he learned Patwa from his nanny. Others acquired it later in life, often by requesting help from a grandmother or other elder, and some had training in linguistics during education abroad. For them and other speakers who possess standard varieties of English, Patwa is a source of symbolic capital.

KEK appears to have been strongest during the decade from its inception to the publication of the first English-Creole dictionary in 1992. Its defining moment took place within the context of two conferences held in St. Lucia in 1981 and 1982 on the standardization of Lesser Antillean Creole orthography. Like language planners in St. Lucia, Dominican activists were concerned that English literacy was associated with the elite and urban educated classes, but not available for the majority who spoke Patwa, an oral language. They adopted the orthography proposed in the St. Lucia meetings due to close similarities between Dominican and St. Lucian Creole. KEK's key goals in establishing this orthography were to legitimize Patwa as a written language, to allow preservation of Patwa oral genres as documented texts, and to teach Patwa literacy. The orthography received some criticism in Dominica, ranging from complaints that more speakers were not involved in its creation to complaints that Patwa was written down at all. But short Patwa lessons in the newspaper and "spelling competitions" on the radio helped to introduce it to the public. Since then, KEK has published a dictionary (including a second edition), folk stories, poetry, traditional songs, and "teach yourself" Patwa handbooks.

KEK members cite many obstacles to their efforts that are familiar to endangered language planners: obtaining funding, overcoming negative attitudes toward the language, updating it to reflect contemporary life, introducing it into the education system, and dealing with organizational and membership problems within KEK itself. Related to these obstacles, KEK's literacy efforts have not reached far into rural areas. In the late 1990s, there was not one English-Creole dictionary in Penville, although the school library had a list of Patwa lexicon and English translations handwritten by a former Peace Corps volunteer. Patwa literacy so far belongs to the more educated urban classes for whom it is typically not the first language. In general, the most fluent speakers of Patwa are the least likely to be literate in any language.

When Patwa appears in written form, like in newspapers or the occasional store advertisement, it is rarely written with anything resembling the standard orthography. In 1998 Rabess reported that about 2,000 copies of the dictionary were sold, mostly to Dominicans living abroad—many of whom wanted to introduce their children to the language. Other consumers of the dictionary are foreigners wanting to learn Patwa, such as Peace Corps volunteers, tourists, and anthropologists. Few rural peoples had seen the other publications, and some even told me that there was no accepted way to write Patwa. The creation of literacy in Patwa actually may have served to accentuate the social divisions between urban/rural and educated/non-educated Dominicans by rendering this new register inaccessible to most of the public.

This conflict is symbolized in the changing of the name "Patwa" (from French *patois*) to "Kwéyòl" among urban activists. This was done in part to signal an affinity with other creole-speaking nations, several of which had chosen similar names in pro-creole movements. It also represented a shift from an oral language to a written language recognized as having grammar, and an attempt to erase negative connotations of slavery, colonial origins, and European debasement. Henderson (1988) explains:

> Although the language is well known as creole today, it was not always known by that name. In fact, for many, many years, it was referred to as patois, a word which only helped portray the language as a dialect of common people. However, it was changed to creole after a Dominica delegation attended a workshop which was organised by the St. Lucia Committee in St. Lucia. Creole has all the established qualities of a fully developed language, its own grammar, syntax and orthography.

Thus, the negative aspects of Patwa's history could be erased with a name change, while retaining positive associations with a romanticized version of rural life prior to the mid-twentieth century. Use of the name Kwéyòl plugs Dominica into a larger pan-Caribbean movement and smoothes out power differences internal to the nation; however, rural villagers continue to refer to their language as Patwa, reinforcing rather than minimizing differences.

There has not been a significant focus on purism in Patwa speech or writing to date, in contrast to other multilingual or language shift settings where the standardizing discourses of minority language activists critique hybrid language practices (e.g., Hill and Hill 1986; Jaffe 1999, 2007b). Dominicans of varying ages told me that people increasingly speak "broken Patwa," but this is of little concern compared to the widespread desire to speak "good" English.[19]

Rabess expressed a deeper concern regarding English and also Patwa in my interview with him:

> We feel that the problem is really how English is actually taught in the schools, rather than Creole. ... Because at the end of the day, we don't speak proper English. When I say proper English, what is referred to as standard English or - or grammatically correct English. And um, and we don't speak Creole properly either, so we end up speaking no language properly. ... That's the problem we have.

This perception of not speaking any language properly underlies discourses about language in both urban and rural settings, but is rarely articulated in everyday life.

KEK has tried to bring Patwa into more active use in public contexts. Members view as one of their greatest accomplishments the establishment of the annual *Jounen Kwéyòl* or Creole Day preceding independence celebrations, when the speaking of Patwa is encouraged in all domains from which its use would normally be restricted, as in schools, government offices, businesses, and banks. *Jounen Kwéyòl* occurs on International Creole Day, a celebration held in French creole speaking areas in the Caribbean and Indian Ocean (such as Réunion, Mauritius, and the Seychelles), and in countries where residents of these islands have migrated. A guide to Dominica's cultural events and organizations describes it as "a day when Dominicans go back to their roots and dress in the national wear, speak a lot of Kwéyòl, and cook mainly traditional foods in traditional style" (Cultural Division 1993: 9). It was reportedly so successful in the 1980s that it was expanded to *Simmen Kwéyòl* or Creole Week, leading up to Creole Day on the last Friday in October. During the week vendors sell creole foods and clothing made from creole madras cloth on the streets of Roseau. On Creole Day everyone in the country is called upon to speak Patwa in all settings, including children at school where it is otherwise strictly forbidden. Children perform Patwa songs and short skits, although the focus tends to be more on traditional dance and music. There are competitions for best creole dress and children are offered a creole lunch, such as roasted breadfruit with salted codfish.

Despite continuing national rhetoric that Patwa is "spoken everywhere" on Creole Day, KEK members and other observers have pointed out that the focus has shifted from the language to other markers of creole identity. Rabess explained: "But you have a de-emphasis now on the language. There is a lot of emphasis on the cuisine, the dress, and so on. But the language aspect of it in terms of Creole Week celebrations has sort of declined so we would want to put it back to the fore." Another member pointed out that "we're losing our focus" on the language (Sonia Akpa, Creole Language Component of the First World Creole Music Festival, speech given October 30, 1997). However, there is also some question as to how many people actually spoke that much more Patwa on Creole Day.[20] Perhaps even more significant is the contradiction involved in having only one day acceptable for speaking Patwa in all settings. Christie (1969: 24) also noted this: "The dilemma is reflected in Dominica in official policy which on the one hand bans the use of Creole in schools and on the other offers prizes for Creole stories and songs on an important national occasion." One education official told me, "To me, it's just a day. I mean it doesn't continue after that. … It hasn't reached the point where we let it permeate, you know, the rest of our lives and so on for the rest of the year."

Many rural villagers, on the contrary, claim that English needs to be the focus. The Penville nurse highlighted a continuing disjuncture between rural and urban experiences. She explained that for Roseau residents Creole Day is fun because "it's strange to them." For rural villagers, however, "Creole Day is every day":

Because for us, we always speak Patwa. So Creole Day is no new thing. But if you go to Roseau on creole day, it's an excitement. All the places, if you go to the banks, these young girls they never spoke Patwa but you hear them talking, you know? So it's strange, and it - it - it sounds better than even we here because we so used to Patwa. So [here] it's like every day is Creole Day.

While villagers generally express positive or neutral attitudes toward KEK's efforts, most claim they have little impact on their daily lives. Ultimately, celebrating Patwa once a year may contribute not to its continued active use, but perhaps more to its "museumification" as a cultural artifact for display and memory.[21] The affective saliency and even subversive power of the language in village life—to be explored in the following chapters—may be neutralized as it becomes a form of cultural heritage to be preserved rather than lived.

Despite the sentiments of rural villagers, KEK plans to introduce Patwa into the formal education system, paralleling efforts elsewhere in the Caribbean (e.g., Migge et al. 2010). There is no concrete procedure for implementation yet, though there have been recent discussions regarding funding and curriculum. Suggestions range from teaching Patwa songs and games in the primary grades to teaching Patwa literacy at the secondary level. KEK faces at least two significant obstacles: securing limited funding from the Ministry of Education to develop a program, and dealing with objections from rural communities where Patwa was until recently the dominant language. KEK carried out two surveys among teachers and secondary school students to explore attitudes (Fontaine and Leather 1992; Konmité Pou Étid Kwéyòl 1997). The surveys generated mixed results, with students expressing more positive views than teachers, who were divided roughly in half on whether it should be introduced in schools.[22] During an interview Ronald Green, then Minister of Education and Sports, expressed positive attitudes toward this project, describing Patwa as "our national language"—quite a change from earlier education reports that claimed it was "of no cultural value" (Hammond 1945). Yet he said that one of the first priorities for the ministry is not developing a creole curriculum, but teaching all primary children to read by the third grade. He explained: "So some would say that to bring in the issue of Creole at a time when we're looking at quote unquote more substantive matters. ... You have to prioritize." Like most teachers, education officials, and rural parents, he expressed the strongly held view that learning English is the top priority. He articulated the central question that KEK will have to address: "What can we do to introduce Creole in a way that allows us still to advance significantly in English but also to make sure that our national language doesn't get lost somewhere along the lines?"

"Resuscitating" the Culture: Village Cultural Groups and National Performances

In addition to KEK, the Cultural Division promotes selected creole forms. The National Day celebrations started by Leblanc have been expanded into several months of cultural shows and events leading to Independence Day on November 3. Many activities are aimed at young people, including youth rallies, athletics competitions, dances, art exhibitions, parades, Creole Day, and a three-day World Creole Music Festival since 1997. There are several rounds of cultural competitions, usually beginning in mid-September, during which community cultural groups from different districts compete in dance, music, song, and story (Figure 1.2). The cultural competitions include four categories in which Patwa is used: *kont* (Patwa folk story);[23] individual song; group song; and *bélé*, an African-influenced dance performed to Patwa lyrics and a drum beat. There is also a *Kokoy tory* (Kokoy story) category, analogous to the Patwa *kont* and added in the 1990s. One winner from each category participates in the Cultural Gala, a grand finale held in Roseau on November 3 after a day of parades, awards, and speeches (in English) by the President and Prime Minister. The following day is National Day of Community Service when villagers are encouraged to come together in *koudmen* style to work on community improvement, such as fixing roads. The government contributes financial aid and/or supplies for approved projects. Independence activities are very popular and are broadcast on radio and television.

Figure 1.2 The Penville Cultural Group performs in Roseau

A main function of the cultural competitions is to display and preserve traditional Dominican cultural forms. In the speeches that precede the performances, activists and local politicians frequently employ a discourse of cultural and linguistic endangerment, and charge rural peoples with the task of maintaining traditional culture. In 1997 speakers repeatedly lamented the "death" of Dominican culture. One speaker called for a return to "the old days":

> What has happened to the musicians? What has happened to the performers? And while I admit the Cultural Division has been trying its best, doing what it can, but we have to go one step further (pause) so the people can go back to the old days of practicing the culture and performing, because our culture represents us. And when our culture dies, we die as a people. (Reginald Austrie, Parliamentary Representative, Cottage Constituency, speech given September 28, 1997)

Another speaker similarly employed metaphors of life and death, referring to the participants as "those of you who recognize the demise of culture in this country and you want to resuscitate it" (Matthew Walter, Parliamentary Representative, Paix Bouche Constituency, speech given September 28, 1997). Raising his hands in the air, he encouraged participants not to give up if they did not win because, "We want to uplift culture. We don't want to kill culture in Dominica." There was a sentiment that people should unite to save the culture, rather than being interested in their own personal advancement or failure: if they give up, they will "kill" the culture.

Anxieties about national development and the global market also permeated discussions that season. Of particular concern was the World Trade Organization's (WTO) decision to dismantle the preferential European market for Windward Caribbean bananas, thus opening up competition from Latin America and threatening Dominica's monocrop economy. The Mayor of Portsmouth considered this in his speech:

> By now you must be very familiar with those terms, WTO, globalization, and what have you. What we are seeing, it is having adverse effects on us as a people. And it is also reflective in the fact that our culture now is under attack. And it is even more so important for us to recognize that in this - the world out there, our culture should be a source of *strength* to us. We should use our culture (pause) to give us that resolve to (pause) to attack and to deal, to address some of the difficulties that we are facing. (Julien Brewster, speech given September 28, 1997)

At the point when the mayor claimed that the culture was under attack, several audience members applauded loudly and called out in support.

American television programming was also blamed for the demise of Dominican culture. Pierre Charles, then Parliamentary Representative for the South and later Dominica's Prime Minister (2000–2004), highlighted this:

> [W]e're a developing country struggling to maintain our own identity. We're struggling against about twenty U.S. TV channels beaming at us everyday, and one of the ways to control you is through cultural domination. And therefore I say hats off to the people who continue to maintain our cultural stand. (Pierre Charles, speech given October 14, 1997)

This sentiment that Dominican culture is threatened by cultural domination from external forces continues to circulate. During return visits in 2006 and 2008 I was told by Cultural Division personnel, teachers, and parents that children, especially boys, are more likely to imitate the dances they see on the American television station BET (Black Entertainment Television) than Dominican forms. I observed this in Penville in 2006, as several groups of teenage boys performed hip hop music and dances rather than traditional ones at a cultural competition during Carnival. Earlier that day, however, a traditional *jing ping* band composed of adults of all ages had led a group of children in a carnival procession down the main road. Villagers enjoyed both events as they participated in a blending of cultural forms, rather than mounting a "cultural stand" against outside influences popular with their youth.

The Independence speeches are full of national sentiment and calls to persevere by developing the nation, uniting the people, and saving the culture. This concern with national and personal development is reflected in the slogans chosen to represent the Independence celebrations each year, for example: "Serving with Pride and Dignity" (1996), "Work to Achieve" (1997), "Building Country, Celebrating Heritage" (2007), and "Celebrating the Journey Together" (2008, thirtieth anniversary of independence). Language is subsumed within this broader discourse on culture. Patwa represents the "true" identity of the people and is a potential force for fighting off external pressures. For example, Pierre Charles continued his call for Dominicans to express their unique identity:

> Let us continue to participate in the cultural exchanges and activities so that our own identity can stand out. What it is to be Dominican. You know some Dominicans they talk like /jay/ [Jamaican] people. They want to move around and talk like Jamaicans. Jamaicans don't try to talk like Dominicans. We are Dominicans, we are who we are. And therefore we should continue to exhibit what we are. (Pierre Charles, speech given October 14, 1997)

He was met with a loud round of applause. He continued:

Some people afraid to talk Kwéyòl. I talk Kwéyòl anywhere in the world, wherever I go. I do not look back to see who is there, because it is ours. Nobody taught me how to speak Kwéyòl you know. It was part of me, and therefore I cannot be ashamed to speak Kwéyòl anywhere. (Pierre Charles, speech given October 14, 1997)

Here, "Patwa" becomes "Kwéyòl," and Kwéyòl is something to be proud of, an innate part of what it means to be Dominican. While many villagers agree, most continue to restrict their children from using Patwa in favor of ensuring their English acquisition. Even in his speech extolling the value of speaking Kwéyòl anywhere, Pierre speaks English to his audience of Dominicans. Ultimately, one can still be Dominican without speaking Patwa; local varieties of both English and Patwa are acceptable in practice, particularly when contrasted with the languages of "outsiders" like Jamaicans as well as a recent wave of Spanish-speaking immigrants from the Dominican Republic.

This disjuncture between national rhetoric and everyday practice becomes evident during the cultural competitions. Despite the four categories that focus on the performance of Patwa, almost all communication takes place in English. The speeches, prayers, national anthem, and most of the talk between performances are in English, aside from sporadic Patwa jokes. Further, the Cultural Division finds that it often needs to teach cultural group members so-called traditional cultural forms, especially the dances, for the shows. Yet when the performances are put on, they are portrayed as "natural," "authentic," and the way rural peoples have always expressed themselves, overlooking the months of lessons and practice required.[24] When Penville villagers founded their cultural group in 1991, none of the members—adults in their twenties and thirties—knew any of the older dances, not having seen them performed in the community. They repeatedly asked community elders to instruct them, but all refused. The members perceived this as the elders feeling "something negative" toward the dances or toward interacting with young people. The group founder explained:

Well it was (pause) is really our group who really brought back the culture into Penville. It used to be very alive in Penville, but for some years ago, for some reason or another, it just stopped. So we never saw Penville people dance. You know? We never had an idea of - So when we went to the other areas there and Vieille Case is there, and Capucine is there, we said but why, why can't we not give it a try? ((laughs)) And we just went forward.

The members participated in workshops organized by the Cultural Division to learn how to do the dances and to perform Patwa songs and stories. The Penville Cultural Group flourished in the late 1990s when its founders were

Figure 1.3 The Penville Children's Cultural Group dances at a Cultural Gala

active members, including twelve adults and a newly established children's cultural group with eight members (Figure 1.3). By 2010, however, I found that the group had disbanded altogether due to lack of participation.

The performances during cultural celebrations also include subtle changes from how such forms were performed generations ago. *Bélé* and *kont* adhere most to their traditional forms, although both contain code-switching into English (often for rhetorical impact in *kont*). The overall context has changed dramatically, however, in that the dances and stories traditionally were performed with the audience as active participants, rather than watching people perform on stage. In contrast to the spontaneous, orally transmitted Patwa work songs, children's songs, and Christmas carols recalled by elders, most cultural groups write their songs so they can be practiced and refined. Further, the songs, while using Patwa lyrics, generally focus on content that is not related to enduring concerns like family life and morality, as found in *kont* and *bélé*. Many address the theme of national development and those that deal most directly with this theme tend to win the prize. This was the case with the Penville Cultural Group's winning 1996 Patwa song, "*Jenn jan lévé*" (Young People Rise Up). The chorus urged young people to contribute to society and to participate in cultural events: "*Jenn jan lévé. Pa wèsté size. Fo pa ou gadé asi moun ki ja tonbé*" (Young people rise up. Don't stay sitting. Don't look to people who've already fallen). The song encouraged youth to emulate several Dominican men who participated in the 1996 Summer Olympics in the U.S. It continued: "*Gadé kò'w kon donmnitjen. Fè kéchòz ki positive. Pa kité drugs pwen lanmen ou. Ou ké igwété dèmen. É sé pa pou fè fenyan. Sa ki dèyè ké soufè"* (<u>Look at yourself as Dominican. Do something</u> positive. <u>Don't let</u> drugs <u>take your hand. You will regret tomorrow. And don't be lazy. He/she who is behind will suffer.</u>). While the lyrics are predominantly in Patwa and do comment on morality, particularly regarding drugs and laziness, the main content concerns national development, progress, and the cultural competitions for which this song was created. Despite this shift in content, the organizers see these categories as beneficial to maintaining Patwa in that they encourage it to be used at all. Raymond Lawrence, head of the Cultural Division, explained: "It keeps both the folk song, and *kont* and thing alive, and at the same time it helps the Creole language to stay alive."

The Commodification of Language and Culture

One way in which this "national language" is taking on new relevance is in deliberations about how to market creole culture as Dominica seeks to diversify its economic base and increase its tourism sector. There is a growing discourse about culture and language as commodities to be packaged and sold in the ecotourism industry and on the international music scene, utilizing discourses of consumerism, heritage tourism, and development (Bully 2003; Henckell 2007). Tourism is discussed as an alternative to the floundering banana industry, but in this discourse, language and culture are becoming remarkably similar to bananas as objects of exchange. They must be cultivated, cared for, and brought to maturity through practice and then offered to foreign buyers who may accept or reject them. This includes performances by average people and professional musicians, principally through popular contemporary Dominican forms like *kadans* and *bouyon*.[25] Patwa is performed for cruise ship and other tourists and is exported through recorded music and tours to other countries such as France and the United States. The government has a vested interest in encouraging the maintenance of creole linguistic and cultural forms that distinguish Dominica as a tourist site and in the music industry. Here Patwa no longer threatens national development, but becomes part of the project.

Lacking the white sand beaches and amenities of other Caribbean islands, such as large hotels and an international airport, Dominica is promoted as "the Nature Island of the Caribbean"—an exotic, unspoiled, untamed ecotourism destination with rivers, waterfalls, rainforest, and a boiling lake. It is described in tourism advertising as the only island that Columbus would recognize today (see Sheller 2003). A major recent project was the completion of a 115-mile hiking trail system linking villages as tourist sites, known as the Waitukubuli National Trail. But increasingly there is a discourse about selling creole culture along with the environment. Through such events as the annual World Creole Music Festival (WCMF), aimed at drawing an international audience, Patwa is being transformed from a symbol of the nation into what is called a "heritage culture product." Here, a discourse of language endangerment serves well to validate government intervention in language preservation and revitalization efforts. In such discussions, language planners, cultural activists, and national developers converge in promoting Dominican culture and language as well as generating revenue.

The WCMF was first added to *Simenn Kwéyòl* (Creole Week) during my fieldwork in 1997. It is a creole music festival held on the three nights leading to Independence Day. Several bands from Dominica and other creole-speaking regions perform on each night. It has since grown in popularity, attracting more international bands and a larger audience, although many Dominicans complain they cannot afford admission. Cultural activists, KEK members, and musical performers were involved in the creation of the WCMF; however, a significant role was played by the National Development Corporation (NDC) at all levels. The NDC's General Manager made clear the reasons for its involvement in the 1997 WCMF program guide:

> The National Development Corporation (NDC) has established the Dominica Festivals Commission (DFC) as a new and dynamic Division to ensure that there is carved out a greater space for Dominica's art, music, and culture in our socio-economic agenda for the new millennium. ... We are witnessing a re-birth—a renaissance—of the arts in Dominica, and this will play a pivotal role as a major component of Dominica's tourism product.

The NDC seeks to promote the arts in Dominica, but with the goal of expanding the tourism industry and hence the development of the nation. Patwa is described as "a world class product" to be marketed internationally through music. The goal is to put Dominica on the map as a tourist destination, a source of creole music, and part of a wider creole world.

The 1997 event began with an all-day workshop entitled the "Creole Language Component of the First World Creole Music Festival." It was by invitation only and was attended by KEK members and other activists, Cultural Division personnel, entertainers, invited guests (like me),[26] the radio, and the press. The workshop was divided into three parts entitled "Creole Language Positioning in the 21st Century Antilles," "Language/Music Synthesis," and "Copyright" (in music). Though a main focus was on the use of Patwa and its role in society and music, practically the entire workshop was conducted in English. The workshop began with KEK member Marcel Fontaine, meeting chairperson, welcoming and thanking the attendees in Patwa. He asked if everyone understood him and received a loud "No!" from one audience member. There was some laughter, and people made comments about not being able to speak creole at a workshop about the creole language.

Fontaine continued in Patwa, but soon stopped and said: "Okay, basically can we just stand and - for a minute and I'll probably just recite something in Creole, okay?" He recited a short prayer in Patwa. After a brief pause, he said, "At this point, I'll be code-switching alright?" There were a few murmurs in the audience, but he proceeded in English.

KEK members utilized the festival as a forum to discuss the status of Patwa and its potential for strengthening links to Martinique and Guadeloupe. Rabess later told me that such events help to "reinforce the creolism, the creole identity of the country." But while this has been a common theme in discussions on language and culture, a new discourse emerged in full force during this workshop: how to market Patwa to tourists. Sheridan Gregoire, Manager of the NDC, explained to the audience that the creole language and culture are "tourism products" that can become "a very, very important component of an entire economic framework":

> So, it appears to me that we are on track in seeing a rebirth and a rejuvenation of the culture in all its expressions. And obviously in order to express it you—you are *bound* to have the language. So we need in fact to develop that language to the fullest in order that we can express the culture to its fullest extent and in order also to ensure that the culture can become (pause) a very, very important component of an entire economic framework. What we have done in the NDC is we have recognized that culture is an important aspect of our tourism product. Because for many years now we have heard visitors say that Dominicans are a warm and friendly people. They're *friendlier* than many other peoples that they've been to in many countries. I think for too long we've taken that fact for granted, and I think we need now to ensure that that is packaged and promoted and exported, because in fact, it sells.

Culture is a "product" that can be packaged to "sell." Language figures in this as an expression of culture and marker of authenticity. It is not necessary in terms of communicating with visitors from the U.S. or Europe, but is a symbol of Dominican identity that can be used to cultivate an exotic image for profit. While in other situations Patwa is a form of symbolic capital for connecting to one's heritage, in this discourse it becomes a commodity—an object of exchange—in itself (da Silva et al. 2007; Heller 2003; Irvine 1989).

These discourses remain strong in Dominica today where, as in communities around the world, local flavor is being marketed to support a struggling economy. In his 2007 Independence Day address to the nation, Prime Minister Roosevelt Skerrit made this explicit: "With respect to product development, the government wishes to draw on the natural and cultural heritage of Dominica to create wealth and employment." This message is highlighted throughout the year in other events, news reports, and political speeches, during which speakers use economic metaphors to encourage performers to "exploit," "develop," and "market" their "unique" practices for profit and to "save" a "dying" culture. In 2008 I attended a Panel Discussion on Village Feasts and Cultural Renewal in the village of Paix Bouche, which was broadcast by radio and television throughout the nation. It was part of a series of meetings by representatives from the Cultural Division and other government ministries to engage with the public in preparation for Dominica's thirtieth anniversary of independence. During this panel discussion the five speakers and several audience members employed the discourse of cultural loss and revitalization, and the discourse of development and culture/language as commodities. In talking about the need for cultural renewal, participants mourned the loss of traditional creole foods, dress, *jing ping* music, folklore, and children's ring games. Complaints included the commercialization of village feasts and cultural activities, the use of Patwa only on Creole Day, declining feelings of community, and a "gradual breakdown in family and society." At the same time, however, some suggested that "change is inevitable" and that a primary strategy for keeping these activities in use should be to increase their value as "products." Cultural Division head Raymond Lawrence spoke of them as "cultural heritage assets" and "tourism products" that could be "packaged" to bring economic benefits to communities and the nation. All agreed that "tradition" should be maintained as close to its "original" form as possible, but that it also must be updated and sold to keep it from slipping further into "decline."

Discussion: Shifting Discourses and Identities

The discourses surrounding Dominica's languages and cultures have changed over time and reflect processes of inclusion and exclusion. Once rejected as backward and divisive, representing the conflicting interests of two colonial powers as well as urban/rural groups, Patwa is now considered part of a national identity cultivated for the outside world through performances and export to richer countries. But while recent efforts toward national unity have promoted more positive attitudes, especially in urban settings, since the 1960s most villages have been evidencing a shift away from Patwa to varieties of English. Despite national rhetoric valuing Patwa symbolically, and increasingly materially, it remains largely an oral language and rural peoples are conflicted about the teaching of Patwa in their schools. Many villagers participate in annual independence celebrations and other cultural events as performers or audiences, but practices such as Patwa songs and storytelling, and traditional dances and music, are becoming further removed from the everyday as something to be performed on particular occasions. Villages are encouraged to form cultural groups to preserve them, but instructors must be sent by the Cultural Division to teach these practices that are supposedly part and parcel of Dominican culture.

Further, language and culture are becoming objects of exchange in the local and global economy. For a small geographically bounded island nation reeling from the collapse of the banana industry and struggling to develop tourism with limited amenities and financial resources, a creole language can be played with as an economic and political tool for connecting with a larger pan-Caribbean identity and African diaspora. While such commoditization of cultural practices may offer alternative means of economic survival, it further marks them as special activities for events like the Cultural Gala, Creole Day, and WCMF. The commodification and championing of Patwa in national discourses may reflect changing attitudes, but these efforts remain distinct from everyday practice and are largely limited to certain times of the year.

For those in power, Patwa is a linguistic emblem of national identity that comes from "the people." This is paradoxical, however, as the rural population struggles to bring English into their communities and teach it to their children, and English remains the only official language of the nation. English is associated with modernity and progress, while Patwa becomes ever more associated with agrarian life, the past, and cultural heritage performances. Patwa activism exists alongside rather than as part of the daily reality of people's lives as they struggle to make ends meet. Research on reversing language shift suggests that creating literacy is a critical step toward preservation. However, Patwa literacy seems to further validate the social hierarchy, which used to be more clearly dichotomous—English for the elite, Patwa for lower classes. Now, Patwa is becoming stratified as well—written, anglicized Patwa for urban elites, oral Patwa for rural lower classes. Calls to preserve the nation's "shared" traditions obscure differential access to valued things like education, jobs, and linguistic resources.

It is critical to note that centuries of negative attitudes and policies toward Patwa did not squelch it, although they significantly impacted Dominicans' views toward it. In the chapters that follow, I describe the everyday lives of villagers who continue to speak it. I explore the complex language ideologies and language socialization practices of one community, as these suggest that both languages remain necessary in everyday life, though in ways that often differ from nationalist and revitalization discourses.

Notes

1. For example, Arteaga (1994), Ben-Rafael (1994), Blommaert (1994), Duchêne and Heller (2007), Errington (1998), Fierman (1991), Heller (2010), Irvine and Gal (2000), Jaffe (1999, 2007a, 2007b), Kroskrity (2000b, 2004), Maguire (1991), Philips

(2000), Stroud (2007), Tollefson and Tsui (2004), Urciuoli (1995), Urla (1993), and Woolard (1989).

2. See Bonner (2001), Gilroy (1987, 1993), Olwig (1993), Safa (1987), Schnepel (2004), Thomas (2004), Williams (1991), and Young (1993); also studies on folkloric performance and cultural authenticity in Quebec (Handler 1988), Greece (Herzfeld 1982), and Bolivia (Rockefeller 1999).

3. For critiques of these stereotypes, see Alleyne (1985), Bebel-Gisler (1976), Jourdan (1991), Garrett (2006), Holm (1989a), Le Page and Tabouret-Keller (1985), and Schieffelin and Doucet (1994).

4. Most slaves came from the larger trading centers of Martinique (the main seventeenth-century French slaving entrepot), Guadeloupe, Barbados, Antigua, and St. Kitts. When the British took control, the transport of slaves directly from Africa became common.

5. The Kalinago held control of the Windward Islands until about 1700, when they retreated into the virtually inaccessible forested interiors of Dominica and St. Vincent to escape Europeans.

6. Important amongst these early settlers were "free colored" peoples from the French islands. They came to Dominica to acquire land and escape social barriers as the French islands intensified the sugar industry. Many owned slaves and identified more with the white ruling class. These early settlers "set the stage for the emergence of a mulatto elite whose values reflected those of the white ruling class" (Baker 1994: 53), including deprecation of Patwa as a language of slavery and backwardness.

7. However, the percentage of citizens identifying as Catholic has decreased over the past three censuses in relation to growing influences from evangelical religions (76.9 percent in 1981, 70 percent in 1991, and 62.5 percent in 2001). The percentage of those identifying as Seventh Day Adventist, Pentecostal, and Baptist nearly doubled from 8.4 percent in 1981 to 15.7 percent in 2001. The category "Other" also increased from 8.9 percent in 1981 to 17.4 percent in 2001.

8. Administrators discussed bringing indentured servants from India as was done in Trinidad, Guyana, and Jamaica, but these plans were never carried out (Myers 1987: 12).

9. See Baker (1994), Myers (1981), and Trouillot (1988) on the formation of a peasantry.

10. Dominica became the first and only British Caribbean colony to have a black-controlled legislature following the abolition of slavery.

11. Dominica became the largest producer of limes in the world at the start of the twentieth century. New technologies were introduced at this time, including the telephone, electricity, and a coastal steamer ship service connecting to Roseau. By 1930, however, the lime industry was all but destroyed by disease, hurricanes, and falling prices.

12. Historical accounts call them the "mulatto gros bourg" (Honychurch 1995[1975]: 235), and villagers still refer to "rich people" as *gwoboug*.

13. Bananas became known as the "green gold" when the British transnational company Geest contracted with the Banana Associations of the Windward Islands to create an advantageous preferential European market for their crops.

14. Universal adult suffrage was granted in 1951.

15. Another early cultural activist was Mabel "Cissie" Caudeiron (1909–1968).

16. The date was moved to the anniversary of Columbus's "discovery" of Dominica, November 3.

17. Two additional radio stations now broadcast Patwa programming.
18. It was first created as an exploratory group, the Standing Committee for Creole Studies (SCCS), to develop an orthography for the oral language (see Stuart 1993).
19. Some prescriptive ideologies occasionally do emerge in public discussions and the media. Further, those who use Patwa in non-traditional domains are challenged with deciding what word to use when no Patwa term exists. Activists often speak the English form with Patwa phonology, whereas villagers tend to code-switch into English. In a KEK workshop in 1997, one activist said: "*pou fè an pwézantasyan an konfwans la*" (to make a presentation in the conference). If Patwa is introduced in schools, standardization will become a more pressing issue.
20. Honychurch (1993[1991]: 118) states: "The national radio station broadcasts in Creole for the entire day and in theory everyone should go about their business in Creole, although in practice, after a few jovial Creole salutations, just to make the point, most people lapse into English for more complex business transactions."
21. Thanks to Daniel Hieber for suggesting the term "museumification."
22. The teacher survey represented slightly less than a quarter of all teachers employed at the time. Penville teachers were given the survey and all responded, but no one returned to pick them up and thus they were not counted in the analysis.
23. For examples of Dominican *kont*, see G. Smith (1991).
24. Thus many rural peoples are taught these cultural practices by people from the city, for whom they then put on the show.
25. *Kadans* is a Dominican form comprised of three musical styles: *calypso, mazouk,* and *beguine. Bouyon* is attributed to the popular Dominican group W.C.K., and is a fusion of *kadans* and traditional *jing ping* music. Both employ Patwa and English lyrics.
26. Other invited speakers included Hubert Devonish, a linguist at the UWI Department of Linguistics at Mona, Jamaica, and Kennedy Samuel, a Kwéyòl activist from St. Lucia.

CHAPTER 2

Childhood in a Village "Behind God's Back"

Located on a winding road in northern Dominica, Penville has approximately 750 residents in just over two hundred households.[1] Approximately one third of its population is under the age of fifteen years with about eighty children under the age of five years. Residents describe their community as *dèyè do Bondyé* or "behind God's back," referring to its remote location and lack of development. A metaphorical framework of "bringing in" things from the outside shapes how villagers conceive of their community and languages. Despite these perceptions of isolation, however, villagers are thoroughly integrated in the national and global speech economies within which their languages are continually evaluated. To understand the shift from Patwa to English, we must examine the interrelations between Penville's location, the continual movement of people, objects, languages, and ideologies in and out of it, and residents' perceptions of tradition, change, and community identity. While much has changed, particularly their expectations and goals, much remains the same, like how most villagers struggle daily just to eke out a living.

In this chapter I sketch out this historical background and describe the social organization of village life. I explore how residents have incorporated new technologies and ascribed meaning to them, particularly roads, schools, electricity, piped water, processed foods, and religion. The importance of English is discussed in depth in chapter 3. These represent a complex of things "brought in" to Penville, but as the modern is introduced and embraced, it is also blended with the traditional in syncretic and socially distributed ways. Further, symbols that have long marked Penville villagers as "rural" and "backward" at the community level—their homes, clothing, foods, occupations, and language—now differentiate people within the community. After describing the village I provide portraits of the six focal children and their households as representing a range of family types. These ethnographic descriptions contextualize the language shift within people's interpretations of their changing community and nation. The portraits also introduce the next sets of actors who play with language and who are the focus of the following chapters—the children and their families.

Locating the Village

Penville is perched on a mountainside facing east toward the communities of Vieille Case and Thibaud. There is evidence of Kalinago presence prior to European settlement (Jefferys 1768; see also Honychurch 1997: 190) and many villagers claim some Kalinago ancestry. Like other post-emancipation villages, however, Penville grew up around small French coffee and cocoa-producing estates dating to the 1700s.[2] Most adults told me that their forefathers were French planters and enslaved Africans who came from Guadeloupe and dominated the area for a long time. It is recognized that Patwa was in some sense imported by these early settlers and created under conditions of slavery and forced transplantation of African peoples.[3] However, villagers see Patwa as being "natural" to them. English was brought in later by the British who remained in Roseau and did not settle as far north as Penville. In the mid-1800s, a Scotsman and his French wife purchased several estates, but their offspring had abandoned them by the early 1900s.

As in other agricultural communities, homes and buildings are constructed along a main road while farmland is located on the surrounding hillsides. Penville is separated into five hamlets: Lower Penville (*Lod Bò*), Upper Penville (*Anho Mòn*), Galba (also *Ovan*), La Haut, and Delaford (Map 2.3). Upper Penville is the central gathering place. It has the largest shops, a disco, several rum shops, a Village Council meetinghouse, a Credit Union, and a recently built arts and crafts center. It is the site of the Government Primary School serving children from all five hamlets from grades one to seven and an independently funded preschool.[4] Just below the primary school is the health clinic where a doctor from town visits every fortnight, and below that is a large field where children play at recess and villagers hold cricket matches and rounders games on Sunday afternoons. Both Upper and Lower Penville have post offices and bread bakeries. People identify with specific hamlets, but share kinship ties that traverse geographic boundaries. There is a strong sense that they all belong to one community.

Most residents depend on the land for their livelihood and survival (Figure 2.1). All six of the focal families engaged in farming in addition to other work. Villagers complain of the labor required to plant, harvest, and transport their produce since much of the farmland is located along the steep slopes of Morne aux Diable, which rises 2,826 feet above sea level. But with fertile volcanic soil and abundant rainfall, Penville is well suited to subsistence and small-scale market gardening (Figure 2.2). Related to this, land is a common topic of discussion and there are frequent contestations over land rights, obligations, and intentions. Land ownership secures a place of residence and means of subsistence, but also is central to the construction of social identities, kin networks, and affective ties.[5] As

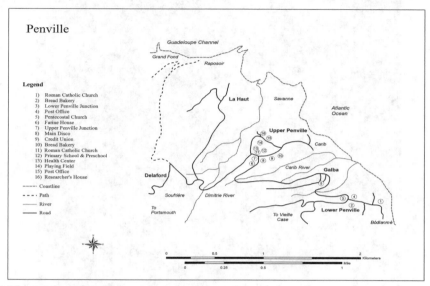

Map 2.3 Penville Village

Figure 2.1 Farmers cut and carry bananas to pack for export

Figure 2.2 Villager carries a basket of produce harvested from her garden

elsewhere in the Caribbean, a predominant inheritance practice is "family land," whereby a parcel of land is owned jointly by descendants of the original owner, either male or female, and its use is determined by consensus or family tradition. Oral agreements over access and compensation frequently lead to disputes. People who do not own land rent from individual owners or simply squat.

The family is the locus of village social relations. I was frequently told that in Penville, "we all one family." This refers to a sense of community connectedness and the fact that most people can trace at least some kin relation to others in the community. Kinship is reckoned through consanguineal and affinal ties, although godparents and close friends often are treated as family. Three principal types of unions are found: extra-residential visitation, consensual union or cohabitation, and legal marriage.[6] These often proceed in this order, with marriage being the professed ideal after age thirty for many. A basic common household structure is difficult to demarcate as this varies widely and can be fluid over time. A household may be composed of a single person living alone (usually a male of any age or an older female), a woman with her children (perhaps "visited" by her boyfriend), a nuclear family (married or by mutual consent), or an extended household or "houseyard" including several generations. Many young people have children, often with multiple partners, and may cohabit for years before legally marrying despite discouragement from clergy and healthcare professionals. A father is expected to contribute financially to his children regardless of his relationship with the mother, but this does not always happen in practice.

Despite their perceived rootedness, kinship ties extend beyond the immediate household, village, and even island. Migration occurs regularly within Dominica and transnationally to other Caribbean islands, England, the United States, and Canada. Often villagers migrate to where there are Dominican communities, as in Guadeloupe, Martinique, St. Lucia, and St. Marten. Many obtain a six-month visa and work in construction or the service industry (e.g., restaurants, hotels, childcare). Some overstay and either obtain residency or are detected and return to Dominica. Through transnational migration, extensive networks of exchange and mutual support reach across geographic boundaries. In Penville such networks are sustained through child fostering, remittances, return migration, visiting relatives overseas when "on holiday" or to work, and frequent narrative activity about where people are and what they are doing there. Many households depend on remittances as a primary or secondary source of income. Children of various ages are left with relatives by their transnational parents. Some children visit family on other islands when the school term ends, or live with relations in town to attend a better school. Of the six focal children, one resided with his grandparents and three others had an immediate family member emigrate during the main fieldwork period (two fathers and a sister). All six families had past transnational experience and kin living abroad. People frequently and fluidly undergo major life changes—migrating to another village, town, or country; moving in with a family member; alternating between their parents' home and a partner's home; switching occupations—in other words, doing what is necessary at the time.

A Changing Community: The Impact of Roads, Schools, and Electricity

Like many villages, Penville was relatively isolated until the mid-twentieth century. Most social connections were with the neighboring community of Vieille Case and across the channel in Guadeloupe. Villagers had to travel a path over a mountainous area known as Soufrière to reach Portsmouth to sell their produce or to take a steamer ship to Roseau. They referred to this path as "the old French road" from when French planters inhabited the area in the eighteenth century.[7] Older residents recall how they or their parents carried sacks of vegetables and fruit on their heads for the long two to three hour walk each way, returning with supplies after they sold their produce. Most walked and some led donkeys; rarely, they traveled by horse, a symbol of wealth. Villagers were by necessity largely self-sufficient. They grew and traded food for what they needed, gave birth with the help of a local *chasfanm* (midwife),[8] and worked cooperatively with handmade tools and local materials to build each other's houses and do other large projects, a practice known as *koudmen*. There were no local schools, electricity, or piped water, and commercial goods were limited to what people could carry over the mountain. Purchased staples included salted codfish, sugar, kerosene, and clothing, though most people reportedly used *siwo* (cane juice) instead of sugar and made their own clothes. Villagers describe these times as difficult, but speak of them nostalgically as "simpler" and "better" than today. People treated one another as "brothers and sisters" and helped anyone in need. Residents of all ages gathered on moonlit nights to share stories and jokes in Patwa. The introduction of new technologies and amenities in the late 1940s brought rapid changes, including more privatized communication in the home and a shift from Patwa monolingualism toward English.

Village adults cite the introduction of the following as catalysts for social and linguistic change: the village school in the late 1940s (improved in the 1980s), roads in the 1950s and 1960s, and electricity in 1986. Descendants of the French-Scottish family who owned land in Penville initiated many of these changes. Hugh and Beryl Harris moved from Roseau to their family's estate in 1939, although they had returned to town by 1950.[9] While formal education was compulsory, attendance rates for Penville children were low and sporadic (the closest government school was three miles away in Vieille Case). The Harris couple became concerned about their own seven children making the daily six-mile roundtrip walk and utilized their personal connections to secure government support for a new school in Upper Penville. This "bought in" the first English domain. Initially it was a small infant school funded partly by the government, partly by the Harris family, and supplemented with a penny a week by the students' families. Later the wooden building was expanded to accommodate classes from Stage 1 (now Grade 1) through school leaving at Form 3 (now part of junior secondary school), following the national curriculum. The school provided a new venue for accessing English and was the first context in which Patwa was forbidden, to the extent possible, from being spoken by children. Mrs. Harris told me that within just a couple years of the school's construction, "English was being spoken by almost everyone at Upper and Lower Penville." While this may be exaggerated, villagers claim they intentionally began encouraging English after the school was built. Often this entailed speaking Patwa to children but only permitting them to respond in English. In 1979 Hurricane David flattened the wooden schoolhouse. For four years, the children attended school in Vieille Case again until the government completed a new larger concrete-block school in 1983. The two-room preschool was built next to it. Villagers cite this vast improvement in educational facilities as central to community development.

As the school provided English, new roads began to open up the countryside and usher in more changes to rural communities. The Harrises were instrumental in ensuring that a road connected to Penville from the east by the 1950s. The construction and ongoing maintenance of the winding road, with its switchbacks and proneness to landslides and washouts during heavy rain, has challenged generations of residents. But villagers pinpoint the road as essential to community accessibility and growth. Soon after its completion, a periodic bus service linked the formerly remote area to other villages and the towns. Service to Roseau increased from one bus making two trips a month, to two buses going every day except Sunday. Out-migration also increased dramatically in the 1950 and 1960s, especially to Roseau. But as many people went out, the road made possible the bringing in of new technologies, amenities, and ideas.

In 1986 electricity reached Penville. Villagers say it brought dramatic changes, allowing new conveniences and altering intergenerational patterns of social interaction and cultural transmission. It immediately created new rifts as more prosperous villagers began service while others could not (using candles and kerosene lamps instead). Electricity made possible a myriad of appliances that residents could only dream of before, though they were aware they existed. The most frequently cited impact of electricity is on leisure time. Before, adults say they gathered by candlelight or lantern at the homes of friends and family to listen to and participate in the telling of Patwa *kont* (folktales) and *timtim* (riddles) by elders. This was the main form of entertainment after work and a site of community gathering and unity, with children included. Since electricity, villagers claim this has been replaced by (English) television. One woman in her late thirties told me that on moonlit nights when it was easy to see the road,

> People would go and sit at a neighbor's home. Three, four neighbors would go together, and the elderlies would take out those stories. We would listen. It would get exciting! But now you hardly find those things happening. You know? So it's like it's not passed on. ... Now everybody has their TV, so instead, people sit and look at "The Young and the Restless" and stuff like that.

Young parents today talk about *kont* and *timtim* as part of the past, something their parents and grandparents did but they are not doing with their own children. Employing the discourse of cultural decline, a woman in her forties explained nostalgically how her children enjoyed hearing riddles one night when the electricity went off:

> I remember at one time Penville was so rich in culture. And everything, or almost everything, has died out. Because I remember we would listen to *kont* and *timtim* and all these thing. And some time ago well, we had no lights. The lights went. So we were just sitting around the table with a lamp and so. So then now, my mother started to tell the children some *timtim* and they were so excited! So happy to hear these things.

People in their sixties and seventies told me that they once knew many *timtim* and *kont*, as well as the dances and music celebrated at Independence time, but now they can no longer remember them and are not teaching them to new generations. While these traditional forms have taken on value at national events, in the village they have come to index poverty, lack of education, and inability to afford a TV and DVD player. When much-awaited cable television finally reached Penville in the early 2000s, all six focal families connected as soon as they could despite that several could not afford indoor plumbing.

Six Family Portraits

The following portraits of the six focal families further illustrate the changing nature of daily life and communicative practices. All were working families like other Penville residents. Some, like Tamika and Kenrick's families, were barely scraping by day to day. Others, like Reiston's grandparents, had accumulated some savings and received financial support from the parents of the children they fostered. The others had varying incomes that fluctuated in the period of one year, as in Jonah's family. His father worked on another island for half a year but then was hospitalized for a serious illness and could not earn for months. In this farming community, many families prosper until their livelihood is devastated when a hurricane destroys their banana plants or other crops. There are only a handful of professionals and they tend to own the shops and bread bakeries as well. Thus there is not extensive variation in socioeconomic status or education among the focal families, like among villagers overall.[10] They differ, however, in their aspirations for themselves and their children. Several invested heavily in markers of higher socioeconomic status like concrete-block houses, amenities like indoor plumbing, and

Table 2.1. The focal children and their families and playmates

Focal child	Age range recorded (year;month)	Sex	Household members	Non-resident child playmates
Alisia	1;11–2;10	Female	Mother: Grace Father: Clement Sisters: Josette, Natalie Brothers: Tedison, Lestrade	Neighbor: Roselia Other: three cousins from down the road
Jonah	2;0–2;11	Male	Mother: Marlena Father: Jude Sister: Theodora Brother: Aaron Cousin: Roma	Brother: Abraham Cousins: Claudette, two neighboring cousins Other: three cousins by maternal grandfather
Kenrick	1;10–2;10	Male	Mother: Tessa Father: Felix Brothers: Daniel, Nicky	Cousins: Tamika, Henry, Vanessa, Glenda, Samuel, Robert, Abigail
Tamika	2;3–3;2	Female	Mother: Lorna Father: David Sisters: Glenda, Vanessa	Cousins: Kenrick, Henry, Vanessa, Glenda, Samuel, Robert, Abigail
Reiston	2;9–3;9	Male	Grandmother: Josephine Grandfather: Cornelius Cousins: Kenneth, Marcel	Cousins: Sherona, Alex, Junior, Helen, Julius, Hannah
Marissa	3;4–3;10	Female	Mother: Patricia Father: Reynold Sister: Sonia Brothers: Nicholas, Oscar	Neighbors: Henrietta, Aaron, Albert

practices such as attending a certain church, even when such things challenged their economic means. Five families identified as Catholic, and one Pentecostal family (Marissa's) was included to get at variation that may be linked to religion and related social networks. Table 2.1 provides information about the focal children, their families, and regular playmates.

The children had extensive and dense social networks (Milroy 1987) that they engaged with on an everyday basis. Women were the primary caregivers, staying home with preschool children while men worked on farms or periodically in construction. Women also worked part-time in the garden or sold produce at the Portsmouth outdoor market, when they would leave children in the care of aunts and grandmothers. Men also played a significant role in the socialization of children, talking and playing with them after work or when home due to injury, illness, or unemployment. Significantly, there were other children living in all six households. Older siblings and cousins play an important role in the caretaking and socialization of small children. The six focal children stayed close to their adult or child caregivers throughout the day, observing them interact, work, and care for others. They accompanied them to social visits, church, and occasionally the garden when no one was available to watch them, such as during planting or harvesting time. They went with caregivers to the shop, bakery, or health center for a booster shot or "worm medicine." Few children travel farther than the other side of Penville or to Vieille Case before they begin school, yet much of the talk between adults and children concerns other places like Roseau.

In terms of language proficiency, none of the focal children or their siblings spoke Patwa exclusively or fluently. All were being raised English dominant—a pattern representative of children in the community at large. There were individual differences among the children related to how much Patwa they heard and produced, but the families had strikingly similar language ideologies—namely, that Patwa "interferes" with children's acquisition of English. Caregivers firmly stated that for children to learn English, they must be spoken to in English and forbidden from speaking Patwa. Yet most of the children code-switched, especially when interacting with peers, as explored in chapters 5 and 6.

Alisia and Her Family

Alisia was a very active child. She was frequently scolded for running, jumping, breaking things, and inevitably falling down. She lived with her biological parents, Clement and Grace, and four siblings: Josette (twelve years), Natalie (ten years), Tedison (four years), and Lestrade (three months).[11] Her parents had been living together since Alisia was born, and they later married. Josette, Natalie, and Tedison were Grace's children with other fathers, and Clement had an older child who lived with her mother. Lestrade,

Grace and Clement's second child together, was born twenty months after Alisia. The family identified as Catholic, but only sporadically attended services because of Alisia and Lestrade's young age. When I first visited Alisia, her parents reported that she was "talking so good," including cursing in Patwa (*jiwé*) when someone wronged her. Grace frequently said, "That Alisia not easy you know," or simply, "Aye Alisia." She called her "troublesome" and "naughty," but often followed this with a laugh. Despite some complications at birth, Alisia's verbal and physical strength were taken as evidence that her challenging start in life had not held her back developmentally.

Clement was an established small-scale farmer growing bananas, root crops, and vegetables to sell at market in Portsmouth and to hucksters. He farmed family land in Soufrière where he also kept several goats. He would leave soon after dawn and return home from work at 2:00 or 3:00 P.M. each day, a typical work schedule for men. When he returned, he would eat lunch and then lie on a small rug on the floor and sleep or play with the children, or he would frequent a nearby rum shop to play dominoes or checkers with his cousins. Grace cared for the children and was often at a nearby public standpipe washing clothes. Grace also did the cooking, though Clement sometimes made a meatless stew that he called "Rasta food." Grace was always struggling to manage the children and the daily chores, which included cleaning up after Alisia's frequent food spills and "accidents," as she frequently urinated on herself and whatever she was sitting or standing on. Grace regularly made comments like, "More you have, more you get work to do *wi*."

Both Clement and Grace were raised in Penville and Clement built their house on a piece of his family land. Houses (*kaz*, also *kay*) are generally constructed of wood or concrete, commonly called "wood houses" and "block houses," respectively. Small wood houses with galvanized metal roofing predominate (Figure 2.3), although residents who can afford it increasingly prefer to build larger Western-style block homes (Figure 2.4).[12] Villagers claim that block houses are better because they are more hurricane resistant than wood houses, but they are more expensive to build and have become a visible marker of socioeconomic differences. Block houses with modern amenities like indoor plumbing, electricity, and telephone are the most desired and symbolically valued.

Alisia lived in a block home with a veranda and a "basement," an open area underneath the house used for storage and drying laundry during rain. The house had two bedrooms: one shared by the children and the other by Grace, Clement, and the baby. Each bedroom had one large bed under which their clothing was stored in duffle bags. The house was sparsely furnished with a wooden table and two matching chairs in the large living room. Families often invest all their savings in home construction and then are "strapped" for everyday items and cannot afford paint, furniture, or utilities. Clement complained that his house remained unfinished because money was "too

Figure 2.3 Wooden house with a neatly maintained yard

Figure 2.4 Residents build concrete block homes if they can afford them

tight." He had many plans, including installing indoor plumbing to replace the outdoor slab toilet. Grace did most of her cooking in what she called "the African way": outside in a large pot or on a sheet of galvanized metal over a fire. Like types of houses and the objects inside them, ways of preparing and serving food have become associated with ideas about tradition/modernity. In the past all villagers cooked over an open fire or in a coal pot, and served food in handmade calabash bowls. Today these practices are devalued as old-fashioned and signifying insufficient resources to do it the more modern way—using a propane gas cylinder stove inside a kitchen.[13] While villagers make calabash bowls and baskets for sale to tourists, they generally prefer to buy manufactured dinnerware and other goods and to store them in nice cupboards in their homes.

As is common in the village, Alisia's home was surrounded by a yard (*lakou* or *douvan lapòt la*). The yard is considered an extension of the home and is distinguished from the surrounding bush and other yards by planted vegetation or makeshift fences of metal roofing and other materials. On the slope of his yard, Clement grew tomatoes, cabbages, and other vegetables for their consumption. There was an array of fruit trees, and colorful flowers and bushes marked the yard's perimeter. Most yards are cleared of all grass and vegetation within their boundaries and thus consist of packed brown dirt. Many people prefer to pave their yards with concrete, clearly marking them from the surrounding bush and gardens as human space. It is important to keep one's yard neat and free of debris or other objects, and not only for avoiding gossip[14]: messy yards are inviting to snakes and witches. Women and older female children, like Grace and Alisia's older sisters, are primarily responsible for the upkeep of the home and yard, and are expected to sweep inside and out every day.

Alisia played with a variety of children including her siblings, three cousins, and preschool-age neighbor, Roselia. Her favorite playmate was Tedison and the two played outside nearly every evening until dark. She began to play with Lestrade more often as he learned to walk, but she was frequently scolded for being too rough with him. Josette and Natalie were too busy with schoolwork and chores to play for extended periods and they were required to monitor the younger children. Grace sometimes complained that the older children's fathers did not provide for them; however, Josette's father's sister who lived in St. Lucia "sent" for her during the study. Josette had started secondary school with its expenses of books, uniforms, and transportation. As things were financially difficult, Grace agreed. Natalie was in sixth grade and Tedison attended preschool; both advanced to the next grade, but school was more of a struggle for Tedison than for his sisters.

Grace and Clement spoke Patwa and English with each other and with friends. Grace claimed that Patwa "doesn't sound nice" like English, despite that she was raised speaking Patwa. She had finished primary school but did not attend secondary school, while Clement did not finish the primary level. Sometimes they spoke only Patwa with each other, but almost always switched to English to address the children. Grace told me, "We do speak Patwa but, you know for our children we speaking a lot of English. Mostly English for them." During the day, Grace often scolded them in Patwa, such as calling Alisia *malpwòp* (nasty) for urinating on herself. Both Josette and Natalie understood Patwa well though they rarely spoke it. Clement and Grace claimed that Alisia and Tedison did not speak Patwa, but were sure they understood it. Grace paid careful attention to their speech, correcting their English grammar and translating Patwa uses into English. Alisia's parents and siblings occasionally read children's books in English to her and let her draw with their crayons and pencils.

Jonah and His Family

Jonah's parents, Jude and Marlena, were very concerned with their children's education and made speaking English a top priority. Jonah lived with them, siblings Aaron (eleven years) and Theodora (five years), and one fostered cousin, Roma (eleven years), whose parents had left Dominica. Jonah's brother Abraham (nine years) resided with a relative in another hamlet. Marlena and Jude became a couple as teenagers, had all their children together, and were legally married five years earlier. Jude traveled to two other islands for occasional six-month periods of construction work. Jonah's family shared a yard with Jude's parents, who they called "Papa Eustace" and "Ma Dora" (or just "Papa" and "Mama"). Jude's adult brother Francis and niece Claudette (thirteen years) shared their home. Francis owned a pick-up truck, a rare and desired possession. Jonah also spent a considerable amount of time at his maternal grandfather's home, as Marlena frequently cared for her ill father. Jonah enjoyed those times as he could play with three young cousins who lived next door.

The two houses were at the end of an offshoot from the main road with several other houses along it, including Eustace's brother's home. Jude was one of twelve children, but was the only to build near his parents. This reflects one of two main types of house arrangements in the village. Many families build their houses clustered around one another in a family compound, usually near a mother or both parents as Jude did. Family members have separate homes, but share a common yard and outdoor kitchen. Jude and Marlena's home was situated on one side of an outdoor kitchen and standpipe shared by the whole family, with Jude's parents' home located on the other side. The second type of arrangement is to build one's home on a single lot of property separate from kin, as Alisia's family did. Regardless of which pattern villagers adopt, financial and material resources are usually shared beyond the bounds of house and yard.

Family membership provides material and affective support and is integral to community inclusion; as such, it entails duties, obligations, and rights, including willingness to offer food, money, or aid to family members in need.

Jonah's family recently finished their block house and it remained unpainted. It had one floor with a partial basement, a veranda, and five rooms, including a bathroom (although the plumbing often failed to work properly). They had several pieces of furniture and a coffee table that was covered with lace doilies and greeting cards sent by relatives overseas. A shelving unit displayed ceramic and plastic trinkets, including a statue of the Virgin Mary. The indoor kitchen had running water, a small fridge, and a gas cylinder stove, although Marlena preferred to cook using a coal pot in the outdoor kitchen. A soda crate filled with empty bottles rested on the floor where, as in most households, it remained empty until the family paid to refill it for the Christmas holidays. Jonah slept in a wooden crib that Jude brought from his time abroad when Theodora was a baby. A crib is unusual in rural areas, with most babies sleeping with caregivers from birth. An English alphabet chart on the wall by the crib indicated the family's attention to education. Jonah's grandparents had a telephone and television that they permitted Jonah's family to use. The yard immediately surrounding their house was paved with concrete.

Jonah saw many different people on a daily basis. His primary playmates included the children he lived with, especially Theodora, Roma, and Claudette, plus two cousins near his home and the three cousins near Marlena's father's house. He spent much of the day with Marlena and Papa Eustace while Jude and Ma Dora were at work and the children at school. Jude played with Jonah almost every day when he returned home. Unlike other children, who were subdued around teachers, Jonah liked to visit a schoolteacher who lived nearby. Jonah also interacted with people employed by Dora to shell coffee beans, including Clarice who spoke only Patwa. Many people came to purchase coffee or cocoa, or to rent one of Dora's donkeys. Jonah knew most regular customers and his mother smiled proudly when he greeted them by name. When Jude was in the hospital, the house was flooded with visitors bringing food and help with chores, a common practice when a family member falls ill or dies.

Jonah's household was supported by farming in addition to wages Jude earned from construction. When Jude returned from six months of construction work abroad, I noticed new toys, knickknacks, and a glass window with a screen, a novelty for the village. With one of the older French family names, the couple claimed they had an obligation to be role models and were active in community affairs, including the PTA and village council. They encouraged their children to participate in school and extracurricular activities, including the 4-H Club and Cultural Group. The family attended church regularly and the children attended Sunday school. Jonah frequently sang religious songs and attempted to lead prayer on his own (see chapter 6).

This family also spoke the most English of the focal families. Both Marlena and Jude were raised primarily in English, claiming they learned Patwa as a second language from peers. Jude told me that he only really began to use Patwa when he lived in Guadeloupe and that if, "Somebody ask me ask me a question in English, to have to translate it in Patwa? I might not be able to do it ((laughs))." Marlena spoke more Patwa than Jude, but rarely to the children. The couple spoke mostly English with each other, occasionally code-switching with adult visitors or for discussing private topics when the children were present. However, both parents occasionally joked, issued imperatives, and scolded the children in Patwa, and Ma Dora and Clarice often teased Jonah in Patwa. At each monthly recording, Jonah and his sister said some new formulaic teasing phrase used by the family, such as "*Ou fou* man" (<u>You're mad</u> man) or "*Ou bèl la*" (<u>You're good there</u>). But when Jonah was two years and five months, Marlena reported to me that he corrected his grandmother to say "coconut" in English when she said the Patwa word *koko*. She beamed at this, saying, "You think Jonah not smart?!"

While they did not consider themselves highly educated (Marlena completed primary school and Jude the junior secondary program), they frequently received advice from their neighbor and Jude's sister, both teachers. They obtained several books that they often read to Jonah. Unlike in other families, Jonah's literacy events (Heath 1982) extended beyond reading the text to relating things in books to real-world objects and events and creating extended narratives out of storylines. By the age of two years, nine months he frequently initiated narratives related to books on his own. In addition the family performed many routines with him, some of which were practiced by the other families but not to the same extent or variety. They encouraged singing, word games, and object play with toys Jude bought, including showing Jonah how to call people on a Fisher-Price telephone, build houses with Legos®, and play music on a guitar. He was encouraged to talk and was rewarded with claps, kisses, and other praise. His family taught him to "make a sweet eyes" (to look at someone and blink exaggeratedly) and "send a kiss" (to blow a kiss to someone) before he was two years old. When he answered something correctly, family members asked him, "Who smart?" to which he responded, "Me!" The family was quite child-centered and accommodating. Jonah regularly became moody when he did not get his way, and usually would be appeased unlike in other households. He even had his own child-size plastic lawn chair that he carefully guarded from the other children. Yet, his caregivers also tried to teach him to take responsibility for his actions; if he did not speak much during a recording session, Marlena would tell him that he "failed to talk" or simply "failed" for the day.

Kenrick, Tamika, and Their Families

Kenrick and Tamika are cousins, the children of sisters Tessa and Lorna, respectively. The two families lived on separate plots of land connected by footpaths in an area owned by one large family, with ten houses in all. Tamika's family shared a yard with her grandparents, while Kenrick's family lived near the boundary of the family land. The children were almost always around many family members and the multiparty interactions could become quite complex. Lorna and Tessa had three sisters and one brother with all but one living in Penville (one sister moved to St. Marten). Kenrick was relatively quiet—his grandmother described him as "*sèwyé kon pen*" (serious as bread)— while Tamika was talkative and frequently got in trouble for getting into things and wandering outside "under the big sun," thus making me follow her.[15]

Kenrick resided with his parents, Tessa and Felix, and two brothers, Daniel (twelve years) and Nicky (nine years). Tessa and Felix were in their early thirties and had been together on and off for thirteen years. They had moved from Felix's grandmother's home into their own house a few months before the study began, but Felix often left to work with his brother in Guadeloupe (his sister and mother lived in Canada). The Catholic Church donated the two-room wooden house to the family. There was a separate outdoor kitchen where Tessa cooked on an open fire. Without plumbing, Tessa had the daily chore of hauling buckets of water from a public standpipe on the road to her home. Like other women Tessa had a small kitchen garden, and Felix planted some banana trees down the steep slope behind their house. Kenrick's parents made their living by farming carrots and yams. They often lived off the money Felix made in Guadeloupe, but that usually disappeared quickly.

Tamika lived with her parents, Lorna and David, and her twin sisters, Glenda and Vanessa (six years).[16] Lorna and David grew up in Penville and were in their late twenties. Lorna had lived in several other villages as a teenager while working as a nanny for relatives. Her main occupation since having her own children was homemaker, but she also had her own garden on land she received from her *pawen* (godfather). She harvested vegetables to sell biweekly at the Portsmouth market and occasionally to local customers and hucksters. She also wove baskets and mats for sale in Roseau. David farmed their garden, harvested bananas for a cousin weekly, and periodically obtained work in town as a construction laborer. He had gone to a nearby island several times where he lived with his sister and worked in construction and carpentry, learning skills that helped him secure occasional work in Dominica. Both Lorna and David left primary school before seventh grade and they did not focus much attention on their children's education (partly due to lack of time and literacy materials like books). Tamika's sisters were repeating first grade, along with their cousin Samuel (six years) who lived with their grandparents next door.

David and Lorna lived together since having the twins, at first sharing David's deceased grandmother's house with his brother. The arrangement did not work out, so Lorna asked her father for a piece of land to build a house in their yard. He gave it to her and David built their home himself, not more than six feet away from her parents' wooden house. There were two one-room outdoor kitchens on either side of the yard. There was no electricity or running water and the family shared the chore of filling buckets at the public standpipe and carrying them to the kitchens. Tamika's grandparents' home always housed more than just her grandmother and grandfather. Lorna's sister, Jane, lived there with her son, Samuel, though she left twice during the study. She spent three months working as a nanny in St. Marten, returned for Christmas, and then went to live with Samuel's father in Guadeloupe, leaving Samuel with his grandparents both times. Another sister, Cynthia, also periodically lived there with her one-year-old son, and later with her newborn baby when she and her boyfriend argued.

The families relied on one another for scarce material resources. Food was a perennial topic of discussion; in addition to obtaining enough food for everyone, discussions also concerned which types of foods were possible to get, hinting at broader social change. The families did not run out of food, as they grew numerous crops and had access to many kinds of fruit and wildlife. When they lacked money to purchase meat, rice, or bread from the shops, however, they complained of having nothing to eat. Like shifting ideas about food preparation, types of foodstuff are becoming ideologically linked to notions of tradition/modernity and emerging socioeconomic differences. Diets of rural villagers have long consisted of foods they could grow or catch themselves. Staples in Lorna and Tessa's families included green bananas, plantains, root crops (dasheen, tannia, and yam varieties known as "ground provisions"), and other local produce. Land crabs, river crayfish, opossum, agouti, and fish are caught when and where available.[17] Some store-bought foods like salted codfish, flour, sugar, and salt have long been staples. Since the road was constructed, these and other manufactured foods like rice, tinned milk, and processed cheese have been sold in small shops. However, imported frozen chicken and turkey parts and tinned sausages are growing components of daily meals, replacing local meats. Similarly, packaged snacks and Kool-Aid, instead of fresh-squeezed fruit juices, are very popular. In the past a typical meal included boiled green bananas, a root crop, and fresh or dried fish or a locally caught meat, all seasoned in a broth using local spices. This is still done, but now having chicken or turkey instead of local meats, rice or flour dumplings instead of root crops, and packaged Goya Sazón seasoning indexes higher status.

Further, Western-style bread bakeries with large electric ovens have opened all over the island. With bakery bread easily available, few families continue the subsistence activity of processing manioc into *fawin* (farina) and *kasav* (cassava bread). Kenrick and Tamika's families occasionally did this activity that brings together people of all ages in a shared two-day social event (in contrast to sending a single child to buy bread from the bakery). But the electric-oven bakery has come to symbolize convenience, modernity, wealth, and change. People continue to eat local foods and meats, but if a person cannot also serve bread or macaroni and cheese, particularly to guests, it is assumed they cannot afford it. In contrast to urban discourses increasingly promoting local foods, villagers (including the focal children's families) perceive a lack of more cosmopolitan processed and imported fare as indexing poverty.

Tamika's yard was a central gathering place for socializing most times of the day, often with many people present. Tamika's great-uncle lived next door with his wife, their daughter, and her four young children. His son had built a small house between their house and Tamika's yard where he lived with his girlfriend and their two children, Abigail and Henry. Tamika's cousin Robert, the son of the sister in St. Marten, lived with another relative nearby. All the children—Tamika and her two sisters, Kenrick and his two brothers, and their seven cousins—played together almost every afternoon, often starting in a large group and then dispersing into smaller ones. Kenrick and Tamika usually stayed together, sometimes playing alone or with three-year-old Henry. The school-age children meandered into the yard at 3:30 P.M. when school ended and were immediately told to change from their uniforms into play clothes. After a snack of tea and bread they played until dusk. According to Lorna, "Whenever one of them want to do something, they all have to do it."

Aside from socializing in the yard the women and children spent a great deal of time doing chores together. They usually washed clothes in a group, bringing the children with them to the public standpipe to wash in large pails or to a nearby river when there was not much mud. They often gathered wood for cooking or went in a large group to the garden where the children played while the women gathered green bananas and ground provisions for their meals. Sometimes they traveled to land owned by a relative to pick mangos, or to another river where they caught crayfish to eat. Lorna, Jane, and their mother wove baskets and mats together. Tessa complained that her sisters had yet to teach her how to make them—they had learned this "traditional" skill at a workshop held by the Cultural Division, and it earned them some additional income. The women and children attended the Catholic Church regularly, while the men went mainly on special occasions and holidays.

In the context of these extended gatherings of adults, the children were exposed to a great deal of Patwa. The adults tried their best to speak English with the children but conversed amongst each other almost strictly in Patwa. The grandfather spoke very limited English and often used Patwa with the children, although they always responded in English. Lorna spoke the most

Patwa of any primary caregiver in the study even though David was adamantly against it. More than once she told me, "Their father don't want people to talk Patwa for them." She was the only caregiver in the study that I observed using Patwa with her children in public. The teachers repeatedly advised her to speak English, as she explained:

> Sometime the teachers tell me don't speak Patwa for them, speak English. She'll tell me don't - don't curse them. Don't tell them *salòp* (dirty person) those thing there. Don't call them *bouwo* (scoundrel). Is about school for me to tell them, then to sit down and make them to learn. To ask them their homework or take a book and make them read what they don't know.

Lorna's sisters also spoke Patwa with their children, but mostly to scold or criticize them. Despite sharing concerns about her children's language learning, Lorna unequivocally responded that she preferred to speak Patwa: "You can say the Patwa *better* than the English. Maybe you have to talk the English twice, but the Patwa is once."

These adults were sure that their children understood Patwa because of their exposure to it. Both families said, however, that their children only spoke English even when addressed in Patwa. Lorna claimed that her children did not even want to hear Patwa and ignored her when she spoke it to them:

> Cause if I call them and I tell them go in the shop *èvè* (pause) *ay an boutik la* (pause) *ay ganyen an liv sik ba mwen* (and (pause) go in the shop (pause) go buy a pound of sugar for me), they will tell me they don't going. They don't understand what is that. So they'll tell me talk in English for them. So after I'll tell them well, go in the shop and go and say you want a pound of sugar. They don't raise up in Patwa.

There were often times that the children appeared to not understand what was said to them in Patwa. Lorna doubted that her children would speak Patwa as adults; Tessa said her boys might with their peers. Yet in both families, the children's English responses to adult Patwa speech indicated a greater comprehension than their Patwa production around adults suggested.

Reiston and His Family

Reiston and his two cousins, Kenneth (thirteen years) and Marcel (eleven years), were fostered by their grandparents, Cornelius ("Papa") and Josephine ("Granny"). The couple had been married for twenty years and had three children together, plus Josephine had three children prior to their relationship. All of their offspring, including the boys' parents, had left Penville for other villages and islands. The family lived in a mint green block house with a basement, concrete-paved yard, and a small veranda with several plastic lawn chairs where Cornelius and Josephine enjoyed sitting in the late afternoon. The three boys shared one of two large bedrooms in the home. The living room was well furnished with a soft oriental-style rug, a settee, two wooden chairs, a cabinet full of glassware and trinkets, a black and white television that could only pick up two French stations from Guadeloupe (none of them understood French so they watched without sound), and a radio with which the grandparents listened to Felix Henderson's Patwa program *Èspéwéyans Kwéyòl* every day. Neither Cornelius nor Josephine traveled beyond Portsmouth except for a rare trip to Roseau, but their children often sent them goods from overseas. The kitchen area had a large refrigerator, a table with four chairs, and a ceramic tile floor. The kitchen was not used for cooking, however, as there were two outside buildings to serve that purpose. About five feet from the veranda entrance was a small concrete block building with a gas cylinder stove and cooking utensils. Adjacent to that was a two-room wooden shed. One side was used for storage and had a couple of wooden benches where the boys ate their meals, while the grandparents ate at the table inside the house. The other side of the shed had a spot for a fire and was used to store ground provisions, bunches of green bananas, and wood for cooking when the gas cylinder ran out.

Just off the paved yard there was a large rabbit cage crafted from old metal roofing and mesh wire. Kenneth and Marcel were responsible for taking care of the rabbits, but Cornelius continually had to remind them to feed them. Near the rabbit cage was a kitchen garden with a variety of vegetables. A clothesline connected to two metal poles marked the yard's border. A few feet from where the concrete ended a field of banana plants began. The area surrounding the home was family land on Cornelius's side: to their right lived Cornelius's brother Philsbert and his teenage son and daughter, while three other brothers owned homes to their left. One brother had died, but his son, Bertrand, shared the small piece of land with his mother, sister, sister's son Junior (nine years), and brother who had built a house but lived in Roseau where he worked. Bertrand and his common-law wife, Felina, had five children who played with Reiston and his cousins daily: Hannah (twelve years), Julius (ten years), Helen (eight years), Alex (five years), and Sherona (three years). Felina gave birth to another child during the study.

Cornelius was a banana farmer, but he no longer worked bananas as much as when they were known as the "green gold." He grew yams and vegetables to sell to hucksters and for the family's consumption, and raised goats for slaughter on special occasions. His youngest son Carl, in his early twenties, lived in Roseau but frequently came home to work when he needed money or if his father needed help. For many young adults like Carl farming is something they are forced to return to if all else fails. Josephine wove baskets for sale to tourist shops in Roseau, worked part-time with the government-paid road crew, and periodically went to the Portsmouth market to sell produce on Saturdays. Reiston's cousins were in school. Kenneth was unable to pass the Common Entrance Exam for secondary school and instead entered the Junior Secondary Program offered in Vieille Case. Marcel was in sixth grade at the start of the study, but began seventh grade and its intensive preparation for the Common Entrance Exam the next year. Both Kenneth and Marcel took turns babysitting a young cousin for their aunt in town on Saturdays. Josephine and the boys attended the Catholic Church on Sundays.

For Reiston a typical weekday revolved around the comings and goings of the people with whom he lived and played. His grandfather left to work in his garden just after dawn. Reiston would arise soon after with his cousins, watching them prepare for school. Most weekdays Josephine remained at home to watch Reiston, do housework, and weave baskets. Reiston played alone or with his cousin Sherona at either of their homes, on the road in-between, or in the gardens behind their homes. They were not allowed to roam far and would be called back if they disappeared for long. On days when Josephine worked on the road, Reiston was told to stay at Sherona's home. Sherona's mother often worked with her husband in their garden, so Sherona's monolingual Patwa-speaking grandmother would watch them. Reiston's grandfather usually walked down the long hill on his return around 1:00 P.M. Reiston would spot his dog first and get excited, running to the road yelling, "Papa! Papa!" and asking what he brought for him (mangos were his favorite). Cornelius often engaged in conversation with Reiston while relaxing on the veranda after work. Reiston eagerly awaited those times as he was very attached to his grandfather and frequently imitated his speech and actions. When the older children arrived home from school, they quickly changed out of their uniforms, ate, and did their chores so they could play until just before dark.

Like other adults, Cornelius and Josephine spoke Patwa with one another, but tried to speak mostly English to the children. Josephine was very proficient in English and had good reading and writing skills. Cornelius could not read or write, and was much more comfortable speaking Patwa than English. When I first met him, he told me: "*Mwen pa fò an Annglé*" (I'm not strong in English). He frequently spoke Patwa to the children for any purpose, while Josephine used it to scold them. Kenneth explained that he and the other boys understood Patwa well because of their grandparents speaking it to them. When asked if he spoke Patwa himself, Kenneth responded that he mainly spoke English, but that he used Patwa "when my mind tell me to." Marcel claimed that he did not like to speak Patwa, even though he frequently did so with peers (see chapters 5 and 6). The whole family claimed that Reiston spoke English only, but his recorded speech was full of short Patwa utterances. His grandfather and the other male children with whom he played clearly influenced his speech and behavior. He and his older cousins spoke the most Patwa of all the children in the study, and they also had the least adult supervision.

Marissa and Her Family

Marissa lived with her parents, Patricia and Reynold, and siblings, Nicholas (eleven years), Sonia (six years), and Oscar (four months). They resided in a two-story block house with electricity, plumbing, and telephone service, although the latter was periodically turned off depending on their financial situation. Both Patricia and Reynold had worked in St. Marten for several years and the house was well furnished with items they bought while there. They owned a Western-style sofa and recliner chair and a shelving unit filled with dinnerware, decorative items, and children's toys. Reynold was a prosperous banana farmer and he grew root crops on land he inherited near their home. Patricia had a kitchen garden where she grew carrots and other vegetables. They did relatively well for themselves, but things got "tight" when Nicholas began secondary school in Portsmouth and needed money for school expenses.

Patricia and Reynold had converted from Catholicism to Pentecostalism. Religion is another important site of social change in the village, one that increasingly signifies socioeconomic differences. Until twenty-five years or so ago, Catholicism was virtually the only religion known in the area. A man in his seventies explained that when he grew up, "*Katolik sèlman ki té ni*" (Catholicism was the only one). Parishioners attended weekly mass in Vieille Case and visited two small chapels in Penville until two large Catholic churches were built in Upper and Lower Penville in 1986. A few people followed Rastafarianism but they were small in number and largely kept their beliefs to themselves. Belief in *Obeah* (sorcery or witchcraft) was and continues to be widespread, although people rarely comment on it unless something peculiar happens and are evasive when asked (see Mantz 2007b).[18] Evangelical religions made inroads in the late 1980s, initially reaching villagers through congregations in Vieille Case. The Pentecostal church attended by Marissa's family was built in Galba in the early 1990s and had a regular attendance of about fifty people. A Seventh Day Adventist church was constructed in Upper Penville in the late 1990s.

The introduction of new religions, like the other social changes outlined above, impacted local social relations and language use. Attending church is an important social event and factor in community membership, but the introduction of other denominations in this small population has divided families. For Catholics a typical Sunday consists of mass and Sunday school in the morning, a large lunch with family, and a community cricket or rounders match in the afternoon. Now families feel separated, as Pentecostal services take most of the day on Sunday (overlapping Catholic family lunches and sports matches) and Seventh Day Adventists attend church on Saturday rather than Sunday. In addition, church-organized events shape people's social lives. Catholics celebrate feasts to patron saints, festivals like Carnival, and holidays throughout the year that the other religions do not recognize or observe differently, such as Christmas and Easter.[19] Each church organizes its own activities, which sometimes take up every night of the week. One elderly Catholic man explained how difficult it is now that two of his children and their families have converted to Pentecostalism. He complains that it is hard to get together with them because their churches have different schedules, they cannot celebrate most holidays together, and, as he put it, "*Yo pa ka bwè wonm, yo pa ka bwè* this, *yo pa ka bwè* that*"* (They don't drink rum, they don't drink this, they don't drink that). Christmas, for example, was the biggest holiday of the year during which people visited and shared food and alcoholic beverages. Many people still maintain that if a person does not have a drink with their friend, "*Nwèl pa wivé*" (Christmas hasn't arrived). But over the past two decades, this practice, along with the tradition of Christmas caroling in Patwa (*siwennal*), has been decreasing in favor of private celebrations.

Many Pentecostals and Seventh Day Adventists claim that Catholics consume too much alcohol, celebrate too many holidays, and do not "practice what they preach" once they leave church. Many Catholics view the other groups as separatist. Some Catholics remarked that the Pentecostals and Seventh Day Adventists are too "proud" to attend the Catholic Church with the "poor people." The Pentecostal congregation consists of the more well to do villagers including teachers, nurses, small-business owners, prosperous farmers, and professionals who travel to Portsmouth and Roseau to work. They own most of the vehicles and almost all live in block houses, further marking Pentecostalism as the "richer" religion.

There are also language differences according to religious affiliation. While all church activities are conducted primarily in English, I heard more Patwa spoken in the Catholic Church than the Pentecostal church. Roman Catholic priests and nuns were traditionally French and Belgian, facilitating more acceptance of Patwa in the Catholic Church throughout Dominica's colonial history. As Christie (1969: 12) states, "Creole, along with French, has had more status in the Church than in any other sphere of formal public activity." Today Catholic mass is performed in English, but the homily may be in Patwa or English, and songs are sometimes performed in Patwa. In addition much of the conversation among adults when socializing before and after mass is in Patwa (Figure 2.5). During the services I attended at the Pentecostal church, I heard almost no Patwa among these more prosperous villagers. Thus, while the Catholic Church offers a context for Patwa maintenance, the increasing associations between English and Evangelical (and Protestant) religions further solidify ideological linkages between English and socioeconomic prosperity.

Figure 2.5 Parishioners congregate after Sunday services at the Catholic Church

Marissa's parents did not own a business or vehicle and were less educated than many professionals in their church. Reynold had completed one year in secondary school and Patricia had a primary education. However, they did well at farming and had high aspirations that were in line with their fellow church members. They frequently talked about wanting "a better life." Reynold questioned me about advanced degree home study programs based in other countries and asked if I knew of job opportunities for him overseas or if I could teach his wife a skill to earn money in Dominica. He once told me regretfully that he had started a home degree program in accounting before he got married, but did not finish it because he was anxious to have a house, wife, and family. The couple continually encouraged their children to get as much education as possible and frequently read to them and asked questions about their homework. Marissa attended all religious activities with her family and had many friends at church.

Patricia and Reynold spoke some Patwa with each other, particularly for jokes or if they did not want their children to understand something. Otherwise they primarily spoke English and rarely even scolded the children in Patwa. They claimed that the little Patwa their children knew was learned "on the roadside" and from other children like neighbors Henrietta (seven years) and twin brothers Aaron and Albert (nine years). At home the parents often repeated lessons learned in church and made sure the children prayed each morning before school, all in English. Marissa pretended to "make service," as Patricia called it, saying "preach the Gospel" among other things while playing with Oscar. Patricia focused on teaching Marissa to count and spell and praised her when she got things right. She frequently conveyed moral lessons, telling her not to lie because "Satan lying" and "Christians aren't supposed to lie." To coax her, she asked, "How nice girl does be?" to which Marissa responded, "Sweet." Marissa used complex sentences like the following when her mother promised her a lollipop for watching Oscar: "Long time you say you will buy a lollipop for me and you not yet buy it." Her mother laughed and bought her the lollipop. Marissa rarely spoke Patwa and was questioned about what it meant when she did. Patricia once teased her for employing the sentence final tags *wi* and *non*, telling her, "You not a French girl!" By the time she was three years and six months, Marissa was given several responsibilities at home including helping to care for Oscar and buying small items from the shop across the street (although she often brought back the wrong thing, like a pound of rice when she was sent to buy a pound of chicken).

The family's religious life had a major impact on their social interactions and activities, including religious camps during school vacations instead of playing with neighborhood children. Their primary social network was their congregation. The recordings are full of explicit commentary on morality and expectations of children, which both echoed and expanded those of other parents. My discussions with Marissa's parents and observations of their daily life helped broaden my perspective on local social organization and dynamics, particularly in terms of new religions but also in understanding language use with children.

Discussion: Continuity and Change in Village Life

This set of portraits of Caribbean family life illustrates points of continuity and change, commonality and difference. The spread of roads, schools, and electricity made an indelible impact on local social interaction, material possessions, and forms of entertainment, including where, when, and what languages are used. Accompanying these changes has been a valuing of things brought in from the outside, providing symbolic capital to those who have them. Many foods and goods, particularly those that can be grown or made from local materials, and certain practices, such as the preparing or making of these items, are considered traditional or old-fashioned. Things that can be brought in like imported foods, appliances, clothing, automobiles, and languages are considered foreign and costly but also modern and desirable. With increased wage labor, travel, and American television programming, villagers have become aware of "modern" things and strongly desire them. Although Penville residents speak of being isolated, the history of the community seems like nothing but contact.

These changing contexts are by no means eliminating social interaction. They are reshaping it, however, as people move from large groups washing at the river or moonlit gatherings for storytelling to the more private setting of the home for doing laundry or watching television, or by sending a child for bread rather than manioc processing in groups. People do get together to watch and comment on English television programs and movies, but there are fewer activities promoting regular intergenerational communication and interaction. Villagers claim that there are more divisions now, as one woman explained:

> Everybody used to unite like brothers and sisters. You go by that one, you go by that one, you go by that one. What you have you sharing for one another, but now? (pause) Some people now, they want to make as they are more than you. They don't want to deal with you, like to say you poor and they are, they *wich* (rich). Like to say the person have *plenty*, and you don't have nothing, so the person not checking you, because you don't have nothing and is they that have thing, so the person want to check who that have *more*. But you that don't have nothing, the person don't want to deal with you.

Villagers claim there is more materialism, greed, and people being "too proud" to interact with others, even in religious contexts. Activities, amenities, and types of food and food production are marked as more rural or urban, local or foreign, traditional or modern. Older villagers relate that before the introduction of wage labor, they did not think of food and money together—if a person worked their garden, they ate. They claim that people were happier when they did not want manufactured things. "*Lavi la sa té wèd,*" they say—that life was hard. They had to rise early in the morning and did not have modern conveniences, but they always had food. Today, many older folk say that if the younger generations do not have money to buy sugar, they cannot even drink their morning tea. One man in his late sixties laughed and told me: "*Donmnitjen, sa yo ka fè, yo pa ka apwésyé*" (Dominicans don't appreciate what they make/grow). Instead people complain when they do not have money to buy bread, processed foods, televisions, and now cell phones and computers.

The six focal families were struggling with these tensions between tradition and change, community and individualism. All were dependent on the land yet all were influenced by migration. Some used their limited financial resources to acquire homes, goods, and amenities that marked higher aspirations than they could comfortably afford, while others had to rely on extensive networks of kin and friends to survive. Some owned very "modern" things, such as a glass window with a screen or sliding glass door in their home, while others (or the same people) engaged in "traditional" practices, like cooking over a fire outdoors. Other key differences included religion, household structure, employment pursuits, and language use. But despite the various points of differentiation among these families, perhaps the strongest point of consensus was their shared ideology about how to speak to children. All the families, regardless of socioeconomic status, education, or family background, required their children to speak English at the expense of Patwa. The majority of these caregivers tried to speak only English to their children and believed they were doing so. In practice, however, the children were exposed to varying amounts of Patwa in their verbal environments and many gained some Patwa competence. The next two chapters explore the complex language ideologies and linguistic practices of villagers as they socialize these new community members.

Notes

1. Community population estimates are from the 1996–1998 fieldwork, although they have not changed significantly since then. Individual household compositions do change regularly, however, due to circular migration patterns.
2. Land-ownership records and a surveyor map show Penville and Vieille Case as French lands during British victory in 1763 (Byres 1776; see also Honychurch 1997: 187, Figure 9.3).
3. Many also cited Kalinago influence. A few mentioned Spanish influence through contact with the French and Kalinago outside of Dominica (see Christie 1994).
4. The preschool is funded by the Catholic Social Centre in Roseau, Christian Children's Fund (CCF), and fees from the parents of the 3–5-year-olds that attend it.
5. Place names map out a history of land ownership and social ties, as well as important events and geographic features. Every piece of cultivated or built land is named and contrasts with the surrounding area, which is called *hazyé la* or "the bush" (see Paugh 2001 for more details).
6. Since the 1950s there has been extensive ethnographic research on Caribbean family and kinship, particularly "matrifocality" and the pervasiveness of female-headed households (e.g., M.G. Smith 1962; R. Smith 1996).
7. The Soufrière track was expanded to a vehicular road in the late 1980s, but had deteriorated by my initial arrival in 1995. Villagers were ecstatic when it was finally completed in the early 2000s, making travel possible in both directions and opening up the area to tourism.
8. Nowadays most children are born in the hospital at Roseau or Portsmouth, but the village nurse is a certified midwife.
9. I was referred to Mrs. Harris by Dr. Lennox Honychurch and am grateful to both for their help in understanding Penville's history. Mrs. Harris spoke with me in an audio-recorded interview and permitted me to read through her memoirs of her time in Penville.
10. None of the most prosperous villagers had children in the desired age range. Most had teenagers, while some were just beginning their families.
11. The ages of siblings and other children are as of the focal child's first recording.

12. These homes typically have indoor kitchens but many have an outdoor kitchen in addition to or instead of an inside one. Block homes usually have verandas while wood houses have wood or concrete steps to the front door.

13. The 2001 population census shows the shift from wood and coal cooking to use of gas stoves over two decades. In 1981 70.4 percent used wood/coal and only 19.9 percent used gas stoves. By 2001 the statistics reversed, with only 15.7 percent using wood/coal and 80.7 percent using gas stoves.

14. The importance of this is highlighted in the annual community Tidy Yard Competition.

15. She was scolded in two languages: "Tamika stay in one place *non*. The sun hot," or *"Tamika, pw'a las maché an sòlèy la?!"* (Tamika, aren't you tired of walking in the sun?!).

16. David and Lorna legally married in 2007.

17. Locally raised livestock include goats, pigs, and some cows, though these are consumed mainly on holidays and special occasions.

18. They spoke of witches more than *obeahmen* (sorcerers), but even these were talked about only in particular contexts such as walking home at dusk.

19. Raymond Lawrence of the Cultural Division explained that there is good participation in cultural groups among the Catholic, Methodist, and Anglican religions, but not Evangelical ones.

CHAPTER 3

Learning English: Language Ideologies and Practices in the Classroom and Home

But you see, most people see Patwa as an inferior language. Like you can speak Patwa, you are nobody. … So right now everybody want to speak English, English, English. And you see it's not our fault because that is how it was before. Like I remember days gone by, Penville was just a Patwa community. So everybody up here is Patwa, Patwa, Patwa, and when you go out, you feeling yourself as nobody among other people because everybody [says] "*jan Penville, jan Penville*" (Penville people, interpreted as disparaging) and you know?

This quote from a Penville teacher in her late thirties suggests villagers' ambivalence toward their vernacular language. They talk about their historically predominant use of Patwa as being responsible for "keeping them back," both caused by and contributing to their isolation. Many speak of how English had to be "brought in," principally by the school, but also by residents who brought spouses from more English-speaking villages or were return migrants. This metaphor of movement and bringing things in is rooted in the history and location of Penville (see chapter 2). Residents now overwhelmingly cite the shift away from Patwa to varieties of English as one of the most positive and consequential changes in the community's development, at least as important as electricity and piped water. It is essential to them "moving forward," or away from their uneducated Patwa-speaking peasant roots. Educational institutions were at the forefront of encouraging this shift to English and have played a key role in reconfiguring intergenerational activities into age-graded ones.

At the same time, local language ideologies are more complex than simply viewing one language as good/positive and the other as bad/negative; further, such ideologies are not homogeneous, as in any community (Irvine and Gal

2000). Residents of the sixty or so villages scattered around the island's coast express ambivalence toward Patwa: both "shame" and "pride." Patwa and English varieties are functionally distributed across domains. They convey different social meanings and index social categories based on variables like age/generation, class, education, gender, and community identity. They are associated with types of places and people, which relate to local notions of ordering the world. Almost all village adults use varieties of English and Patwa to varying degrees and value both for expressing contextually relevant identities and affective stances. Yet children generally are forbidden to speak Patwa in the presence of adults, except in specific circumstances to be described in chapter 4. Despite outward claims that English is "better" than Patwa, however, villagers indicate that both are needed to create a whole person.

In this and the next chapter I explore these complex language ideologies and the ways they impact the language shift. Language ideologies act as a "mediating link between social structures and forms of talk" (Woolard and Schieffelin 1994: 55) and are vital in negotiating group and individual identities. Although in practice the languages are not so strictly separated, these two chapters are divided according to language: English and Patwa. For villagers, this is the most salient opposition and they employ different strategies in speaking the languages to and around children. English, the focus of this chapter, is explicitly taught to children and considered important for polite or formal domains and speech acts. Patwa, the subject of chapter 4, is more implicitly socialized in ways that highlight its continued importance. When considered together, the chapters provide a nuanced look into how age-graded strategies of language use are leading to reconceptualizations of the languages, including rendering English a "child" language and Patwa an "adult" one (thus giving it power in the community despite its relative lack thereof in the national and international speech economies). This investigation provides a critical backdrop for examining how children play with the languages in their peer interactions.

"Bringing in the English": Language Shift in Penville

Dominicans use rich metaphors to talk about languages and the processes of learning or losing them, often referring to food and drink, life and death, and objects of value.[1] Language is frequently talked about as a commodity, which is likely related to national discourses about heritage tourism. Like other objects of exchange language can be gained, lost, bought, sold, given, taken, and imported like foreign goods and development (see Irvine 1989). I was told that English had to be brought in to Penville, similar to how residents talk about modern goods bought at town and hauled home. But unlike objects such as food and appliances, Patwa and English are described as if they are living entities. Some people described Patwa as "dying" while others said it "thrives" and will "live on." Still others told me that Patwa "interferes" with English and would "kill" children's English if they were allowed to speak it. English is described as "soft" while Patwa is "hard" and "rough." Just as people have to weed their fields to protect their produce and keep their yards clean to deter witches and snakes, they have to protect their children from Patwa. Most, however, are not concerned about English "killing" Patwa. For children, English must be nurtured while Patwa must be suppressed, at least until they are older.

Villagers report that Penville was almost exclusively Patwa-speaking until the mid-twentieth century. Older residents were well aware of negative stereotypes about Patwa in the capital town; many were ashamed of their use of Patwa, but say they could not "get" English for their community. Others claimed that their parents discouraged them from regularly attending school in Vielle Case in favor of working the land instead. Penville was "just a Patwa community." English was foreign and unattainable, but increasingly desired like other modern things. The school brought in the first English domain in the 1950s. The school was rebuilt and expanded in the early 1980s as it became increasingly important in the community (Figure 3.1). Patwa was long disdained and forbidden in Dominica's education system and such ideologies shaped rural education where there was room for English only (Hammond 1945). Adults who attended the first school recall receiving beatings from teachers for speaking Patwa anywhere on school grounds. This began to change with the cultural awareness movement, but well into the mid-1980s, the

Figure 3.1 Villagers watch a cricket match on the playing field below the Penville Government Primary School

headmaster (now principal) would patrol the corridor and playing field with a rod used to discipline pupils who broke the rule of no Patwa in school. For most students this was a difficult transition since Patwa was the home language and English was hardly spoken. Few achieved their school leaving certificates, let alone passed the Common Entrance Exam to attain a spot in secondary school.[2] One of the few students to finish school and become a teacher herself described it succinctly: "Only those who were determined to learn would learn." As in creole and minority language situations worldwide, the school laid the groundwork for the language shift to English.[3]

Many villagers claim that they intentionally decided to stop speaking Patwa to their children and to encourage English as much as possible after the construction of the school. This was already the case among many who brought spouses from elsewhere to Penville. For example, two brothers from Vieille Case married women from Penville and moved there in the late 1940s. Their children say that their fathers forbade them from speaking Patwa and only spoke English to them. The eldest daughter of one explained: "We were never allowed to speak Patwa at home. We learned the language from our peers and community. Daddy would not even allow kids who could not speak English to visit us or come to play in the yard." Their mothers, however, spoke some Patwa to them, and they grew up more bilingual than their own children are now. Today the children of these men are some of the most proficient and "standard" English speakers in Penville, and many have left to take up occupations in teaching, business, and medicine in Roseau and overseas. While they are sometimes criticized for their preference for English, most adults model their speech to children after these more well off individuals.

The purist language ideologies espoused by school personnel and certain families began to mark Patwa as age-graded, non-standard, and even deviant. One women in her forties explained that her father would beat her and her siblings if he caught them speaking Patwa. She will only speak Patwa to him now if he does it first. Other adults express similar ambivalence, like this teacher in her late thirties:

> Um, I don't speak Patwa to my father. Even if I try to, but is just a few sentences. But to *converse* in Patwa? No. We couldn't speak Patwa at home. Because my father would see to it that we speak English in the home and then up to now as big - as I am married, I cannot look at - and he's old! He's eighty-three, yes, and I cannot look at him and converse with him in Patwa. I find it's difficult for me to do because that was not customary.

She expressed shock that she could not speak Patwa to an eighty-three-year-old man, even now that she is "big" and married herself. Her hesitations ("then up to now as big - as I am married, I cannot look at - and he's old!") indicate her strong sentiments. It is not a matter of her assessing her Patwa competence as inferior or underdeveloped. Rather, language choice has become status-marked and age-graded: Patwa is avoided when speaking to authoritative elders, like parents and teachers, even if they speak Patwa themselves.

Out-migration and travel increased dramatically when the road was completed in the mid-twentieth century. Older adults say they felt ridiculed for speaking Patwa when they left Penville. They report that when they went to Vieille Case for church, Portsmouth to sell produce, or Roseau to shop and conduct business, they were stereotyped as "backward," "Patwa-speaking," and "*jan ovan*" (windward people). No parent, they claimed, would want their children to visit relatives in town and speak Patwa in front of them. Of course, Penville residents were not the only ones stigmatized for using Patwa or for being rural—in fact, most Dominicans outside of Roseau were considered as such. In addition to language, it was their means of subsistence, foods, and dress that marked, and continue to mark, the social identities of rural peoples when outside their communities. But it seems that the identity marker most seized upon by villagers as representing their rural roots has been Patwa. Many people told me that Patwa is "just a slang language," "broken French," a "dialect," and not a "real" language at all. English is the "real" language (see also Christie 1994: 14). Such evaluations of Patwa as not "real" or "right" emerge in children's peer interactions as well, as they sometimes critique one another's use of Patwa (see chapter 5).

Thus, there were multiple pressures to shift to English engendered significantly by the schools but also by increasing contact with the rest of the island, by prosperous villagers who had adopted language ideologies similar to those among Roseau residents, and by the linguistic insecurity and shame cultivated among rural peoples when speaking Patwa outside their village. The children who grew up during this time of change, now in their forties to sixties, tended to acquire English as a second language in school, or learned the restricted, non-standard varieties spoken by their parents. As these adults began raising their own children, the parents of the preschool and school-age children that I followed, enough English was spoken for them to forbid children from speaking Patwa in the home. But the village was still so immersed in Patwa that most of these children became bilingual in both languages. Members of this generation, in their late twenties to early forties during the study, say they spoke Patwa with their friends "on the roadside" or on the school playing field but not with caregivers. Because of the school they were able to complete more education than their parents. As they matured this generation could speak and understand both languages and most code-switch when speaking either language with peers. They tend to command a range of English varieties and some degree of productive competence in Patwa. They refer to their code-switched speech as "mixed," "mix-up," and "half Patwa, half English," but most do not view code-switching as negative in appropriate contexts.

More fully bilingual in both Patwa and English, these parents have been able to go a step beyond their own parents as they play with the languages of their community: they are able to forbid their children from speaking Patwa and enforce it. By regularly communicating with them in English and requiring children to speak English in return, they are restricting the direct input that children receive in Patwa. While the extent to which they accomplish this varies, children tend to speak English as their first and primary language. Villagers now make a direct causal link between the English-only strategy and children's increasing success in school, demonstrated in 1999 when for the first time in Penville history all the children in the seventh-grade passed the Common Entrance Exam and several even received financial aid to attend secondary school.

Preventing Patwa "Interference": Learning English at School

The school remains a major socializing institution and it is here that the most rigid and purist English language ideologies continue to be instilled and enforced among children and adults alike. During my fieldwork there were eight teachers including the principal. All were female and six were born and raised in Penville. One teacher was from another northern village but married and had children in Penville, while the principal commuted from Vieille Case. All had formal training at Teacher's College in Roseau (established in the 1970s and now part of Dominica State College) and many participated in programs offered by the Ministry of Education. It is significant that most of the teachers lived and had families in Penville rather than being "outsiders" appointed by administration and not invested in the community or local social relations. Their views on language reached beyond what they said in school or PTA meetings to everyday community interactions. Several grew up with the parents of their students, yet they were also different, being some of the wealthy and most influential residents. Almost all were from families that adopted the "English only" strategy early on and, strikingly, five teachers attended the Pentecostal church, having been some of the first in Penville to convert from Catholicism. As educational authorities and community members, the teachers have a profound influence on how people make sense of language use and the process of language acquisition.

Language Ideologies among Teachers

In my discussions with them, the teachers expressed contradictory perceptions of Patwa. They unanimously agreed that it was "holding back" village development and blamed it for "interfering" with children's English, especially literacy. At the same time, they claimed they no longer employed corporal punishment for children speaking Patwa on school grounds deeming it unnecessary since children come to school speaking English now, albeit not the ideal "standard" the school system expects. "Before times," the teachers claim, "too much Patwa" was the problem. Those who entered the profession in the 1970s said that in the early grades they would spend most of the year teaching English as a second language. The preschool teacher says this has changed drastically during her nineteen-year career as she no longer has to teach her pupils English "from scratch":

> And when people [like education officials] would come in my class I would hide. And I would not let the children talk ((laughs)). Unless the people go ((laughs)). So when the people - when the people would go then the class would just woo::! Then they would be live again. Because Patwa wasn't that special as now. ... It wasn't that special, as though as long as you could speak Patwa you'd be left out.

Nowadays, she continued, children seldom speak Patwa when they start preschool. "That?" she says, "That done. You can't get that again." The first-grade teacher agreed: "English is their very first language now. That's what they hear at home." The second-grade teacher similarly claimed that children speak "only little words, words there and there," but not whole sentences in Patwa. The third-grade teacher said, "Every child speaks English now," although she occasionally has students who answer a question in "half English, half Patwa," so she says she "gives them the correct thing." The fourth-grade teacher explained, "We do not really have that problem now. Long ago." The fifth/sixth-grade and seventh-grade teachers agreed that while it was common before, they now hardly ever hear children speaking Patwa at school, even with peers. In fact, they claim that children laugh at students who speak Patwa in the classroom.

Nevertheless, teachers continue to blame Patwa for children's problems with English grammar and non-standard usages. They describe the English of children and other villagers as ranging from "standard," "proper," "good," and "fluent" to "non-standard," "poor," "bad," and "broken." Laughing, the principal exclaimed, "Standard?! Is far from standard sometimes." They complain that students have a "limited" English vocabulary and "do not use their grammar properly." The fourth-grade teacher described it as "not up to standard":

> They speak a lot of what we call broken English, dialect like. They transfer from Patwa to English, and here is a place that is not reaching English. It's Patwa. ... So then now that is the problem. Speaking proper English. That is the problem we have now. Although they speak English but not standardized English. ... Leaving out verbs and (pause) there is a direct

translation from Patwa to English. And so *"mwen ka alé,"* "I going" [instead of "I am going"].

As indicated by this teacher, the principal reason cited is that children "translate directly" or "transfer" from Patwa to English, even though children supposedly no longer speak Patwa. The third-grade teacher gave an example: "Like in Patwa we say *'mwen ké pété ou atè.'* The children say 'I'll burst you down.' You see? As if they translate direct Patwa to English. And it's not supposed to be so." The most significant areas where teachers find that Patwa "interferes" with children's English are in reading and composition.

Spoken usages are targeted for explicit correction in the classroom. In the following example, a first-grade boy is corrected when he uses the construction "it have" to answer his teacher's question about a book called *Lucky Dip*:

Example 3.1

1	Teacher:	Now. Is the boy and the girl the only people in that picture?
2	Class:	((loudly)) No!
3	Boy:	Miss! It have plenty plenty people.
4	Teacher:	There are ma::ny::
5	Class:	((xxx, children talk at once))
6	Teacher:	People. Say ((speaking slowly)) "there are many people in the picture."
7	Class:	There are many people in the picture.
8	Teacher:	Say that again. ((speaking slowly)) "There are many people in the picture."
9	Class:	There are many people in the picture.
10	Teacher:	Somebody say "it have." I don't want you to say "it have." "It have" is BAD English. Say "there are." Say that everybody!
11	Class:	There are.
12	Some:	Many people.
13	Teacher:	Say that. "There are many people in the picture."
14	Class:	There are many people in the picture.

A pupil answers the teacher's question with a common but non-standard English construction, "It have plenty plenty people," referring to a crowd pictured in the book (line 3). Teachers view this sort of construction as evidence of Patwa interference. In Patwa one would say, *"i ni otan moun,"* translated literally as "it have many people." However, this is so commonly used that even if it was once due to language transfer, it is now an integrated feature of the English variety to which children are exposed every day. The teacher immediately corrects it by first repeating the boy's answer with a substitution of the desired construction (lines 4 and 6), and then by explicitly telling the class to repeat "there are" twice more (lines 10 and 13). She highlights the contrast between language varieties: the student's usage belongs to a variety identified as "*bad* English." Standard English, which she provides in her correction, is the unmarked variety of the school. The teacher's own non-standard use of "is" rather than "are" on line 1, "*Is* the boy and the girl the only people in that picture?", passes by unnoticed.

Another prime example of Patwa interference cited by teachers is children "leaving out verbs" in their sentences. They offer examples like "I hungry" (*mwen fen*), "I fine" (*mwen byen*), and "I going" (*mwen ka alé*) as direct translations from Patwa to English. The fifth/sixth-grade teacher claimed that they "leave out the action word" or "miss out a verb" when they speak English, as is done in Patwa. What is missing in these constructions is the copula "to be." One teacher cited this explicitly: "They don't use 'is.'" She attributed this to their "broken English" and "problems expressing themselves in English." However, copula deletion is a common feature of English creole varieties and is used in informal speech throughout Dominica, even in Roseau. Yet the teachers attribute it to direct translation from Patwa to English by children.

Recently teachers have been taught that there are different varieties of English and that these vary geographically, with common varieties throughout the Caribbean. They are beginning to acknowledge that the Englishes spoken by their students, and by Dominicans generally, differ from the variety privileged by the education system but are similar to varieties spoken elsewhere in the Anglophone Caribbean. Two of them clearly expressed such views. The fourth-grade teacher claimed that standard English "is not something that is widely spoken properly in Dominica," even in the media. The seventh-grade teacher questioned whether Patwa was to be blamed at all:

> But I am not too sure that it's just the Patwa or just the fact that in Dominica we do not speak standard English. So it might not only be the Patwa influence in that - but just the - the way of speaking, because we don't really speak English per se. We have our own quote *English* (pause) which actually comes into the classroom.

The preschool teacher told me that she once encouraged her students to imitate a child born on the island of Montserrat, who she claimed spoke "the real English":

> I had a preschooler, and then she was - she was from Montserrat. And then her accent was so fine. ... It was good. And (pause) when she would repeat something the others - other children would repeat it after her. And then they would all turn, and tell me ((using a high-pitched voice)) "teacher

look what Janine said." ((regular voice)) So I tell them, I'll tell them yes, that's the *real* English, so you yourself say it too.

Thus, Dominicans do not speak English "properly" or even the "real" English at all. They have their "own" English, which is not only different from that spoken by the rest of the world, but is sub par. An ideological extension of this is that teachers and parents alike have come to see proficiency in English as a reflection of a person's intelligence. They frequently describe today's children as "smarter" and "brighter" than past generations and directly link this to their acquisition of English. They describe children who have problems speaking English as "slower" or "more backward" than those who already speak a school-like variety. One teacher bluntly told me, "Children who speak a lot of Patwa are very dense."

Keeping Patwa out of the Classroom

Teachers claim that speaking Patwa is no longer an issue yet they go to great lengths to eradicate it from the classroom. In school children's Patwa usage typically consists of a single lexical item like the name of a food, plant, or animal within an English utterance. It may emerge as a child attempts to answer a teacher's question, such as when referring to a book. Teachers respond by replacing the Patwa word with its English equivalent or calling attention to it in a rhetorical question without explanation. The following interaction occurred in the preschool early in the academic year. The class of eleven students aged three to four years old are discussing what their parents do on a typical Thursday. The teacher asks the students about their mothers' chores and they begin talking about laundry:

Example 3.2
1 Teacher: Where would mommy put these clothes to dry?
2 Girl: [Outside.
3 Boy: [On the *ling*.
4 Teacher: ((to Boy)) On the:?
5 Boy: ((louder)) *Ling*.
6 Teacher: On the *ling?!* On the LINE. She'll put them on the LINE. Where - where will she put the line?
7 Girl: Outside.

The teacher employs a common technique for questioning or challenging something a child has said. On line 6 she poses an emphasized rhetorical question regarding the proposition in question, "On the *ling?!*", and then immediately provides the answer she desires, "On the line." She provides no explanation despite that preschool introduces students to the rule that Patwa is not permitted in school. The teacher does not even offer an opportunity for the children to repeat the correction, instead moving on to another question.

The typical pedagogical strategy in the primary grades is to translate children's Patwa usages into English for them to repeat and presumably learn. Teachers say they occasionally need to do this to introduce new English vocabulary or if a child does not know an English equivalent. The second-grade teacher provided an example:

> Last week we was having a social studies lesson with (pause) different parts of the home like the dining room, the bedroom and whatever, and the child gave me *lasal*. That means the living room you know, so I had to tell him well is not *lasal*. *Lasal* is Patwa, but we call it living room. But the child only know *lasal* because that is what he has been hearing at home. *Lasal*.

As in this self-reported correction, the teachers strive to keep children's relatively rare usage of Patwa out of school, often by drawing attention to the place-related constraints on its use. They also call attention to children's grammatical or phonological errors in English speech.

The following segment from "picture study" in the first-grade class demonstrates such strategies in action (Figure 3.2). There are twenty-six students aged five to six years old in the class. The teacher, who has taught in Penville for thirty years, is holding up a child's book called *Lucky Dip* (the same book as in Example 3.1, but this interaction occurs one week later) and

Figure 3.2 The teacher removes Patwa from "picture study" in the first grade class

is asking the class to describe the events on each page. The book is about a boy and girl who pay to pick a wrapped prize from a barrel, a game familiar to students from school fundraising events. On this page, the boy is looking at the prizes as the game operator walks toward him:

Example 3.3.a

1	Teacher:	Alright. The man is coming to give him ONE. Alright. He's looking at it and he's saying to himself, I want one I want one. But (.5) why do you think he just cannot just PUSH his hand and take it?
2	Boy 1:	Miss!
3	Boy 2:	Miss!
4	Boy 1:	[Because he didn't pay.]
5	Boy 2:	[Because they will call him] *vòlè*!
		(Because they will call him <u>thief</u>.)
6	Teacher:	Because he did no:t?
7	Some:	Pay.
8	Teacher:	He did not pay. Somebody say they would -
9	Teacher:	[They will call him -
10	Boy 3:	[They will call him *vòlè*.
11	Teacher:	They will call him *vòlè*. Now (.5) *vòlè* is a – listen to tha:t! ((speaking slowly)) *Vòlè* is a Patwa word.
12	Girl:	((to teacher)) Miss!
13	Teacher:	((louder)) And when we are in school we spea::k?
14	Class:	English!
15	Teacher:	We speak English.

Two students eagerly answer the teacher's question about why the story protagonist does not take a prize (lines 4 and 5). The teacher implicitly validates Boy 1's answer, "Because he didn't pay" (line 4), as correct by repeating his sentence frame as a question to the rest of the class: "Because he did no:t?" (line 6). When some students reply, "Pay" (line 7), the teacher confirms this (line 8). She then targets Boy 2's answer, "Because they will call him *vòlè*!" (line 5), for correction. In everyday life, *vòlè* would be used to call after a person who steals something, as it is more affectively marked than the English noun "thief." But *vòlè* is not allowed in school because it is Patwa and its usage prompts a correction. The teacher lectures on line 11: "They will call him *vòlè*. Now (.5) *vòlè* is a - listen to tha:t! ((speaking slowly)) *Vòlè* is a Patwa word." This highlights that *vòlè* is the problematic usage because it is in Patwa, not that the meaning is incorrect. She further sets up the contrast between languages when she then asks the class to collaboratively articulate a rule statement: "And when we are in school we spea::k?" (line 13). The class enthusiastically responds "English!" (line 14), displaying that by first grade they are well aware that English is the language of the classroom. The teacher reaffirms this using the collective pronoun "we," which includes her with the students: "We speak English" (line 15). Her correction highlights associations between language and place. The language lesson continues, however, when another child offers an alternative:

Example 3.3.b

16	Girl:	[((loudly)) He have to say /tif/ [thief].
17	Teacher:	[All those (xxx).
18	Teacher:	((to Girl)) Huh?
19	Girl:	/tif/.
20	Teacher:	((to Girl)) You have to say THIEF.
21	Boy 2:	Steal.
22	Teacher:	((to Girl)) Not /tif/.
23	Boy 2:	((louder)) Miss steal!
24	Some:	Thief.
25	Teacher:	Not /tif/ but you have to sa::y?
26	Some:	Steal.
27	Teacher:	Steal. Very good.
28	Some:	Steal.
29	Teacher:	He'll steal. So a person who steals is called a:: (.5) [stealer.
30	Boy 4:	[*Vòlè.*
31	Teacher:	((impatiently)) Not a *vòlè*. We don't say a *vòlè* is PATWA!? ((speaking slowly)) A person who steals is a:: (.5) stealer or a (.5) THIEF. What do we sa::y?
32	Boy 5:	((loudly)) Thief!
33	Teacher:	A thief. All right. So he doesn't - so he doesn't want people to call him *vòlè* - he doesn't want people to call him thief. So then he is wai::ting for the man to::?
34	Some:	Give him one.
35	Teacher:	To give him ONE.

On lines 16 and 19 a female student who has been trying to get the teacher's attention since line 12 offers the English word "thief" instead of *vòlè*. However, her non-standard pronunciation as /tif/, while characteristic of the local English, now singles her out for correction by the teacher (lines 20 and 22). In contrast to *vòlè*, the teacher portrays /tif/ as simply incorrect, not constrained by context or place or part of a particular language variety. Boy 2, the student who originally suggested *vòlè*, then exclaims "steal" (line 21 and 23). As this is another English alternative, the teacher prompts the children to repeat it (line 25) and then praises them with "Very good" after they do it (line 27). But now "thief," the English translation of the Patwa noun *vòlè*, has been replaced by the verb "steal," which no longer fits the original problematic sentence frame, "Because they will call him *vòlè*." The teacher then tells the class: "So a person who steals is called a:: (.5) stealer" (line 29). Now she has gone so far to eliminate the Patwa usage that she suggests "stealer," a word I never heard used during my fieldwork, as people say thief, /tif/, or *vòlè*. Despite her many corrections, Boy 4 again offers the response, "*Vòlè*" (line 30). She rebukes him impatiently, "Not a *vòlè*. We don't say a *vòlè* is Patwa!?" (line 31). She then tells the children, "A person who steals is a:: (.5) stealer or a (.5) THIEF" (line 31). She gives a brief recap during which she says *vòlè* (line 33), though this is likely accidental due to her previous corrections of the children and her immediate self-repair to "thief." She ends the discussion by trying to elicit her initial description from line 1, "The man is coming to give him ONE," again on line 33, "So then he is wai::ting for the man to::?" Some children respond, "Give him one" (line 34), which she confirms (line 35) before moving on.

This example, while distinctly not playful in tone (the teacher becomes quite serious), illustrates how teachers play with the language of their students to convey that Patwa is not to be used in formal settings. In fact, while this teacher went to great lengths to remove a single Patwa usage, it is critical to note her place-related admonishment: "And when we are *in school* we spea::k?" (line 13), "We speak English" (line 15). This implies that Patwa may be acceptable outside the classroom. Through such metapragmatic commentary by adults, children come to recognize the contextual specificity of the languages of their community. This is highlighted in a conversation I had with Reiston's eleven-year-old cousin Marcel about children's language use. When telling me about two boys who occasionally speak Patwa in school and are corrected by their teacher, he said, "The teacher don't want them to speak it." I asked if the teachers ever use corporal punishment when this happens, and he said no. I continued my questioning, asking categorically, "They tell you don't speak Patwa?" At this point Marcel quickly qualified his initial statement with reference to place: "No they tell them not to speak Patwa *in the class*." Teachers do not forbid Patwa in all places, just in the context of the classroom. This suggests that Patwa may be acceptable for children to speak elsewhere—but where?

"Hardening" Children's English: Language Learning at Home

In most homes children are spoken to in English from birth and are expected to do the same once they begin to talk. Teachers have been very instrumental in this process; in addition to correcting children's language use at school, they suggest language-related strategies to parents to help their children improve academically. They instruct parents "how they should say things to the children," according to the principal. The third-grade teacher explains:

> You would always caution them about - do not talk Patwa to their younger children and so. Speak English. You meet them [outside of school], okay the parent is talking Patwa to the child, tell the Patwa - the parent well, speak English to your child and so. And most of them are aware of it. They know how the Patwa itself, is that that keep them back.

Most of the teachers claim that they rarely tell a parent not to speak Patwa at all, but they do strongly "encourage" them to speak English to children. The second-grade teacher instructs parents: "When it comes to success in school the English is more important. You putting English first." To further this goal the principal began adult education sessions so that caregivers could learn to teach their children to read in English before they begin school. Parents have taken this advice to heart. Those who can afford it buy books and others request that relatives overseas, or anthropologists who lived there, send books for their children. One parent asked me to send a *Hooked on Phonics* set for her preschooler.

For children English is an object of correction at home as well. Children are thought to be most impressionable when first learning to talk. Young children's language abilities, like their bodies, are considered "soft" and vulnerable and must be protected and regulated by adults until they mature. Dominicans view and treat children differently according to their age and if they have met developmental and cultural milestones. Babies are considered very soft and helpless, and must "harden" over time. Small children are rarely disciplined, but by the time they start primary school at age five they are given little slack for their mistakes, disobedience, or lack of respectfulness, and are expected to talk and understand English with clear articulation. It is through hearing others and practicing speaking that language skills harden over time, like babies themselves.

It is widely held that children learn language by imitation. A forty-year-old woman explained: "Yes, they like to imitate whatever you do. The way you walk, the way you talk. So that, you know, by imitating they learn." In order to ensure children's acquisition of English, caregivers choose to speak English to them regardless of which language(s) they speak with other adults. Direct instruction is considered essential to learning English. Linked to perceptions of how it had to be brought in to Penville and taught at school, caregivers say they must "show" children English as they learn to talk. Many prompt children to name objects in their environment, asking "what is that?" and answering in English if necessary, or telling them to "look the [noun]." They also engage in some literacy exercises, such as reading books or discussing pictures on alphabet charts. Direct instruction in Patwa is thought to be unnecessary and potentially harmful because caregivers fear that children may not learn the English equivalents once they begin using Patwa. Many claim that Patwa is already *adan yo* or "in them" and in need of being suppressed until they get older. Speaking Patwa and "mixing" codes are acceptable for adults, who have already been "held back"; but children have a future that can be heavily influenced by the linguistic resources they acquire, so parents have adopted a future-oriented language strategy in speaking English to them. Many assume that children will begin speaking Patwa as they get older like children always have and most are strongly against the idea of teaching it in the English domain of the school—posing challenges to KEK's Patwa revitalization plans.

Monitoring Children's Language Use at Home

Like teachers, caregivers often patrol, evaluate, and manipulate children's language use at home. When children begin to talk from roughly eighteen months, adults describe their speech as "babyish" and "not clear" in reference to indistinct articulation of consonants. In response, adults frequently tell them to "open your mouth to talk" or "pronounce properly." Adults strongly disapprove when children talk with their fingers or other objects in their mouths and they direct them to remove them or threaten children with, "You will get trush" (thrush). Most children suck their thumbs and fingers, sometimes three at a time, for years. While it is expected among babies, older children are teased and repeatedly told to stop. Jonah's father frequently criticized him for "sucking finger" at age two. One day he teased Jonah: "You worse than a baby because you sucking finger. Big baby Jonah. Big baby Jonah. You sucking finger." Children are encouraged to speak up and not be shy; if they are quiet when spoken to, they are asked if they are afraid or tired. Tessa scolded her nine-year-old son Nicky for talking with his head down: "I not hearing what you saying *non*. You talking for me, or you talking for your foot?"

During every transcription there were instances when a child's speech was unintelligible. When this happened, caregivers made guesses at what a child said. However, if I questioned them about what they thought the child *meant* to say, they rarely tried to guess, claiming that it is impossible to know what a child really means or if they mean anything at all. Examples of their comments include: "Sometime anything that come into their head children saying"; "I tell you they saying anything. So long they can pronounce the word, it will go"; "She just say it, she don't know." Children are considered to talk a lot of *léko* or "nonsense." This is simply ignored or dismissed with young children, but caregivers appear disturbed when they cannot tell what an older child, especially a teenager, is saying, indicating that expectations for language competence and appropriate behavior increase significantly with age. Jonah's family frequently criticized thirteen-year-old Claudette because, according to Jonah's mother, "She talking too much like a baby." By age five children are expected to talk more adult-like with fewer grammatical errors and clearer pronunciation, and are teased or scolded if they do not.

Figure 3.3 Female caregivers, like Tamika's (left) and Kenrick's (right) mothers, monitor children's speech and actions

Adults closely monitor children's language usage and correct errors in English as they get older. It is typically female caregivers who call attention to children's grammatical errors, nonstandard English pronunciation, and inappropriate speech (Figure 3.3). Their strategy parallels that of the female teachers observed at the preschool and primary school.[4] They repeat the child's utterance but replace Patwa words or ungrammatical English forms with the preferred English equivalents. Here Alisia (two years) makes a grammatical error in English that is common among young children:

Example 3.4
1   Alisia: ((to Mother)) Take out* it for me. [re: a bracelet on her arm]
2   Mother: Take it out for you?
3   Alisia: Yeah.
4   Mother: Leave it on your arm baby.

Alisia's mother rephrases her request with an embedded repair: "take out it" (line 1) becomes "take it out" (line 2) without explanation. She does not call explicit attention to the error or press Alisia for a repetition, and Alisia does not offer one. This correction contrasts with the mother's direct attention to her school-age children's ungrammatical utterances, as in the following example of Alisia's brother Tedison (four years) during the same recording session when I stood on the strap of my bag:

Example 3.5

1	Tedison:	((to AP)) Amy you sit downing* on it.
2	Mother:	((to Tedison)) What?!
3	Tedison:	((to Mother)) Hm?
4	Mother:	Sit downing?! *Tedison kouman ou ka palé la?*
		((clearly enunciating)) Standing up.
		(Sit downing?! <u>Tedison how are you talking there?</u>
		Standing up.)
5	Tedison:	Standing up on it.

Tedison makes two errors here. One is fairly common: he attaches the 'ing' suffix to the adverb 'down' instead of to the verb 'sit.' He also confuses the action, however, as I am standing rather than sitting on the strap. His mother questions him with an indignant, "What?!" (line 2). He requests clarification (line 3), prompting her to correct him explicitly with an other-initiated other repair, using English for the correction and Patwa for the critique of his language ability (line 4). He repeats her without hesitation (line 5).

Similar corrections occur when children use a Patwa word in their English speech and caregivers try to ensure that children know English translations. Here, Reiston (three years and five months) is swiftly corrected by his grandmother when he uses Patwa to refer to a knife she has dropped:

Example 3.6

1	Grandmother:	((drops knife on the floor))
2	Reiston:	*Ga!* Where granny *kouto?*
		(<u>Look at that!</u> Where is granny's <u>knife?)</u> [where did it go?]
3	Grandmother:	Is not a *kouto.* KNIFE.
4	Reiston:	Where the knife?
5	Grandmother:	It fall down. I see it. ((picking up the knife)) I get it.

The grandmother does not explain that *kouto* is a Patwa word and that Reiston should use the English equivalent, nor does she give a reason why "knife" is preferred over *kouto*. In fact, she phrases her correction as if he used the wrong noun entirely, as if he has called it a fork or spoon instead of a knife (imagine, 'Is not a fork. Knife.'). Reiston, who is accustomed to such correction, rephrases his question with the English equivalent (line 4). Only then does he receive an answer (line 5). His use of *ga* (line 2), however, is not corrected; the reasons for this are explored in chapter 5.

In contrast, caregivers rarely correct children's mistakes in Patwa and when they do it is only for a gross mispronunciation that typically engenders a laugh or joke to others. When Alisia (two and a half) incorrectly said *daksé* when she meant *dékatyé* (to tear up, to unfix), her mother did not correct her Patwa error but provided an English equivalent instead:

Example 3.7

1   Alisia: I *daksé** my head. [re: her hair]
2   Mother: You what?
3   Alisia: I going and *daksé** my head.
4   Mother: ((repeating Alisia)) You going and *daksé* your head?
5   Alisia: Yeah.
6   (2)
7   Mother: Not to unfix up your hair you know girl.
8   Alisia: Yeah.

Alisia's mother requests clarification twice (lines 2 and 4), but after a pause, translates directly to English, replacing *daksé* with English "unfix" rather than Patwa *dékatyé* (line 7). She also replaces "head" with the more precise noun "hair." Alisia uses *daksé* twice more later that day, both in questions to her father. He requests clarification, "Hm?", but both times Alisia repeats herself exactly and he simply nods and looks away, highlighting that women rather than men assume the primary role of regulating their children's speech.

Villagers are very conscious of their language choice with children. The village-wide language shift is well recognized and no one denies it; to the contrary, most point it out. Marissa's father, for example, says his children do not speak Patwa because, "Is only English I speak to them." Unlike in other situations of language shift reported in the literature, these young to middle age adults are generally not concerned that children may stop speaking Patwa completely. Some say they do not care or that children will eventually begin speaking it because they hear it around them. Echoing the teachers some claim children would be better off without it as it "interferes" with their English. Most fear that if children hear too much Patwa, it can "grab them" and the English can start to "come out" of them to be replaced by Patwa. The converse, that English can make Patwa "come out," is hardly considered possible and rarely mentioned.

Socializing Respect and Politeness through English

Sociability is highly valued in Dominican society and is maintained through practices like greetings, calling out to people, and general politeness (see also

Mühleisen and Migge 2005). Such practices loom large in child language socialization as children are obliged to be polite and display respect, especially to their elders. It is the responsibility of caregivers, particularly mothers, to ensure that children learn these important cornerstones of community interaction. For adults, both Patwa and English may be used to accomplish any of these basic forms of communication. Children, however, are socialized to learn and produce them only in English. In addition to using conventional forms, it is the age-appropriate choice of code as well as proper tone of voice—subdued and not too demanding—that indicates a polite and respectful demeanor. Young children are exposed to a great deal of English through these key cultural routines and socializing activities. Children learn to link English with politeness, respect, and formality; Patwa is reserved for other social functions (see chapter 4). Adults explicitly teach children important aspects of sociality through direct modeling in English through "say" and "tell" routines. Children are instructed to greet others, call out their names, announce their arrival when visiting homes, use kin terms and addressee names, and verbally recognize important familial and friendship ties. Children are praised in English when they accomplish such routines correctly, particularly when they call out or say thank you without prompting. Jonah's mother expressed pride that her two-year-old always greeted people and called them by name. Once during transcription she said, *"Timoun sala ni natiwèl"* (That child has sympathy/feelings). This is a primary goal of caregivers in socializing their children to be communicatively competent social actors.

Greetings are basic to social interaction. People are expected to greet when they visit, telephone, or simply pass one another on the street. It is polite to inquire how someone is doing and to give adequate notice before leaving a social situation. For adults all three speech acts (greeting, asking "how are you," and leave-taking) may be done in English or Patwa depending on the participants who come across one another.[5] Children, however, are prompted to greet in English, and are instructed to "Say 'hello'" when greeting or "Say 'I going'" when leaving. While adults frequently address other adults in Patwa saying, for example, *Ou byen?* (Are you well?), they switch to English to address children (e.g., "You cool?"). To not greet someone is considered rude or a sign of anger. Children who hide behind their mothers and do not say hello are told they are "making bad" or being "rude." They are shamed in front of others, such as when Tamika's six-year-old sister Vanessa did not greet her father one day. Her mother scolded her, "And Vanessa you don't know when you pass your father on the road you have to tell him good afternoon?" One is expected to greet a stranger, let alone their father. Glenda, her twin sister, then demonstrated her knowledge of this and the potential consequences of not greeting by telling Vanessa, "If he had *hit* you a slap." Vanessa shrugged.

Learning to "call" people in one's social network is vital for maintaining social relationships.[6] Children are explicitly taught calling-out sequences in

English, whereby a caregiver instructs a child to "call [name]," and the child does so.[7] For example, Tamika's mother models for Tamika (three years and one month) how to call her cousin Kenrick:

Example 3.8

 1 Mother: ((calling)) Kenrick!
 2 Tamika: Kenrick.
 3 Mother: Call him hard for him to hear.
 4 Tamika: ((loudly)) Kenrick!
 5 Mother: ((in high-pitched voice)) Say "come."
 6 Tamika: ((loudly)) Co::me.
 7 Mother: ((in high-pitched voice)) Come and meet me.
 8 Tamika: ((loudly)) Come meet me.
 9 Mother: ((in high-pitched voice)) Kenrick!
10 Tamika: ((loudly)) Kenrick!
11 Mother: ((in high-pitched voice)) Come!
12 Tamika: ((loudly)) Come and meet me!

Like other caregivers Tamika's mother speaks English for the instructional sequence. She uses a high-pitched voice to model what the child should say. Tamika tries calling six times, but Kenrick does not hear and the routine is dropped.

Deference to the authority of elders, a critical dimension of communicative competence, is socialized through use of proper terms of address and other politeness forms. Address terms like Mommy, Daddy, Auntie, Uncle, Ma'am, or Sir show respect and recognize social status. The only relationship that is generally named in Patwa by both children and adults is with godparents: *nennenn* (godmother) and *pawen* (godfather). Using proper terms of address is critical in school where children are required to address teachers as Miss/ Mistress or Mister. This is socialized through English and drawn attention to after a breach. For example, when caregivers question or tell a child to do something and the child answers minimally with "Yes," the caregiver then prompts, "Yes, who?" An appropriate response by the child would be, "Yes, Mommy." Similarly, children are told to say "please" and "thank you" (also "thanks" or "ta"), but not their Patwa equivalents *souplé* and *mèsi*, respectively.[8] Adults prompt children by asking, "What (do) you say?" or "You forget, man?", or refuse to release an object until the child uses the politeness form. This often requires no speech at all by the caregiver.

Paying Attention to Others

Children are directed to pay attention to the social activities of others from birth. Adults call children's attention to people driving by their homes by exclaiming,

"Transport!," and asking "Who own?" Children come to recognize local vehicles, which allows them to report to adults: who is going out and when; what people brought home; if a bread, egg, or rum truck is passing; or if strangers such as police, welfare, or tourists are in the area. Children are told from a very young age to "look" at things in their environment and are frequently asked, "who(se) own?" or "who own that?" This is multifunctional, as the act of calling children's attention to objects around them and to whom they belong socializes them to recognize not only what they can and cannot play with, but that such an activity is important in itself. Children are questioned about the whereabouts of people and told to ask individuals where they are going. These routines are in English and tend to fit the same relatively simple frame:

Caregiver: Where [name]?
Child: S/he go [place].
Caregiver: S/he go [place]?
Child: Yeah.

Such routines are ubiquitous in early caregiver–child communication and are one of the first forms of social interaction in which children partake. As they get older, children are told to ask people where they are going, such as when someone passes on the road. The place often indexes the activity to be undertaken; thus, calling and inquiring about someone's destination is a means of gathering information.

In fact, gossip is a primary social activity for adults and is carried out in Patwa and English. Gossip is multifunctional, serving as entertainment, a way to keep track of news and events, and a means of social control, among other things. Adults do not engage in gossip with children but recognize that children are an invaluable resource for providing useful information obtained while going to school or running errands. Older children are purposely sent to find out news or the whereabouts of someone, but adults do not engage in conversation or evaluation about it with them, though they do so with other adults in children's presence. Caregivers frequently clarify vague or incorrect answers and request more details such as place names, descriptions of activities, and the source of children's knowledge. Jonah's family frequently questioned him about people and places, as in this example about his grandmother when he was two years and eleven months:

Example 3.9
1 Father: Where Ma Dora?
2 Jonah: She not there.
3 Father: Where she went to?
4 Jonah: She go.

    5 Father: Hm?
    6 Jonah: She go um she go Grand Fond.
    7 Father: Who tell you is Grand Fond she go?
    8 Jonah: Where there she go?
    9 Father: I don't know. I asking you. Who tell you is Grand Fond she go?
   10 Jonah: ((louder)) She go Grand Fond!
   11 Father: And do what?
   12 (1)
   13 Father: Jonah.
   14 Jonah: Yeah?
   15 Father: What she go and do Grand Fond?
   16 Jonah: And - and see the cow.
   17 Father: Oh mama is a nice lady man.

Jonah's father requests elaboration about where the grandmother went (lines 1, 3, and 5) and what she was doing there (lines 11 and 15). He questions Jonah twice about the source of his knowledge (lines 7 and 9), demonstrating that it is important to know whether the information comes from direct or indirect report. Further, his father provides moral commentary about Jonah's grandmother as "a nice lady" (line 17), thus socializing the relevance of evaluation in narrative construction. This refers to the fact that she was helping Jonah's father because he was ill and unable to go himself. This kind of routine comprises a good portion of caregiver speech with children and socializes them to imagine and report on people and activities in other places, something they will do throughout their adult lives.[9] But unlike children in generations past today's children learn this valued skill in English not Patwa. Children who understand Patwa can figure out what is happening around them, but they are socialized to report back in English, even when questioned by an adult in Patwa.

English as a "Child" Language

English is the language of most social routines with children—it is what children are spoken to and speak in from birth. It is the language used by adults for the most basic of inquiries into children's well-being and needs, and it is the language of the school where children spend a significant part of their childhoods. English is so marked as a child language that even during contexts where Patwa predominates, caregivers typically code-switch into English to speak to a child or to report children's speech. One mother, for example, reported a conversation with her three-year-old to another adult: "*I di mwen* mommy I want piece guava, *mé mwen di* no it too late for you" (She told me mommy I want a piece of guava, but I said no it's too late for you). The adult reports both the child's and her own utterances in English within a Patwa conversation, suggesting either an accurate portrayal of the language used or compliance with expectations that such a conversation should be in English. Adults report adult speech in Patwa or English; however, I never heard an adult code-switch from English to Patwa to report a child's utterance, even for rhetorical effect, providing evidence that Patwa is not a language for children.

Such language alternation extends to turn taking within conversations. When adults are conversing with one another in Patwa, they regularly switch to English to speak to children. In the following example, Tamika's parents alternate languages according to whether the addressee is an adult or child. Tamika's mother had instructed Tamika to wash her hands in a pail of dishwater in the kitchen. Her father added, "And bring some water for daddy yeah," but did not specify that he wanted clean drinking water from a different pail. Tamika (two years and seven months) returns with a cup of dirty water and takes a sip before giving it to her father:

Example 3.10

1 Tamika: ((sips the water, hands the cup to her father))
2 Father: ((looking down at the dirty water)) *Éla:: Ga sa Lorna fè timoun la bwè. Ga!*
   ((interjection expressing pity or remorse) Look at what Lorna made the child drink. Look at that!)
3 Mother: *Ki sa i bwè la?*
   (What did she drink?)
4 Father: *Vyé glo sal la.*
   (The old dirty water.)
5 Mother: ((quietly)) *I py'a bwè vyé glo sal la.*
   (She isn't drinking the old dirty water.)
6 Mother: ((to Tamika)) You drink that?
7 Father: ((to Tamika)) You drink water?
8 Tamika: Yeah.
9 Father: ((sucks teeth in disgust))[10]
10 Mother: ((to Tamika)) That water dirty. Why you drink it for *non?*
11 Father: ((to Mother)) *Poutji ou menm pa té kouvè glo la non?*[11]
   (Why didn't you cover the (dirty) water (tag)?)
12 Mother: ((to Father)) *Glo pou lavé zasyèt wi.*
   (It is water for washing plates (tag).)
13 (2)
14 Mother: ((to Tamika)) Go and uncover the pail and take clean water for your daddy.

The parents speak Patwa to one another (lines 2–5), switch to English to address Tamika (lines 6–10), switch back to Patwa with each other (lines

11–12), and then switch back to English to direct Tamika to get clean water (line 14). When bilingual adults argue or criticize one another, they often choose Patwa over English, highlighting its links to intensified stances and emotions like anger. Tamika, however, only responds to the English questions directed at her (line 8). Children are expected to speak English even when spoken to in Patwa and are portrayed back to themselves as speaking English in reported conversation. All of these practices create a social world heavily filled with English; it also makes the contrast between child language (English) and adult language (Patwa) all the more salient to children.

Speaking English in the Community

Over the past few decades English has infiltrated all contexts of village interaction. While it may be used by any given speaker in virtually any situation, English continues to be more strongly associated with formal contexts and activities like school, church, and conducting business, especially in town. All official discourse is now conducted in English, including village meetings, ceremonies, and cultural shows, which are held on school grounds. Penville does not have a community center, so the school serves this purpose for meetings and events. No matter their function, these events follow a formulaic organization including formal openings, a prayer, speeches, and closings that are conducted almost entirely in the most standard varieties of English that speakers can muster, sometimes with a code-switch to Patwa for humor. Children are brought along to such events and further exposed to English as the language of formality, politeness, and official authority. An end-of-year awards ceremony at the Penville Primary School in 1997 illustrates the common format, which mirrors formal gatherings at the national level. It was conducted in English and included official introductions, a prayer, the national anthem, and multiple speeches in addition to distribution of the awards. The local PTA President welcomed visitors in a standard variety of English:

> Welcome Honorable Parliamentary Representative, Education Officer of the North, our district nurse, um PTA executives, distinguished guests, um, Principal, staff, friends, parents, children. We are honored. On behalf of the PTA of Penville school, I wish to welcome every one of you to this function here today. We are happy that you have taken time out of your busy schedules to be here with us. We hope that you will enjoy every part of this activity. Once again, welcome.

As is customary, each speaker formally welcomed all guests, including special acknowledgment of those in official roles. This was a school-related event, thus the speeches included discussion of how far the community had come in terms of the children's Common Entrance Exam scores that year, with seventeen of twenty-six passing and three earning scholarships. Before praying the local Catholic priest commented on the improved results by reformulating a derogatory phrase reportedly coined by Vieille Case villagers: the "Penville goats," referring to how residents farm the steep land the way goats scale mountains. He likened the changes to them "raising up from Penvillian goat to Penville rabbit":

> And I so much appreciate of what I heard about you in making this great sacrifice of trying to go up from Penvillian goat to Penville rabbit! Which means to say, I will explain to you what that means. Before we had a name hearing ... about Penvillian goats. We put down that name and we rise up to Penvillian rabbit. You know why I'm saying rabbit? Because when I was a young boy, when people used to tell us stories, rabbit is the animal that was most clever. You know? So today see how we are rising up, and I wish you all to keep up with that - that standing all you have.

The event chairperson then drew on the goat reference twice more in his speech, as in the following:

> I see in this classroom here this afternoon maybe a whole government [the children]. People who are going to run this country in the not so distant future. We didn't have those kind of people before. As the um, Mr. Joseph said, we were claimed to be goats. But I tell you, Penville people have been trying, and they will continue to try and strive for success. When you have children of that early age ... thinking so far and wide, I think they will take their village and their country somewhere. Dominica needs to move higher and higher and higher, and I think we are producing the caliber of people to move it from where it is, farther and farther.

As in other events, metaphors of development and moving forward permeated the speeches. I was surprised, however, that villagers would use a pejorative phrase coined by outsiders and I later questioned some people about it. Contrary to my reaction, they agreed with it wholeheartedly and said that "rabbit" indeed suited them well now.

These examples highlight the formal nature of community meetings, and also give further insight into how villagers interpret the changes undergoing in their community.[12] Yet it is important to note that such ways of speaking do not necessarily extend outside the formal meeting place. Once when I arrived too late to find a seat at a Village Council meeting, I stood in the corridor with a group of men observing the event. While the talk in the meeting was in English, this group spent the entire time joking about and critiquing what was said at the meeting in Patwa. The formal (inside) discussion was in English while the informal (outside) discussion was in Patwa, thus highlighting place, contextual, and functional constraints on language choice.

Discussion: "The Patwa Not in It"—Or Is It?

Penville residents struggled to bring English to their community and now they want to keep it there. They claim that Patwa interferes with children's English and prevents them from succeeding in school. Most caregivers do not allow children to speak Patwa in their presence. Adults cite the fact that their children now are performing better than ever in school as evidence that their English-only strategy is working. A mother of a teenage girl described the "progress" made since adults curbed their use of Patwa with children:

> It has improved a hundred percent. Because I can remember in my days when we used to go to school is by accident a child would get to go to a secondary school. And now eleven, twelve, seventeen children [are] attending the secondary school, so it has come out from there. But I know the hold back of our community was the Patwa.

A father of four said that children have "given up the Patwa for education." He pointed out that children "from uneducated parents like us" are even getting financial awards to attend secondary school. He explained that parents are "after them to speak the English, because the Patwa keeps them a lot behind." Many adults told me that they care much more deeply about how their children do in school than whether or not they ever learn to speak Patwa fluently. A father in his late twenties said for children, "English is more important." When they grow up, children are expected to provide for their families and care for aging parents. If children speak English and become educated, they are more likely attain a better job and contribute to the family.

Further weighing against the continued use of Patwa is that villagers say Patwa is not an "international language" or "internationally accepted" like English and it does no good for getting a job abroad or even in Roseau. This is a major concern among young adults who hope to find work outside Penville and out of farming. Several young men told me, "You must have the English to get the job." A young woman explained that if you go to work and your boss tells you "good morning," you cannot reply "*bonjou*" and expect to keep your job. A bus driver in his late twenties told me that during a training course for tour guides, participants were encouraged to learn languages like

French and Dutch to communicate with tourists. They were not encouraged to use Patwa, however, despite cultural heritage tourism promotion. He described it bluntly: "The Patwa not in it."

Of course, not everyone agrees with this and child language socialization practices suggest that Patwa is still very much "in it" as a marker of community identity and belonging. A man in his fifties said the problem is that Patwa has been the language of the home, but when children go to school, they are "forced" to do everything in English. He claims that Patwa is their "mother tongue" and that if schools would teach Patwa literacy, "They could really do something, eh?" While few residents articulate such sentiments, language socialization practices strongly indicate that to be a competent village member, some degree (however minimal) of Patwa competence is expected. English is more powerful institutionally speaking in that it can give access to material and symbolic resources like jobs, money, education, social mobility, and status. But Patwa is an essential part of community identity, solidarity, and belonging, and is symbolically valuable within the village. While someone who speaks mostly English with occasional code-switches is rarely commented on (like Dorian's 1982 "semi-speakers"), a person who speaks only English may be considered "too proud" or at a disadvantage for not having learned Patwa. Return migrants are criticized if they come from an English-speaking country and their children do not speak or understand Patwa. Several villagers in their fifties and sixties once gossiped about a young woman who returned from St. Marten and did not speak Patwa to her children *"pyès pyès pyès"* (at all, at all, at all), and as a result the children could not speak a word of it. They claimed the children spoke "good English," but were appalled that they could not speak any Patwa. Some competence in Patwa—no matter how passive or restricted—is considered an important element for community inclusion. This is the subject of the next chapter.

Notes

1. When I began learning Patwa, I was told that I had much to "swallow." One man said, "*Ou ni pawòl pou apwann jis bouden ou plen*" (You have words to learn until your stomach is full).
2. This exam was phased out in 2005 when secondary education became universal.
3. G. Smith (1991: 59) reports that "Patois, never again" was etched in stone above a school in St. Joseph.
4. See Cavanaugh (2006) for a similar discussion of female responsibility for ensuring children's acquisition of standard Italian, while men are more associated with the use and revitalization of the local vernacular Bergamasco, in Bergamo, Italy.
5. For examples, see Paugh (2001: 291, 339 note 13).
6. Calling sequences are multifunctional, used for greetings, attention getting, checking if someone is home, requesting permission to enter, summoning passers-by, locating

people, and socializing children to these functions. Caregivers also use calling routines to distract small children when they are upset or getting into trouble, telling them something like, "Look Papa calling you. Come and see Papa," even if the person is not really there (also see Kulick 1992; Schieffelin 1990: 81–86; Sidnell 1997).

7. In calling routines, names may be marked with the vocative suffix -o (e.g., "Kisho!").

8. Such routines start soon after birth. When a newborn baby burped, its caregiver would immediately say "Sorry" with a rising intonation, as if the infant was saying it.

9. This is also a significant means of remembering and maintaining relationships with people who have migrated. Practically every recording contained references to other villages, islands, and countries, so much so that I kept a list of the place names mentioned in each session.

10. David draws air through his teeth to make a sharp sucking sound that is known as "suck teeth." This common Caribbean gesture commonly indicates disgust, annoyance, disappointment, etc.

11. David further scolded Lorna a few minutes later: "*Lè ou vwè glo la sal, ou ja sav i ké ay adan i. Sé kouvèy*" (You know she will go in the dirty water. You should cover it.).

12. It also indicates how relations with other villages impact their own self-definition.

CHAPTER 4

Becoming "Good for Oneself": Patwa and Autonomy in Language Socialization

Alisia's mother and I are sitting at the table while she peels carrots for lunch. Alisia (one year and eleven months), who frequently urinates on herself, suddenly leaves the room and returns a few minutes later without her shorts on. This follows:

Example 4.1

1	Mother:	((slams down the bowl of carrots and glares at Alisia, speaking loudly in a deep voice)) Who tell you take it out [the shorts]? For me to beat you, eh?
2	Alisia:	No.
3	Mother:	Yes!
4	Alisia:	Yes!
5	Mother:	((in a low deep voice)) I'll beat you.
6	Alisia:	You lying.
7	Mother:	Huh?
8	Alisia:	You lying.
9	Mother:	((loudly)) I lying?!
10	Alisia:	((points at Mother)) You!
11	Mother:	Who lying there?
12	Alisia:	You *malpwòp*.
		(You are <u>nasty</u>.)
13	Mother:	((laughs, turns to AP)) You hear what she say Amy? She tell me I lying. *Malpwòp*. You know what is *malpwòp*?
14	AP:	What?
15	Mother:	Nasty!
16	AP:	Ah! *Malpwòp*.

17 Mother: *Malpwòp* is Patwa. She tell me I lying.
18 AP: ((laughs))
19 Mother: You see how - you think she don't good for herself?
20 AP: Oh yeah. She's good for herself.
21 Mother: She's VERY good for herself.

The mother's aggravated stance and threats to "beat" Alisia suggest that the child is in for a punishment for wetting her shorts (line 1). Alisia has heard this threat from her mother before, however, as the family struggled to toilet train her with limited success. She boldly replies, "No" (line 2). Her mother then threatens her in a more serious tone (line 5). When Alisia confidently challenges this with the accusation, "You lying" (lines 6 and 8), her mother does not punish her for what could be interpreted as insolence; instead she rekeys the scold into a playful teasing session with a rhetorical, "I lying?!" (line 9). Alisia points at her mother and fearlessly asserts, "You!" Her mother prompts her to continue (line 11). Alisia retorts boldly, "You *malpwòp*" (line 12), using a Patwa adjective that her caregivers call her when she urinates on herself. Her mother laughs and proudly recounts the incident to me to ensure my comprehension as it is one of our first recordings, thus framing Alisia's retorts in cultural terms: "She's VERY good for herself" (line 21). That means that Alisia can verbally defend and assert herself, a highly valued social skill. She is able to recognize that her mother is not (entirely) serious and provides a strong-willed response, to her mother's delight. In other contexts, such as a real scolding, her boldness, use of Patwa, and accusation that an adult is lying would be negatively sanctioned, but here it is a positive sign of Alisia's growing ability to keep up in a routine teasing session.

In this example and others in my corpus of videotaped caregiver–child interactions, the tensions involved in socializing both obedience and autonomy, and the role of language choice in this process, become evident. Caregivers in Dominica, like the world over, employ relatively predictable routines to socialize children into culturally intelligible subjectivities, including expected ways of being and interacting with others.[1] Through language use with those around them children acquire culturally specific ways of communication that are age and status appropriate, including how to display culturally recognizable and contextual affective stances, and when and how to demonstrate politeness and accommodation versus assertiveness and control. Caregivers also socialize children how not to behave and feel (Fader 2009; Kulick and Schieffelin 2004). How adults interact with children, or do not interact with them, is culturally organized.[2] Like other Caribbean children, Dominican children are socialized through common routines how to be polite and respectful (see chapter 3), but also to be bold and able to stand up for themselves—and these stances can be accomplished in part through language choice. Despite individual differences among households, the languages are increasingly divided according to functions, affective keys, and age/status differences in interactions between adults and children. While adults tell children not to speak Patwa, they simultaneously socialize use of the language for particular functions. Local theories of child rearing and expectations of children shape the transmission and reproduction of culture but also play a key role in change.

Children's language use at home and at school is highly regimented by adults. Yet children do manage to acquire variable degrees of Patwa competence. But how do children who are expected to speak English around adults and largely hear English spoken to them acquire any Patwa at all? As in other multilingual societies, there exists a "gap between explicit discourses valorizing a particular language variety and the implicit evaluation constituted by socialization practices" (Howard 2008: 189). There is a complementarity to English and Patwa that becomes clear in language socialization practices.[3] Both languages are needed for expressing valued community identities, affective stances, and social relationships despite a privileging of English in metalinguistic reflections. Adults use Patwa with children to convey affective meanings that English is not considered able to express adequately. Many aspects of sociality, including greetings and politeness, are explicitly taught through pointed instruction in English, which is considered more "calm" and accommodating than Patwa. Other valued qualities and demeanors associated with individuality and autonomy, like how to stand up for oneself, are socialized more implicitly through participation in and observation of everyday interactions among adults and children. This chapter analyzes situated activities in which adults socialize children to assert themselves appropriately as they develop age-graded "bilingual subjectivities" (Garrett 2007).

Language and Affect: The Power of Patwa

In contrast to English, which was "brought in" to Penville, Patwa is described as something that always has been with villagers and is simply *adan yo* or "in them." A woman in her early twenties explained that Patwa "is not even learned, it just comes naturally." The nurse described it as "a root in Penville," as if physically part of the area. It emerges from the inside while English must be imported from the outside and protected from the influences of Patwa. Further, adults describe Patwa as distinguishing Penville from other villages and English-speaking urban communities. They claim that "Penville people love their Patwa," and I was told that any adult who says they do not speak or at least understand it is lying or putting on airs. People who want to seem *gwan*, "big" or proud, often those with a prominent family name or experience traveling, use English to act "different." That Patwa serves as an emblem of community identity is seen in how villagers compare "their" Patwa to that spoken in other areas, particularly the south. When I first explained my research, I was told that I had chosen the right place because Penville's variety was "better," "easier" to learn, and "more clear" than the Patwa spoken in the village of Grand Bay and elsewhere. Several people assert that Penville's variety is the *vwé* or "true" creole passed down from their African ancestors. Villagers similarly claim that Penville itself is more safe, fertile, "real," "traditional," and simply "better" than communities closer to town, especially southern villages that have a reputation for crime, drug trafficking, and gun use. Patwa is a positive emblem of village identity and the good aspects of being rural: cooperation, simplicity, and little crime, or at least nostalgia for these things.

When asked about their languages, villagers identify Patwa with places outside the human-built area of the home, yard, and school. They say it is best for socializing in the banana field or garden, at the river or standpipe, and "on the road." The road serves important social functions as a site of community interaction (Figure 4.1).[4] It is a gathering place where people stop to exchange gossip and catch up on news. All along the road men and women pass on foot to and from work, usually alone or trailed by a small dog and carrying large sacks of food on their heads and a cutlass in one hand. Children make their way to and from school, often traveling in small groups. Two main "junctions" in Lower and Upper Penville serve as bus stops, meeting spots, and play areas for children, who often "drive" handmade wooden toy trucks or play cricket after school there. These are gathering places for the sale of pig or cow meat, especially for holiday meals (such as Christmas). On the road one can buy fish, meat, bread, eggs, fruit, cask rum, homemade sweets, and anything else an individual is selling from a truck, basket they are carrying, or blanket in their yard. The road becomes the site of festivals during Carnival and other holidays. Villagers can be heard interacting in Patwa all along the road, exposing children to routine ways of speaking it.

English is viewed as an important key to success but Patwa has its own symbolic value. Patwa is associated with intimacy and solidarity while English is the language of education, distance, and official activities. Patwa is considered appropriate for informal contexts, like talking and joking with friends, or for inserting a degree of informality and solidarity into more formal speech situations (such as meetings) through brief code-switches.[5] In everyday social interaction each choice of code or variety signals an "act of identity" (Le Page and Tabouret-Keller 1985) positioning the speaker and hearer in particular, though not always in intended or even conscious ways. Code-switching (both intra- and intersentential) is integral to village language use and in many ways is preferred to either English or Patwa monolingualism. Patwa and English are widely believed to be two very separate language systems yet code-mixing goes on constantly and sometimes the boundaries

Figure 4.1 The road is an important site of community interaction

become quite fuzzy, particularly with well-integrated borrowings such as *fig* (banana), calques such as "there I going" instead of "I'm going there" (from Patwa "*la mwen ka alé*"), and other forms of bilingual simultaneity (see Christie 1982). Even the use of Patwa place names (*Anho Mòn* instead of Upper Penville) and borrowings commonly heard and relatively unmarked in local English varieties (*koko* instead of coconut) indexes a more informal community identity and marks a person's rural origins in urban settings.

Villagers talk about how Patwa is disempowering outside Penville, but there is an unspoken sense that it is very powerful within the community and in particular circumstances outside the village to be discussed below. English is regarded as "soft" or "gentle"—like small babies and young children—while Patwa is considered "rough," "vulgar," "raw," and better for emotionally expressive speech acts such as joking, cursing, gossiping, assessing others, arguing, teasing, and telling colorful stories. All are integral skills for a communicatively competent adult. Patwa is regarded as more "commanding" and forceful than English, and despite fears of Patwa interference with children's English is considered ideal by many adults for dealing with disobedient children. Similar adjectives are used when talking about personality traits. A person who is "hard" or "rough"—*bon pou kòy* or "good for him/ herself"—is able to stand up for themselves, walk where they please (even at night without fear of witchcraft), and make their needs or wants known. Someone who is *mòl* or "soft" is considered meek, shy, and not good for themselves.[6] An outgoing person is called "bold" and "not nothing soft" while a reserved person who keeps quiet may be called a *moumou* (a mute person) or interpreted as being "stupid," "slow," or "too proud" to interact with others. A man who is too soft may be considered effeminate and called a *mako* (homosexual male). To be bold and outgoing are positive qualities for both men and women, and generally people prefer their children to be bold rather than shy. Women and girls are expected to be more polite and reserved than men and boys but also strong-willed and able to stand up for themselves when necessary, such as when joking or responding to an insult. At least some proficiency in Patwa is desirable for such functions, which require confident stances and high affective expression.

According to adults, Patwa is particularly effective when used as a "secret" language around people who cannot understand it, such as outside Penville or Dominica. I was told that a person who cannot understand Patwa in Dominica would be *mawé* (tied), though villagers similarly said that children would be "tied" if they *only* knew Patwa when going to school. One man in his twenties explained that it is bad to not understand Patwa, "because *lè ou gadé ou ay an koté, moun ké kwititjé ou. Ou pé ké sav* yeah?" ('because <u>when you go somewhere, people will criticize you. You wouldn't know</u> yeah?'). Others liked speaking Patwa when they knew people could not understand it, as a police officer told me, "It's fun to talk over people's heads." Caregivers often speak in Patwa to one another when they do not want their English-dominant children to understand them. Additionally, Dominican visitors to Guadeloupe or Martinique said it greatly helped them in communicating with their French neighbors.[7]

Patwa for "Intimate" Communication and Baby Talk

Many adults describe Patwa as a more "intimate" language for communicating with close friends and family.[8] The school principal explained that she had to learn Patwa when she came to Penville from Vieille Case to bond with the teachers:

> [I speak Patwa] with the teachers cause I don't have a choice. And when I came here at first I really felt funny because um most times when they communicate - especially when they're relating very closely um they speak Patwa. So I didn't have a choice. I didn't want to be seen as you know always speaking English, so most times - I mean, when we're doing school business we speak English, but then otherwise [Patwa].

Even when proficient in both languages, many adults claim to feel "more comfortable" speaking Patwa than English. English is considered polite but less expressive than Patwa. Yet when I asked men and women involved in romantic relationships what they spoke when alone, they gave a variety of responses from "mostly English" to "mostly Patwa." This did not fall clearly across socioeconomic or other lines although age played a part, as younger generations speak more English. Several couples spoke primarily English with their children but I observed them switch to Patwa with one another in emotional, urgent, or conflict situations.

The associations between Patwa and intimacy become clear in that despite the privileging of English with children, Patwa baby talk forms have been retained and are frequent in speech directed at infants and children under age five. This baby talk register is grammatically English but employs a large Patwa lexicon, highlighting its associations with intensified affect. There appear to be fewer English baby talk lexemes than Patwa ones, but caregivers do employ reduplication of English words as in "shoe-shoe" and "tea-tea." There is some phonological modification in both Patwa and English speech such as /fanfan/ for *zanfan* (child), /titing/ for "sleeping," and use of higher pitch.[9] Though used within English utterances, Patwa baby talk lexicon refers to the earliest and most salient things in children's lives (see Table 4.1).

Table 4.1 Examples of Patwa and English baby talk lexicon

Baby talk term	English gloss	Language
tété	breast, to suckle	Patwa
nana	food, to eat	Patwa
dodo	sleep, to sleep	Patwa
sisit	sit (down), from *sizé*	Patwa
bobo	sore, injury (akin to English 'booboo')	Patwa
ba toutou	give kiss (common routine with small children)	Patwa
kaka	feces, to defecate	Patwa
poopoo	feces, to defecate	English
peepee	urine, to urinate	English
ta	thank you (usually with a rising intonation, "Say ta:::")	English
peep-peep	vehicle	English

Children are encouraged to use the baby talk lexicon to describe their wants and needs when they are beginning to talk until they start school. One mother described such words as, "Just a little slang. Those children say it when they learning to talk." Another mother clarified: "But only for children, yeah." Caregivers report that these are among the first words children speak in addition to "mama" or *manman*, which many interpret as Patwa even though all the young mothers referred to themselves as "mommy" and to children's grandmothers as "mama."

Adults and older children also use Patwa terms of endearment in addressing children and when trying to console them or engage their interest. Common examples include *kòk*, *doudou*, *toutou*, and *koko*, all of which are described by speakers as "little nicknames" for children and roughly translatable as "darling" or "sweetie."[10] When caregivers try to soothe babies or small children, they call them these "pet names," as several mothers referred to them, in addition to English ones such as "baby," "sweetheart," and "darling." Children are called *timoun* or *zanfan* (child), *tibway* (little boy), and *tifi* (little girl) in Patwa, and may be cajoled by being called *zanfan mwen* (my child). Within months of learning to talk young children address baby siblings with these terms. Adults do not negatively judge children's use of these words as they are considered harmless. By the time they enter school, however, children are expected to use the correct English equivalents in most contexts.[11]

In addition to baby talk lexicon and terms of endearment, there is a performative aspect of Patwa that is explicitly encouraged through lullabies and other routines. The following is an example of a common Patwa lullaby:

Dodo ti bébi. Mama pa la. Papa pa la. Si ou pa dodo bèt la ké manjé ou. Si ou pa dodo bèt la ké manjé ou.

(Sleep little baby. Mommy's not there. Daddy's not there. If you don't sleep the creature will eat you. If you don't sleep the creature will eat you.)

In a similarly themed routine, caregivers pretend their hand is an animal that runs up and down the child's body until it stops and "eats" them through tickling. Adults usually pretend to be a rat (*wat*) or cat (*chat*), but children have begun substituting *bèt* (creature).[12] Here, Kenneth (thirteen years) performs it to amuse Reiston (three years and three months) while their grandparents are working:

Example 4.2

1 Kenneth: ((with rising intonation, walking hand up Reiston's side))
            Bèt la mouté mouté mouté. Bèt la mouté mouté mouté. Bèt la mouté mouté mouté.
            (The creature is going up, going up, going up.) [three times]

2 Reiston: ((laughs))

3 Kenneth: ((with falling intonation, walking hand down Reiston's side)) *Bèt la désann désann désann. Bèt la désann désann désann.*
            (The creature is going down, going down, going down.) [twice]

4 Reiston: ((laughs))

5 Kenneth: [((speaking fast and tickling Reiston)) *Bèt la manjé'y la. Manjé'y la! Manjé'y la! Manjé'y la!*
            (The creature is eating him there. Eat him! Eat him! Eat him!)

6 Reiston: [((laughs hysterically))

Reiston then performs a shortened version with Kenneth:

Example 4.3

1   Reiston: ((to Kenneth)) *Bèt la mouté mouté mouté* ((tickles Kenneth)).
2   Kenneth: ((pulls arms together tight, smiling))
3   Reiston: ((laughs))

This routine entertains Reiston while socializing positive affective associations with Patwa and his relationship with Kenneth. Further, it gives him an opportunity to practice the routine and employ Patwa forms that would not be acceptable in conversation with caregivers. The use of baby talk, child-oriented routines and lullabies, altered voice quality, and reduplication key positive affective stances in interactions with small children. They also function as a resource for appealing to children, as their frequency along with exaggerated intonation increase when trying to persuade them. Use of such features emphasizes age and status differences between adult/older child speakers and infant/young child addressees. Further, it highlights that Patwa is associated with affective stances that complement or intensify those expressed through English, and this is transmitted to children as such from their very first encounters with language.

Joking and Teasing

The intensified affect indexed by Patwa carries over into verbal play and humor, including short jokes, double entendre, and lengthier teasing. Adults say that Patwa is preferred for this banter because it is considered "rougher" and more "vulgar" than English. One woman explained that Patwa was fun. "Speaking Patwa," she said, "will more convey the message. If you have to give a joke, it will sound better in Patwa." Another man told me, "It makes the joke better." Joking between men and women is often of a sexual nature although this occurs within the sexes (like among friends and co-workers) as well. Men and women often "throw" joking comments at one another and it is preferred that these be in Patwa rather than English. For example, I once overheard a woman telling some men in English about how she had stayed up all night listening to a cricket match on the radio. One man then said to her in Patwa: "*Oh, ou enmé jwé bol la?*" (Oh, you like to play ball/cricket?). She replied with an emphatic "*Wi!*" (Yes!) and later explained to me that although he explicitly asked if she likes to play cricket, he was really asking if she likes to have sex. There are also many jokes that play with the boundaries between codes and are told by adults and children. For example, a mother and her eleven-year-old daughter taught me the following in which the addressee is told to respond *li* after each line of the joke:

Speaker:	*Addressee:*
I was walking down the road past the river	li
And there was a man in the river	li
He was washing his big toe	li

The joke here is that *toli* is "penis" in Patwa. Thus the person saw a man washing his big penis (toe-li/*toli*). The mother considered the joke very funny and appropriate for her daughter.

Bilingual villagers say they prefer Patwa for common speech acts like teasing, cursing, and arguing with people (see Garrett 2005 for St. Lucia). In this example from Tamika's family half-serious teasing banter serves as a greeting when Irving, Tamika's grandfather, returns from tending his cow to find that his wife Eugenia is not home and there is no lunch prepared for him. His daughters Lorna and Cynthia are inside Lorna's house:

Example 4.4

1 Irving: ((calling from the yard)) *O Eugenia té alé?*
(Where did Eugenia go?)

2 Cynthia: ((yelling from inside the house)) *An Piton.*
(To Piton.)

3 Irving: ((speaking loud and fast, outside)) *Zò tout lé dé tapé kò zò anlè an Piton pou zò - pou zò pa bouyi an fig mété la ba mwen.*
(Both of you found yourselves in Piton for you (plural) to not boil a banana to put there for me [for lunch].) [re: Eugenia and Cynthia]

4 Lorna: ((laughs))

5 Cynthia: ((laughing, yelling outside)) *Ola ki - ola ki ni manjé la daddy?!*
(Where is - where is the food daddy?!) [i.e., she doesn't have food to cook]

6 Irving: ((speaking fast)) *Zò dé dyablès ka fè mwen PÈ la mandé zò sa zò vini aché.*
(You two she-devils made me FRIGHTENED to ask you what you came to get.) [re: earlier that day in Piton]

7 Lorna: [((laughs loudly))

8 Cynthia: [((laughs))

9 Irving: ((from outside)) *Èben zò modi asi latè.* ((walks past the door of the house)) *Mm!*
(Well you are bad on the world. Mm!)

10 Lorna: *Bondyé::!* ((laughs))
(God!)

11 Cynthia: ((looking at Lorna, smiling)) *M'a té ni manjé.*
(I didn't have food.)

12 Lorna: ((calling loudly to Irving)) *M'a té ni manjé non* daddy.
                Zanfan! An sèl liv fawinfons mwen té ni la. Mwen météy an
                difé. Manjé David ki la.
                (I didn't have food daddy. Child! One pound of white flour
                alone I had there. I put it on the fire [to cook]. David's
                food that is there.)

After Cynthia answers Irving's question about his wife's location (line 2), he
retorts with a half-joking complaint that the women went to Piton in lieu of
making lunch for him, an expected female chore especially for wives (line 3).
His lament is emphasized as he complains that they did not even boil a
banana for him. Lorna and Cynthia's laughter in response (lines 4 and 5)
suggests that Irving is not fully serious. Cynthia retorts with a rhetorical
question demanding the whereabouts of the food she is supposed to cook
since the family struggles to provide enough food for everyone. In fact, she
and Eugenia were gathering green bananas and other crops for the household
when they saw Irving in Piton earlier. Her joking response is mitigated with
use of the English "daddy" (line 5). Irving continues teasing his daughter,
however, calling her and her mother "she-devils" that made him afraid to ask
what they were up to—and might want from him—in Piton (line 6). Both
daughters laugh at this, especially Lorna (lines 7 and 8). He then tops off his
teasing as he walks past the open front door of the house, "*Èben zò modi asi
late. Mm!*" (line 9). Lorna explodes with the exclamation "*Bondyé::!*" followed
by laughter (line 10). Cynthia then looks at Lorna and quietly says that she
did not have food to prepare (line 11). Although she is smiling her comment
indicates recognition that there is some truth to the teasing. Lorna follows this
by defending herself for not cooking Irving's lunch: she needed to prepare the
little food she had for her own husband David (line 12). Irving does not
appear angry, however, and goes in the kitchen to eat some bread left from the
night before. Soon after he is joking with his daughters again. This family
frequently employs Patwa to tease and subtly criticize one another's actions
and ethics, especially regarding shared material objects and work obligations.
The children often are present to overhear them.

Conversation and Gossip

Village adults frequently code-switch between English and Patwa in their
everyday casual conversation with one another. Considered more expressive
and vulgar, Patwa is particularly favored for gossiping among bilingual adults.
Commonly called *bèf*, gossip occurs anywhere but especially on the road, in
rum shops, and in the yard (Figure 4.2).

Villagers despise yet simultaneously delight in gossip. They frequently
complain about "bad-talking people" or *malpalan*, yet savor every tidbit they

Figure 4.2 People socialize outside a village shop

manage to obtain (or create). Gossip acts as a mechanism of social control, as people say they avoid doing particular things, like wandering the streets or stealing fruit, because they will be talked about if detected. People complain that there is too much gossiping in the community yet most engage in it. For example, two close friends in their late twenties, Elma and Serena, complained one afternoon that their neighbor was always "in their business." Elma exclaimed brusquely, *"Elsa sala enmé mandé. I anni vwè mwen pasé èvè pail mwen, i ka mandé mwen sa i ni adan i"* (<u>That Elsa likes to ask questions. She sees me pass with my</u> pail, [and] <u>she's asking me what's in it.</u>) But not two minutes later they began gossiping about other local women while Serena combed her five-year-old daughter Yasmina's hair. Using mostly Patwa they criticized the actions, comportment, and morals of those in question. Serena's angry tirade about Tina, Yasmina's godmother, is prompted after Elma mentions Tina's daughter Doreen:

Example 4.5

1   Serena: *Tina yo pa pyès moun non. Tina di mwen Norma pa moun pou ba nonmé zanfan, èvè i pwen douvan mwen, i pwen douvan mwen.*
<u>(Tina and them are not good people at all (tag). Tina told me that Norma wouldn't be a good godparent [to Yasmina], and she was in front of me, she was in front of me [talking badly about Norma].)</u>

2 Elma: Hm hmm.

3 Serena: *I fè mwen pa ba Norma nonmé Yasmina èvè atjwèlman i kay*
           ba Norma nonmé ((waving the comb)) *bébé Doreen.*
           (She made me not have Norma christen Yasmina and then
           she had Norma christen Doreen's baby.) [re: Tina's
           granddaughter]

4 Elma: Hm hmm.

5 Serena: ((shaking head back and forth)) *Pa TI biten wi? I di mwen.*
           (Not LITTLE thing yeah? She tell me.) [re: speaking badly
           about Norma]

6 Elma: ((nodding head)) Hm hmm.

7 Serena: *Vlé i té vlé Yasmina pou mwen té ba'y nonmé Yasmina ou sav.*
           (She [Tina] wanted me to ask her to be Yasmina's godmother
           you know.)

8 Elma: *Sé mandé sa'y ka ba Yasmina atjwèlman.*
           (Ask what she is giving to Yasmina now.) [Implies that
           Tina, who became Yasmina's godmother, does not provide
           for her like a godmother should]

9 Serena: *Atjwèlman mi konsa i yé èvè Norma. Sé yo ki* ((crosses two
           fingers)) best friend. Mm. Norma *ka genyen lèt, sik,*
           arrowroot, *tout biten ba bébé la. Lè i fini vann, sa'y pa vann*
           i genyen ba'y li.[13]
           (Now look how she is with Norma. They are best friends.
           Norma buys milk, sugar, arrowroot, everything for the baby.
           When she finishes selling [her produce at market], she gives
           what she doesn't sell to her.)

10 Elma: Hm hmm.

11 Yasmina: ((climbing on Serena's lap)) Mm! Mm! Mm!

12 Serena: *Mélé èvè jan Penville. Jan Penville ka tiwé pen la an bouch ou*
           ba an lòt.
           (Get involved with Penville people. Penville people take the
           bread out of your mouth to give to another.)

13 Elma: *Tiwé pen la ba an lòt.*
           (Take out the bread to give to another.)

14 Serena: ((to Yasmina)) You self. Sit!

15 Yasmina: ((continues wiggling on Serena's lap))

16 Serena: *Sizé non ou menm!* ((sucks teeth))
           (Sit yourself!)

The women criticize the intentions, morality, behavior, and gossip of other
village women. Serena complains that Tina repeatedly told her negative things
about Norma when Serena considered asking her to be Yasmina's godmother

(lines 1, 3, and 5). She suggests that Tina bad-talked Norma so that Serena would choose *her* as Yasmina's godmother, which Serena eventually did (line 7). Elma agrees with Serena (lines 2, 4, and 6) and then strongly critiques Tina's behavior as godmother by suggesting that she has not fulfilled the expectations of this role through giving things like food and clothing to Yasmina (line 8). Serena then contrasts this to Norma's behavior as godparent to Tina's grandchild, claiming that she frequently gives things to her goddaughter. She also morally critiques Tina as two-faced: despite Tina's previous bad talk about Norma, she now acts like they are "best friends," illustrated non-verbally by crossing her fingers (line 9). Serena sums up her experience with reference to *all* Penville residents as looking out for themselves (line 12). Elma aligns with her by repeating most of the statement (line 13). Note that the heated gossip session is conducted almost entirely in Patwa. There are two brief code-switches to English, both by Serena: "best friend," a common English phrase, and "arrowroot," which tends to be said in English rather than the Patwa alternative *toloman* (line 9). Adults often employ even more code-switching into English for interactional functions like rhetorical effect and reported speech, however, there is a small child present and older children nearby who know the women being talked about, hence Patwa use helps obscure the content. Serena switches to English to issue a directive to her young daughter, demonstrating the common pattern of speaking English when addressing children (line 14). When Yasmina does not obey, however, Serena switches back to Patwa and sucks her teeth to highlight an escalation in seriousness (line 16), a common control strategy among adults to be explored below.

Managing Children: Patwa as a Strategy of Control

Language choice with children is shaped by culturally specific ideas concerning sociality and individuality, authority and autonomy, and adult–child status differences. Children acquire knowledge of status and role through language use with others around them. In Penville there is a rough "division of labor" between the languages in speech to children. English is the language for explicit instruction and socialization, used for greetings, calling routines, socializing politeness, and routines directing children to look at and name objects, as well as most other interactions concerning children's wants, needs, or feelings. Patwa, on the other hand, stands out as a moral discourse used by adults to make negative evaluations through assessments, insults, and curses. It is used to issue directives to children as a last resort when adults have told them to do or not do something several times in English with no response. When adults code-switch into Patwa it indicates that things have escalated and become more serious. Children are extremely sensitive to such switches and typically do what they are told immediately. If not, the next strategy usually employed by adults is to threaten and then carry out a physical punishment.

Children are considered naturally messy, rude, and in need of control to make them behave and *lévé* or "raise up" to be good persons. They are scolded for "dirtying up the place," playing in other people's things, and disrupting the orderliness of the home and yard. Marissa's mother explained: "When you have children in a home? The place doesn't stay how you want it. You have to satisfy with that." Similarly, Tamika's mother complained: "*An douvan lapòt pa ka wété nèt èvè sé zanfan sala, eh? Bondyé*" (A yard doesn't stay clean with those children, eh? God.). Adults spend their days trying to keep children under control and their homes tidy. Children are highly cherished but generally not treated in a child-centered way. Adults do monitor children's behavior and speech, including where they go, what they play with, and if they are in harm's way. In line with these goals, speech to children consists heavily of imperatives (e.g., "come here," "don't do that," "put it back") and evaluations or questioning of their behavior.[14] Under calm circumstances when it only has to be said once, this speech tends to be in English. But adults will use Patwa to keep control through directives and negative assessments as it is considered more emotionally charged and effective in driving a point home with children. Its use marks a change in affective stance and signals that the stakes have increased. Through their play with the two languages in speech to children, adults reaffirm links between Patwa and adult status/control.

Language and Discipline

Children are expected to be obedient, respectful, and deferent to their elders. Disobedient children are chastised for wanting to *koumandé* (command) or "rule" themselves. A child who does what they want or talks in a way that is considered too grown up is criticized for acting *two nonm* (too mannish) or *two fanm* (too womanish), explained to me by one parent as: "*ni mannyé gwo moun*" (to act like a grown up).[15] There are age-appropriate ways of speaking and children are criticized if they violate these expectations. For example, children are expected to respond immediately when they are called. This should be in English and with a tone of voice that is respectful and not whiny (too babyish) or demanding (too womanish or mannish). While it is good to learn to defend oneself under the proper circumstances, such as when mistakenly accused of something, it is a serious trespass to intentionally disrespect one's elders in an inappropriate interactional frame (when being serious rather than playful). A child who does so is called *hadi* (rude) or *mal élivé* (badly brought up) in either Patwa or English. This sometimes comes with implicit encouragement, however, depending on the seriousness of the trespass.

When a child misbehaves caregivers try a range of options before it escalates to use of Patwa and ultimately corporal punishment. They use bargaining tactics like conditional promises of rewards such as going somewhere ("Eat for us to go on James bus") or receiving a treat ("I'll buy sweetie for you eh *kòk?*"). They also threaten to withhold objects or activities. Some caregivers caution that they will call the police or an adult the child fears. Shaming is another tactic, and may include warnings of what another person will do if the child does not comply ("Amy going to laugh at you"). This may be accompanied by threats of physical punishment in English and/ or Patwa, such as "I'll beat you" or "*Mwen ké kwévé ou.*"

Significantly, caregivers use language choice as a means to indicate an escalation in seriousness by switching from English to Patwa in their directives or assessments. Caregivers are explicit about how powerful code-switching is in such situations. According to many, such switches express their frustration when their patience has run out and they are "fed up." One woman explained that Patwa "brings out the message better, especially when you are angry." Kenrick's mother answered the question "do you ever speak Patwa to your children?" with this:

> Yes, as though if I have something to say fast. I will say *"Daniel pwen sa ba mwen. Nicky ay mété sa la. Nicky pa fè sa"* (Daniel take that for me. Nicky go put that there. Nicky don't do that). Something they make me vex, I'll make a rage and talk Patwa to them but I don't - that is not something I really do to talk Patwa for them. My talking is English for them.

Other caregivers agree that Patwa better expresses one's "rage" than English. Even teachers say they sometimes speak Patwa to children in and outside of school, like the second-grade teacher:

> Yes sometimes I do [in school]. Even at home I do that you know because when you see I speak *twice* in English and they do not - um, not to say they don't understand, but as in the Patwa word comes out more (pause) you know. And then it's harder, its *rough* you know so as if they *listen* to me better ((laughs)) when I give it to them in Patwa.

The third-grade teacher says she uses it in the classroom to "scream after a child," stating, "Sometimes you tell them something in English, to me they did not take heed. When you tell them in Patwa, to me they understand." Other teachers agree.

These caregivers qualify their statements, however, by claiming that they otherwise do not speak Patwa to children. But disciplinary contexts are considered appropriate, or at least justifiable. During preliminary fieldwork in 1995, I audio-recorded my friend Odette speaking Patwa to her children—for my benefit—while she was washing clothes in her yard. After a few minutes, her sister Victoria called from her house:

Example 4.6

1	Victoria:	((calling to Odette)) *Sé bon?*
		(Is that good?) [re: speaking Patwa to children]
2	Odette:	We:::ll (1) *mwen ka palé pli Patwa pasé Annglé.*
		(We:::ll (1) I speak more Patwa than English.)
3	Victoria:	*Lé ou faché?*
		(When you are angry?)
4	Odette:	*Népòt mannyé.*
		(For anything.)

This reaction to hearing a mother speak Patwa to her children indicates how strongly English has become associated with child rearing while Patwa is appropriate for expressing anger. By asking if it is "*bon*" (line 1) and thus implying it is not, Victoria negatively evaluates Odette's language choice. Her follow-up question suggests that it would be acceptable in certain circumstances but not in regular conversation (line 3). Odette exaggerates in her response by claiming she would speak Patwa to them for any reason (line 4), as she normally speaks English to children.

The Escalation to Patwa

In their efforts to ensure obedience from their children, caregivers transform Patwa into an adult register and a potent means to manipulate and control others. Usually when adults switch to Patwa, their speech shifts to a deeper, harsher, louder, more urgent tone than in regular conversation or previous utterances, and includes dramatic paralinguistic cues such as a sharp nod or shake of the head, or lifting of a hand as if to slap the child. The marked use of Patwa is multifunctional, fulfilling an intensifying function as an emphatic, rhetorical device in addition to transmitting a message (i.e., not only referential or a translation). Usually adults have issued a command more than once in English, thus it is hard to tell if young children understand what caregivers are saying in Patwa or if they simply recognize the implications of the switch. The scolds "*ou pa ka tann?*" (you're not hearing?) and "*pa fè sa!*" (don't do that!) are particularly familiar since most children hear them on a regular basis when they refuse to comply.

Often caregivers switch to Patwa to issue imperatives during goal-oriented activities such as bathing, dressing, and feeding, or when they have commanded a child several times in English with no result. The following example between Tamika (two years and nine months) and her mother exemplifies the escalation to Patwa. Her mother wants to bathe her while Tamika wants a cup of juice:

Example 4.7

1	Mother:	Well go and take the soap for you to bathe.
2	Tamika:	Where my own mommy? [re: juice]
3	Mother:	It there. Go and take the soap for you to bathe and come for your own.
4	Tamika:	Take it for me. [re: the juice]
5	Mother:	Come and bathe.
6	Tamika:	((does not move))
7	Mother:	((yelling rapidly)) *Fè vit pou mwen ay fè twavay mwen! Mwen ni pou jis lavé.* (Hurry up for me to do my work! I have to wash [clothes].)
8	Tamika:	Leave me alone.
9	Mother:	((screaming)) Tamika go and take the soap!
10	Tamika:	((gets the soap and goes to bathe))

Before switching to Patwa the mother issues four directives in English for Tamika to take her bath (lines 1, 3, 5). She then code-switches to Patwa with a rising tone and faster speech, implying that she should have finished washing clothes already and is behind in the day's chores (line 7). Tamika dares to challenge her by employing a common sentence frame among children, "Leave me alone" (line 8). Her mother then switches back to English, again creating a rhetorical contrast and indicating further escalation by screaming her directive, "Tamika go and take the soap!" (line 9). At this point Tamika does what she is told (line 10). Children are very sensitive to code-switches and the possibility of a more serious punishment to follow.

Such Patwa uses index intensified, often negative affect and affirm adults' rights as more mature, culturally knowledgeable members to direct children's actions and speech. Sometimes caregivers explicitly refer to this in their metapragmatic comments. For example, Reiston (three and a half) was taking a bath under the outside pipe when his grandmother told him to move so she could wash clothes. After twelve English utterances she lightly slapped him on the arm and he began to cry. She continued with Reiston crying throughout her monologue: "Boy move yourself from there eh? Take your - tell Kenneth take your bath towel to wipe you and put clothes on you. Go and wipe yourself and put clothes on you. Go! You bathe enough. *Ou toujou vlé koumandé kò'w* (You always want to rule yourself)." Reiston finally complied. Notably, the grandmother's evaluative commentary on his actions was in Patwa despite an otherwise English interaction. The shift in language highlights the contrast between adult/child roles and authority. Other caregivers made similar comments, such as Tamika's mother when Tamika refused a directive:

She too bad. Is so. If you see you leave her so, *i ka* take over *ou.* You understand? She TOO small for her to want to rule me. *Mwen di ou sòti la, sé sòti la.*

(She's too bad. It's like this. If you let her do what she wants, <u>she'll</u> take over <u>you.</u> You understand? She's TOO small to want to rule me. [<u>When</u>] <u>I tell you to come out from there, you come out from there.</u>)

Caregivers generally prefer verbal control to corporal punishment, but the situation can escalate to physical threats and actions if a child continues to disobey. This occurred in even the most child-centered families like Jonah's. Once when Jonah (two years and eleven months) refused his father's directives to go in the house, his father threatened him, "I'll slap you in your *boumboum* (bottom) eh?" He continued, "You not *koumandé*ing (commanding) me, *kon di Lola* (according to Lola [a neighbor])." The code-switch to Patwa intensified its negativity and highlighted the contrast between their statuses and rights. However, the scold was mitigated through partial displacement of responsibility for the utterance by revoicing another adult's reported speech. When Jonah still did not comply, his father asserted his will by exclaiming, "Daddy will not let you do whatever you want," and physically carrying Jonah into the house.

Patwa for Moral Evaluation and Reaffirmation of the Status Hierarchy

In addition to intensifying directives, caregivers utilize negative affectively marked Patwa adjectives and nouns in English utterances to issue moral judgments and negative evaluations of children's behavior or demeanor (also see Durbrow 1999). Use of these terms provides a potent commentary on children's comportment and censures unsociable qualities or actions. Children soon begin calling other children these disparaging terms (see chapter 5). These examples appeared in my recordings of all six families:

anbétan (troublesome)	*hadi* (rude)
ochan (impatient, busy)	*sòt* (stupid)
mal élivé (badly brought up)	*tèbè* (idiot)
malpwòp (nasty, dirty)	*défo, vowas* (greedy)
salòp (dirty person)	*filozòf* (self-important, a show off)

Caregivers direct such terms at children, as in "You (are) too *anbétan*" or "*Mal élivé!*" often accompanied by a shake of the head or sucking of the teeth. Adults also critique children's behavior using third-person reference as Alisia's mother did multiple times in a span of fifteen minutes when Alisia (two years and four months) was acting particularly troublesome:

"Alisia modi." (Alisia is bad.)
"Ga kalité Alisia non." (Look at Alisia's character traits (tag).)
"Woy! Alisia sala anbétan." ((Interjection!) That Alisia is troublesome.)
"Sé zanfan sala mwen ka pété yo atè mwen menm." (Those children, I'll burst them down on the ground myself.)

While such comments often are directed at other interlocutors, here only Alisia, her mother, and her infant brother were interacting. I was nearby but not part of the conversation. Children do not need to understand all of what is said in such commentary, as the use of Patwa and exasperated tone lends pragmatic saliency and indexes that an adult's patience is running out.

Caregivers also employ other formulaic phrases such as *"ou ka sanm (an vyé) ..."* (You look like/resemble (an old) ...), either alone or with a disparaging noun phrase, such as *"an gwo makak nwè"* (a big black monkey) or the name of some unusual or antisocial person in the community. Adults refer to children's behavior and actions with belittling terms like *kochonni* (nonsense) and *makakwi* (foolishness), warning them not to *kasé* (break) or *dékatyé* (tear up/break) something they are touching. Children hear these intensified verbal insults on a daily basis and use them to critique the actions of others, especially other children. Sometimes they apply them to their own actions, as Alisia (two and a half) did by repeatedly calling some scribbles she drew *"kochonni."* These single Patwa lexical usages tend to be incorporated into completely English sentences or conversations.

When children neglect to greet, do not say thank you, or act "greedy" (see Paugh 2001: 313–326 for extended examples), adults frequently code-switch into Patwa to evaluate, shame, and teach them a lesson. Here, Jonah (two years and four months) did not greet Clarice, a close family friend in her late sixties, when she arrived at his house. He later calls to her:

Example 4.8

1 Jonah: Clarice!
2 Clarice: ((in a deep tone)) *Sa ki palé ba'w?*
            (Who spoke to you?)
3 Mother: Mm ((laughs)).
4 Clarice *Ou ka pasé mwen. Ou pa ka di mwen bonjou. Apwézan ou ka kwiyé mwen?*
            (You're passing me. You're not telling me hello. Now you're calling me?)
5 (2)
6 Clarice: Huh?
7 (1)
8 Clarice: Huh?

9   (2)
10 Mother: ((to Jonah)) You vex with Clarice man?
11 Jonah: Hm hmm.
12 Mother: You vex with her?
13 Jonah: Hm hmm.
14 Mother: She shame you?
15 Jonah: Hm hmm.
16 Mother: Okay.

Clarice teases Jonah by challenging his call to her (line 2) and scolding him for not greeting her properly when she first arrived, suggesting that it is inappropriate to greet at this time (line 4). Jonah is taken aback, perhaps because he is surprised not to be greeted in return, or that Clarice speaks only Patwa to him, or that she scolds him if he comprehends it (although her tone makes it evident even without comprehension of the words). His mother questions why he does not respond to Clarice, asking if he is "vex" with her and if she "shamed" him (lines 12 and 14). These questions frame Clarice's actions and Jonah's responses in cultural terms, helping him understand what went wrong. Specifically her question on line 14 announces the activity that occurred in place of a return greeting—that Clarice "shamed" him.

Adults use Patwa to reaffirm the status hierarchy when children are judged to overstep the bounds of appropriate childhood behavior. Here, Alisia (two years and five months) responds inappropriately when her mother demands a fork with which Alisia almost poked her younger brother's eye:

Example 4.9
1   Mother: ((holds hand out for the fork))
2   Alisia: No girl!
3   Mother: ((speaking fast)) *Kilè ou ka kwiyé* girl *la?* Give me the fork.
             (Who are you calling girl there? Give me the fork.)
4   Alisia: ((brusquely hands the fork to her mother))

Alisia enacts an assertive stance by using a common form of address among children with their peers—"girl" ("boy" is similarly used)—in an emphatic refusal of her mother's directive (line 2). Use of this form implies that Alisia's mother is of the same status as her. Her mother swiftly sanctions this breech with a code-switch to Patwa, "*Kilè ou ka kwiyé* girl *la?*," and a repetition of her directive, "Give me the fork," all in fast-paced speech (line 3). Like other caregivers, Alisia's mother employs the contrast between English and Patwa speech as a means of contrasting adult/child roles and expectations, and reinstating the hierarchy (Paugh 2012a). Patwa serves as a conversational resource for controlling children, a "voice of authority" (Farris 1992) more commanding than English for imperatives, scolding, and moral critique.

Socializing Boldness through Patwa

Adults praise children for being deferent, sharing, and using English vocabulary. But only speaking English and being polite does not make a complete and competent communicator. Independence, personal autonomy, and self-sufficiency are highly valued qualities and in order to attain these, one must become *bon pou kò'y* or "good for oneself." As the above examples indicate, a child who is viewed as too assertive will not be tolerated by an adult. But there are times when it is better to be womanish or mannish. A fundamental tension is thus to socialize obedience and respect while simultaneously pushing children to become independent and bold, all part of a larger constellation of sociability. This is largely accomplished through the division of labor between Patwa and English. Children are directly socialized into important aspects of sociality and politeness through English, but are socialized explicitly and implicitly through both languages to verbally defend themselves. Not surprisingly then, some speaking of Patwa is expected if not encouraged in children's speech, and other than baby talk, its use for this function is one of the few acceptable times for children to speak it. It is in this way that caregivers facilitate the development of age-graded bilingual subjectivities, whether intentionally or not. This is critical to understanding how Patwa can be best maintained in the face of other community and societal changes.

Explicit Socialization of Boldness

As a baby it is acceptable to be "soft." But as a person matures they should become increasingly "hard" and able to assert themselves. This partly entails intentional toughening up of children. Babies are bathed in warm water at first, but after a couple of months they are bathed in cold water straight from the pipe so as to toughen and not spoil them (also see Krumeich 1994: 125).[16] Adults generally do little to pacify children when they get upset or cranky, letting them cry until they stop on their own. If a child does something that a caregiver warned them against and gets hurt, adults have little sympathy and comment "*sé bon pou'w*" (that's good for you) or "*ou vwè?*" (you see?). They do not want their children to be *kapon* (cowardly) and encourage them to verbally defend themselves and use language for expressive purposes and verbal play. They explicitly praise children, usually in English, for bravely calling out to people and not crying when they injure themselves.

Adults also purposely provoke children by calling them derogatory names, falsely accusing them, or lying about something the child would know to be untrue.[17] This usually keys a playful affective frame, but a child who cannot stand up for him/herself may become angry or upset, stop talking, or cry. They are then told by their caregivers to respond with a curse such as *tèt papa'w* or its English equivalent "your father('s) head" or an emphatic "leave me alone." To varying degrees children demonstrate awareness at a young age of when adults or older children are kidding or falsely blaming, threatening, or taking advantage of them, thus highlighting the salience of these routines.

Adults often choose to use Patwa when "troubling" children in the presence of other adults. They initiate or pull young children into teasing sessions between themselves and others. One adult tells the child to say something to the other adult, and then that person will retort by doing the same. This often begins in jest, primarily to entertain, but can be used to criticize others who are present.[18] While it can take place in English adults often switch into Patwa as the interaction becomes more focused on teasing. Children typically repeat the adult in Patwa if they can but it is rare that a young child contributes new material, and unlikely even for older children. Through guided participation in such routines (Rogoff 1990) children learn how to tease and to indirectly critique others. Here Tamika (three years and two months) and her mother are sitting in the doorway of their house counting and adding numbers. Tamika is not doing very well at the exercise and her mother repeatedly prompts the correct answers. Tamika's aunt Cynthia then yells from the yard:

Example 4.10

1   Cynthia: ((to Tamika, from outside)) Tamiko!

2   Tamika: ((from inside)) Yo:

3   Cynthia: ((laughing)) When your mommy tell you one and one (.5) say *kay mama'w plen tout* ((laughs)).
     (When your mommy tells you [to add] one and one (.5) say <u>your mother's house is all full</u>.)

4   Lorna: ((to Tamika)) Tell her *mach.*
     (Tell her <u>scram</u>.)

5   Tamika: ((to Cynthia)) *Mach!*
     (Scram!)

6   Cynthia: ((to Lorna, speaking fast)) *Pa di i mach. Mach ka biten anlè sa. Pa di i mach!* ((laughs)) *Amy - ou vwè Amy kay matjé'y. Mach.* You mustn't say that. Lorna. You hear? *Kon di Felix Henderson* ((laughs)).
     (<u>Don't tell her scram. Scram thinging [recording] on that [the video]. Don't tell her scram. Amy - You see Amy will write it. Scram</u>. You mustn't say that. Lorna. You hear? <u>According to Felix Henderson</u>.)[19]

7   Lorna: *Cynthia lè ou vwè ou ka di sa sé pou tann kouman ou ka palé fò fò fò anlè sa wi.*

(Cynthia you should hear how loud loud loud you sound in that yeah.) [on the video recording when Lorna and AP transcribe]

8   Cynthia: [((laughs))
9   Mother: [((laughs))
10   Cynthia:.   *Mé kw'a di mach. Chyen ki mach.*
      (But you're saying scram. Dogs that scram.)

Both adults employ the "say/tell" frame in English but then provide the teasing utterance for Tamika to repeat in Patwa. Tamika does not get the chance to respond to Cynthia's prompt—which was a sexual reference according to Lorna—but does tell Cynthia "*mach*" at her mother's prompting. The imperative *mach* is used with animals and is interpreted as very derogatory when spoken to a human. Cynthia seems concerned that Lorna is teaching her child to say this expression to a person (and that I will transcribe it), which is considered by many to be worse than cursing. The example demonstrates how more competent members guide children through common routines and that there are boundaries in both form and content.

Implicit Socialization of Boldness

Children learn how to verbally defend themselves not only from the direct input they receive through guided teasing and joking sessions but also from observing adult behavior during everyday interactions (Lave and Wenger 1991). As adults play with Patwa—joking, poking fun, gossiping, criticizing, chastising, and ordering others around—children come to associate the language with such a demeanor and when they do use Patwa, it is to accomplish similar pragmatic functions. Further, adults employ Patwa to indirectly praise children's bold behavior through comments to themselves and others in contrast to how they employ English to directly praise polite behavior. Here Tamika (two and a half) and her grandmother are walking home with other family members from a long day of work in the garden:

Example 4.11

1   Grandmother: ((to the group)) *Annou annou. Wen mwen ka fè mwen mal.*
          (Let's (go), let's (go). My waist is hurting me.)
2   Tamika: ((repeating her grandmother)) *Annou no:n. Annou. Annou.*
3   Grandmother: *I di annou!*
          (She said "annou"!)
4   AP: ((to Grandmother, laughing)) *Mwen sav.*
          (I know.)

5   Grandmother: *Tann Tamika!* ((in a high-pitched voice)) *Annou annou* ((laughs)). ((in normal voice)) *Sé sa ki fanm wi. Timoun sala! Éla.*
(Hear Tamika! "Annou annou." She is womanish. That child! (interjection).)

Rather than correcting Tamika the grandmother repeats and highlights the Patwa directive for the group (lines 3 and 5). Here it is womanish in a good sense: bold and purposeful to get people moving.

Children learn socially valued interactive skills through participation in and observation of such interactions. When children begin defending themselves on their own, they often respond with Patwa curses or short phrases, even in English conversation. Adults rarely correct such uses within particular constraints: they cannot occur too regularly, in the wrong place (namely home or school), or in a way that is judged to overstep the bounds of appropriate childhood behavior. Adults implicitly praise bold speech and actions with comments like, "She good for herself you know" or "That child not nothing soft *non*," even when in the process of telling children not to do something (as in Example 4.1). This is typically accompanied by laughter or a shake of the head. In certain contexts a child is even allowed to direct an adult's actions if they are interpreted as being bold but not rude (as in Example 4.11). Children are scolded only if they are viewed as trying to "rule" themselves, or if they curse at an adult outside of playful teasing (also Garrett 2005). Children are thus permitted, and sometimes even encouraged, to play with Patwa as an adult register—as long as a balance between being respectful and being confident is maintained.

Discussion: Enregistering Patwa as an Adult Language

Children are socialized to be English dominant and are monitored by adults for Patwa usage in most contexts. This strategy, however, relates to more than the future-oriented goal of providing children with English so that they may succeed in school and the job market as so many adults claim. As this chapter demonstrates, it is embedded within local theories of personhood and expectations of children, who are considered "naturally" disobedient and in need of control. These theories mesh well with ideologies about the languages that associate English with education, accommodation, formality, and official settings, and Patwa with boldness, autonomy, informality, and community. English represents qualities and demeanors, like politeness and obedience, that make it an ideal language for children, who are socialized to be respectful, deferent, and accommodating to elders. Patwa, on the other hand, has become linked to adult status, roles, and authority, something that children are not supposed to obtain until they are older and have their own children. Not allowing children to speak Patwa suppresses not only the language but also children's will and autonomy to the authority of adults, thus paralleling broadly held cultural ideas about the status of children. When adults catch older children speaking Patwa, they typically highlight age, status, and place-related restrictions on their usage.

Yet children are exposed to a great deal of Patwa in their everyday social environments as adult caregivers use it for conversation, teasing, and gossip with other adults and speak it directly to children, especially when trying to control their actions. Both sets of functions serve to mark it as an adult register, which most adults expect children will produce later in life. Once children's English becomes "strong" caregivers become more lax with their own Patwa usage, but still do not permit children to speak it. When Alisia was two and a half, I noticed her mother speaking more Patwa to and around her, particularly when she got into trouble, which was also happening more frequently. I questioned her about it. "Now she's harder," she replied. "Now she's getting hard." She told me that Alisia's English had gotten "strong" so to hear a little Patwa would not harm her. But even when adults speak more Patwa as children get older, it is as though they are speaking Patwa *at* them— telling them what to do, disciplining them, or assessing their behavior—rather than speaking it *with* them. Adults do not have conversations with children in Patwa and children are expected to respond in English even when addressed in Patwa. These patterns of "intergenerational unreciprocated language choice" (Makihara 2005: 744) undoubtedly will impact the level of Patwa competence that children are able to achieve in childhood and adulthood.

An attention to both language ideologies and language socialization practices, however, indicates that rather than a wholesale abandonment of Patwa, adults continue to socialize children to use Patwa for pragmatic functions and expressing intensified affective stances. Adults employ multiple strategies to control children, including imperatives, negative evaluations, warnings of corporal punishment, and threats to withdraw affection, goods, or other rewards. These speech acts are intensified when adults employ Patwa, which indexes their rights to control children's lives and actions, particularly in adult-dominated places like the home and school. A code-switch to Patwa when children are disobedient keys increased seriousness, although it also is used for playful teasing. Children are implicitly and sometimes explicitly pushed to be bold and to use Patwa, thus encouraging the emergence of bilingual subjectivities over developmental time. As caregivers and teachers use Patwa in pragmatically salient ways to tell children what to do based on the power associated with their social roles, children learn specific ideas about Patwa and how to use it as an authoritative "adult" register. Most children begin using Patwa in similar ways in child-controlled contexts, specifically in play with peers. This is the focus of the next two chapters.

Notes

1. As Schieffelin (1990: 19) states: "Socialized in the early years and keyed by predictable metacommunicative devices, routines are extremely important in helping to create a semblance of predictability and providing a framework for contingent responses."

2. Including when infants or children are considered to be conversational partners and persons, which is a long-standing concern of language socialization research (de León 1998, 2005; Kulick 1992; Ochs 1988; Ochs and Schieffelin 1984; Paugh 2012a; Schieffelin 1990).

3. This brings to mind notions of cultural duality—contrasting white colonial and Afro-Caribbean values and practices, including language—that have been posited in studies of West Indian societies (Sutton 1974; also Burton 1997), such as Herskovits's (1971) "socialized ambivalence," Wilson's (1973) "reputation" and "respectability," and Abrahams's (1970) and Reisman's (1970) work on Caribbean languages and ambiguity.

4. Anything that happens on the road is public knowledge and people may be judged for it. To avoid conjecture, residents conceal items in dark plastic bags or cloth as they travel to their destinations. Both men and women socialize on the road, though women can be severely criticized if judged to be spending too much time "wandering" the community.

5. Stuart (1993: 59) suggests that Patwa is used for "the oral and the informal," while English is used for "the written and the official" (also Christie 1990: 67).

6. A person can become soft through illness. Tamika's mother once described Vanessa as "*tou mòl*" (too soft) to go to the shop because she had been sick for two days.

7. Some adults said their Patwa knowledge helped them learn French, while others claimed it "interfered" and prevented acquisition. As French is only taught at the secondary level, the primary schoolteachers were unsure if Patwa influenced children's learning of French.

8. Christie (1982: 45) described Patwa as expressing "their innermost feelings more satisfactorily than English" and Stuart (1993: 64–65) called it "the language of 'feeling'" for many Dominicans.

9. A prevalent feature of talk to young children is the use of third-person reference by name in English, for example, "Come see Mommy" or "Daddy will help you."

10. *Kòk* and *doudou* are commonly used among adult intimates as well.

11. However, many caregivers use Patwa when referring to private areas of the body when speaking to children. Once Tamika (two and a half) was directed by her mother to "show mommy your (body part)" in both languages as follows: "head," "nose," "mouth," "*tété*" (breast), "hand," and "*kòkòt*" (vagina).

12. Many adults learned this now widespread routine from their children, who acquired it at school during Creole Week. Caregivers also sing English lullabies and songs learned at school.

13. During transcription of this part, Serena described Tina and her family as jealous and "*vyé kalté moun*," which she translated as "bad people."

14. It is once work is done that adults converse or play with children for longer periods of time.

15. Taylor (1951: 48) describes *i (two) nonm* as "a reproach frequently made in reference to little boys who behave too independently for their years."

16. Only cold water is piped to homes. Without water heaters bathwater for babies must be heated in a pot on the stove or fire.

17. See de León (2005) on how Zinacantecos caregivers in Chiapas, Mexico, encourage *k'ak'al* (anger) in young children to toughen their newly emerged souls.
18. Zentella (1997: 236–240) finds that among New York Puerto Rican families, teasing routines using children verge on challenging *respeto* (respect) but also solidify family relationships.
19. Felix Henderson, the host of the radio program *Èspéwéyans Kwéyòl*, frequently says "*Ou tann?*" in Patwa or "You hear?" in English and is often quoted by listeners. This reference helps to keep Cynthia's rebuke of Lorna in line with the playful teasing frame.

CHAPTER 5

Negotiating Play: Children's Code-Switching as Symbolic Resource

Jonah (two years and two months), Theodora (five years), Claudette (thirteen years), and Jonah's mother Marlena are sitting in their outdoor kitchen. The children are discussing if a hen nesting in the corner will lay an egg, while Marlena washes clothes in a basin on the floor. The conversation is in English until Claudette sees an egg that was not there earlier. She is unaware that her cousin Roma (eleven years) put it there to fool her, making her the butt of a joke as Roma often did:

Example 5.1
  1 Claudette: *Ga* there the fowl put the egg.
                (<u>Look at</u> where the fowl put the egg.)
  2 Claudette: ((reaches for the egg but quickly stops as Marlena speaks))
  3 Marlena: [Claudette leave the fowl alone.]
  4 Theodora: [It going and make a other   ] one Claudette. [re:
                                                    another egg]
  5 (1)
  6 Claudette: *An patjé zé i ni an bonda'y* man.
                (<u>It has a lot of eggs in its bottom</u> man.)
  7 Marlena: ((very low)) Claudette!
  8 Claudette: ((looking up)) Yeah?
  9 (2)
 10 Marlena: ((quiet but scolding tone)) *Ou déwò?!*
                (<u>Are you outside?!</u>)
 11 ((no response from Claudette; Marlena continues washing clothes))

This example highlights important themes of this chapter. Claudette uses Patwa in affectively marked ways to signal her surprise and reveal new information to her cousins. She calls attention to the egg with the potent

Patwa attention-getter, "*Ga*" (line 1). Use of this imperative is so common among children that adults rarely correct it and it slides by here. However, after Theodora suggests that the hen will lay another egg (line 4), Claudette produces a full Patwa utterance (line 6). Her declaration is creative and humorous, but is swiftly censured by the adult. First, Marlena utters Claudette's name in a low tone suggesting inappropriate behavior (line 7). This is followed by a short but powerful Patwa scold, "*Ou déwò?!*" (line 10), implying that Claudette has crossed a context-related boundary by using Patwa within the home. At another level, however, Claudette has crossed the boundaries of acceptable childhood behavior by employing an adult register, Patwa, in the presence of Marlena. This key point emerged during transcription when Marlena explained that she chastised Claudette because, "She was feeling so big to use that word there." I asked what she meant by "big," and Marlena explained that Claudette was acting "too womanish" by using Patwa; in other words, too much like an adult. Such metapragmatic reflection indicates recognition by adults that Patwa has become associated with status and authority in adult-controlled spaces.

Claudette may have been attempting to gain the floor and raise her status among the children through a witty Patwa utterance, as she did not realize she had been duped; but as Marlena's scold indicates, such usage threatens the social and linguistic hierarchy when an adult is present. When adults catch children speaking Patwa, they have a range of reasons at their disposal to inhibit its use, including evoking ideas about place and context—but rarely do they tell children not to speak it at all. By demanding "are you outside?!" rather than simply commanding Claudette not to speak Patwa, Marlena suggests that such usage is acceptable outside the confines of the adult-dominated home space. Caregivers consciously try to teach children English but they also transmit ideologies about and ways of speaking Patwa through place- and age-related admonishments and in their own code-switching practices. Children use Patwa in similar ways in their own peer interactions; however, interactions like Example 5.1 stand out in my corpus, as children rarely speak even this much Patwa near an adult.

In this chapter I explore how children employ the multiple linguistic resources available to them to negotiate power relations with peers, organize play activities, mark alignment and affective stances, socialize one another, and construct their own social worlds. Many researchers have drawn attention to the collaborative, relatively egalitarian nature of children's play as compared to the relations children have with parents and authority figures in institutions like schools (Blum-Kulka and Snow 2004). However, children's negotiations of power, hierarchy, and inclusion and exclusion have become increasingly visible in studies examining peer talk-in-interaction. Children utilize symbolic resources such as language varieties, artifacts, physical space, and their bodies to co-construct local hierarchies and social relationships (Bolonyai 2005; Kyratzis 2004; M. Goodwin 2006; M. Goodwin and Kyratzis 2012; Griswold

2007).[1] Switching codes can index symbolic capital, acting as a dramatic device for outperforming other children and displaying "teasing or mocking stances" toward one another (Cromdal and Aronsson 2000: 454; see also Lytra 2007).[2] Further, children's play evidences a resistance to or transgression of adult standards through their exploration and manipulation of adult forms. As a forbidden and "non-standard" language, Patwa takes on subversive power for children in constructing their own cultures and identities. It is particularly useful for acting "good for oneself" vis-à-vis peers. Yet, children's covert uses of Patwa have not been explored as a resource in language revitalization.

I examine children's play in same/multi-age and same/mixed-gender groups ranging in age from two to thirteen years. These "communities of practice" (Lave and Wenger 1991; Wenger 1998) converge around shared play practices and physical spaces. As Lytra (2007: 25) points out, viewing children's play groups in this way "highlights the importance of practices in building group membership and belonging without glossing over inequalities in social relations or difference among members within a community." The common practice of child caregiving creates contexts in which older children socialize younger children both through and to use Patwa without an adult presence. Older children correct, model, and otherwise guide younger children's speech and language activities, providing important scaffolding for learning activities (Rogoff 1990; Vygotsky 1978; Watson-Gegeo 2001). I combine the study of children below age four with those above it, asserting that older children are socialized to be directors of social action and examples for others to follow, while younger children imitate "more competent partners" (M. Goodwin 1990: 12). This contrasts with most studies of peer interactions in multilingual settings, which have focused on school-age children or adolescents.[3] The children in this study vary in their Patwa and English competence and in individual preferences for language choice, but the chapter highlights patterns found across families. Children's role play, an activity during which they use more Patwa than in any other pursuit, is the subject of chapter 6. Together the chapters show that peer play is an important locus of cultural exploration, reproduction, and transformation for children (Corsaro 2005; James et al. 1998; Kyratzis 2004).

The Organization of Children's Peer Play

Sibling caregiving is common as adults rely on older children to watch younger children while they do housework, errands, or outside work (Figure 5.2). Older girls and boys assume this role comfortably and capably, although boys do so more often in homes that do not have older female children. Common play activities for both girls and boys include imitating adult activities, singing and dancing, climbing trees for mangos, "taking spree" on a homemade swing, and tossing a ball. There are some gender differences in children's play. Boys frequently go into the bush to fetch wild fruits, hunt birds with homemade slingshots, and drive "trucks" they fashion themselves from household materials. When they are responsible for tending small animals like rabbits or goats, they often make that a focus of play as well. Like men, boys have more freedom than girls to move away from the home and yard, particularly to the road, bush, or playing field after school.[4] Girls typically are required to stay near the home, particularly if there are household chores or younger children to look after. Their imaginary play includes pretending to be mothers with children, performing domestic tasks like cooking and washing clothes, and role playing nurses or teachers. Girls sometimes have dolls and small children have stuffed animals, particularly when they have relatives living abroad to send them. Children reportedly played ring games before the introduction of electricity, but I rarely saw this activity outside of school-directed activities.

Figure 5.1 Jonah plays with his sister and fostered cousin while his eldest brother does chores

Children learn to monitor how they talk and behave when around adults. But without an adult presence children make noise, scream, talk over and tease one another, make messes, battle for control of activities, and use Patwa. Children usually do not have elaborate imported toys so talk is very important in creating and sustaining play. During transcription caregivers often interpreted children's play and the talk accompanying it as random, purposeless, and out of control.[5] Once when I asked Jonah's mother to interpret what he and his playmates said, she commented, "I don't know. They saying *what* that come in their mouth." Caregivers sometimes claimed they would have scolded their children if they had seen them behaving that way. A transcribing mother once commented, "If I was there I would hit those children one *blas* (lick/slap) yeah!" I explained to parents that I wanted children to behave naturally. I resolved this issue with some families by transcribing play with older child participants, like Reiston's cousins Marcel and Kenneth.

Figure 5.2 Natalie cares for her younger siblings Alisia (in her arms) and Tedison

Adults prefer their homes and yards to be neat and orderly and for children to "behave properly" in them. Groups of children are not allowed inside because they disrupt the household and make too much noise. Adults generally do not take seriously children's speech or actions during play although many recognize that children talk more with peers than adults. Once when Reiston's cousin returned home from school, his grandfather exclaimed with a sigh of relief, "*Marcel vini. I ké fè'y palé!*" (Marcel has come. He will make him talk!). Children spoke much more when interacting within their own age cohorts.

Adults often attribute children's linguistic errors, odd constructions, use of Patwa, and cursing to peer influence on their language development. Many caregivers complain that they try their best to speak "good" English and not Patwa with their children, but that children acquire non-standard English and Patwa forms during peer play. One mother told me, "That is where they start learning." During transcription caregivers frequently attributed young children's cursing to influence from "those other children," thus denying their own input (yet adults often curse in Patwa around and at children—see chapter 4). When Alisia (two years) cursed at her brother Tedison in Patwa, her mother told me, "She hears it from those children. So it just, it just in her." Tedison was frequently blamed for being a bad influence, such as when Alisia began using "big mama" as an intensifier (e.g., "that big mama cow") and when she went through a two-month period of stuttering before turning three. After one use of "big mama" her father responded to her, "Tedison that causing you to say those things there."

Playing in their own communities of practice with little or no adult supervision is thus a primary socializing context for children. Despite adults' interpretations of children's multiparty interactions as chaotic and disorganized, they are in reality highly structured with children utilizing language to organize play, control the floor, and gain resources, both material (such as toys, food, or interesting objects) and symbolic (such as status). Peer interaction is a critical form of language socialization and a means for children to construct their own cultures. As M. Goodwin (2006: 3) states, "By coordinating their talk with others children bring their social world into being." Such contexts are important for the young children observing and taking part in them, socializing them how to relate to peers and what language varieties to use. They learn to judge, criticize, and sometimes report to adults what goes on among them. This is also the most fruitful arena in which children can explore the range of their linguistic repertoires, when they are less likely to be told "less noise" or "no Patwa" by vigilant adults. Here children insert Patwa speech into English interactions through code-switching and language mixing. Such hybrid linguistic practices have been observed among children in other Caribbean language shift situations, including in St. Lucia where children switch between Kwéyòl and English (Garrett 2005, 2007), on

Corn Island off the Caribbean coast of Nicaragua where children mix English and Spanish with the indigenous Miskitu language (Minks 2006, 2010), and in New York where Puerto Rican youth alternate between Spanish and English (Zentella 1997). Such heteroglossic practices are often lamented by parents and in language-planning efforts and purist discourses; however, this kind of language use permeates children's multilingual worlds and can be a strong base for language maintenance and revival.

Indexing Authority and Affect: Patterns in Children's Patwa Usage

Children's earliest language use generally includes the Patwa baby talk lexicon employed by adults and older children to signal intensified positive affect and index the status of infants and toddlers (see chapter 4). In turn, children as young as three years employ the baby talk register with younger siblings. Other usages include Patwa loanwords, particularly nouns that are so integrated within the English vernacular that they are heard more frequently than their English counterparts. Like adults children employ *wi* and *non* as tags, sometimes serving an emphatic function ("I going *wi*", "Don't come *non*"). Other examples include names of foods: *fig* (banana), *penpen* (breadfruit); animals: *mannikou* (opossum), *siwik* (river crab); and lizards and insects: *abòlò* (ground lizard), *myèl* (honey bee). Strikingly, most of these grow or live in the bush outside the human built environment. Caregivers rarely correct such usages whereas they do correct children's use of Patwa to refer to things commonly found in the home or yard, such as *mouch* (fly) and *poul* (chicken). As discussed in chapter 3, teachers supply the English alternatives for any Patwa usage in school. Even though not particularly affectively salient, these lexemes are marked as non-standard—and thus potentially subversive—in institutional settings.

Apart from these more integrated Patwa forms, a sketch of children's Patwa use in otherwise English peer interaction highlights how it has become a potent resource for affective marking and negotiation of power. Children use Patwa lexical items, expletives, and exclamations to intensify their speech, index affective stances, and call attention to what they deem important. These switches to Patwa are typically marked by shifts in prosody, interactional stance, gesture, and bodily orientation, indicating that children are shifting linguistic varieties (languages and/or registers). Children also use English varieties to index changes in alignment or "footing" (Goffman 1981), but their Patwa speech is usually louder and more impatient than their English speech, or, conversely, may be spoken under their breath in annoyance or frustration. Adults at home may not comment on a child's isolated Patwa use unless the child seems to not know the English form or is judged to overstep the limits of appropriate childhood behavior, as in Example 5.1. However, children's most extensive uses occur when out of earshot of their caregivers, especially during imaginary play.

I must highlight again that children primarily use varieties of English for most functions. When they argue, they argue in English with occasional code-switches to Patwa. When they tell stories or talk about one another, it is in English with isolated Patwa lexemes or short phrases. When they negotiate the organization of play frames and pretend play spaces, it is overwhelmingly in English. Children's talk about their emotional states is also predominantly in English while adults use both Patwa and English. Children use English emotion lexicon, such as "vex" rather than *faché*; "afraid" (or its vernacular equivalent "fraid") or "frightened" rather than *pè*; "happy" or "glad" rather than *kontan*; or "like" or "love" rather than *enmé*. However, displaying emotion is a social, situated activity that can be shown by other means than a specific vocabulary (M. Goodwin and C. Goodwin 2000). In multilingual settings, as Pavlenko (2005: 131–132) points out, "Speakers may use these languages to index a variety of affective stances, and they may also mix two or more languages to convey emotional meanings." For example, in Trinidad, Youssef (1993) found that the level of emotionality experienced by young children (especially anger or excitement) could engender a shift from Standard English to Trinidad English Creole.

Every Patwa usage cannot be attributed to a single function such as intensified affect or competing for power, but Patwa has become a potent resource for negotiating authority, autonomy, and social identity, despite or because of the fact that children do not use it as an everyday language in any context, including with peers. Children's speech in play is heteroglossic, drawing on multiple voices and language varieties, including those forbidden in adult-controlled settings. This comes into focus as children assume authoritative roles in telling other children not to speak Patwa and in correcting one another's speech, which I examine at the end of the chapter. For children, playing with linguistic codes can be a powerful conversational resource for expressing emotional intensification and interactional stances.

Curses, Interjections, and Reference to Supernatural Beings

Children as young as two years use Patwa forms that index strongly negative affect, including curses such as *patat mama'w* (your mother's vagina) and *tèt papa'w* (your father's head). They also employ the direct English translations of these, particularly "your father('s) head," indicating that cursing for Penville children is not strictly code-specific (cf. Garrett 2005). Alisia cursed at her siblings, parents, and visitors (including me) in all recordings with its frequency increasing during her third year. Here Alisia (two years and four months) and her brother Tedison (four years) are playing outside under the supervision of their sister Natalie (ten years). They are wrestling when Tedison falls on top of Alisia:

Example 5.2
1   Tedison: ((laughing)) I going back again. ((falls on Alisia))
2   Alisia: *Patat! Patat mama'w* boy!
            (<u>Vagina! Your mother's vagina</u> boy!)
3   Tedison: ((jumps up))

Alisia curses to verbally assert herself, indexing intensified negative affect and condemning Tedison's careless behavior. Similarly, children curse in Patwa at children who refuse them something, tell them what to do, or otherwise frustrate them, further socializing associations between Patwa and self-assertion among the children interacting with them.

Like adults, children produce intensified Patwa exclamations to express surprise or disbelief, such as *Bondyé*, *Mondyé*, and *Papa mèt*, all of which can be translated as "God." For example, Reiston (three years and five months) would not let his cousin Kenneth (thirteen years) have a turn playing with a homemade truck. When he finally relinquished it Kenneth began driving it aggressively near him. Reiston yelled out, "*Papa mèt*! It going and jam me!" He then screamed and ran away, even though Kenneth claimed, "No, I won't jam you" (which he did anyway). Other expressions imply that someone has the right to tease or mock someone, such as *bètj*, defined as "good for you!" by villagers and implying "you got what you deserved." Reiston kicked a ball away from Kenneth later that same day and yelled, "*Bètj* I win. *Bè::tj!*" Like adults children also employ *mach!* (scram) to shoo away dogs, chickens, and other pesky animals. The use of this imperative implies control over another living creature and is a means for sending things that do not belong in the human environment back to the outside or bush.

Children similarly refer to frightening or evil entities associated with the outside using their Patwa forms, such as *soukwiyan* (witch), *dyab* (devil), and *bèt* (an unidentified creature or insect). This is consistent with local patterns as adults tend to refer to these creatures in Patwa even when speaking English. However, it also solidifies ideological associations between Patwa and the natural environment and with powerful supernatural or unknown forces. Caregivers and older children strengthen these associations by threatening disobedient children that a *dyab* or *soukwiyan* will get them. Alisia's caregivers frequently warned that a *dyab* would take her when she wandered off by herself, and her older siblings routinely claimed that a *dyab* would eat her during play. One day Alisia (two years and ten months) repeatedly asserted that one was outside, every so often whispering "*dyab*" apprehensively to her mother and me. She also used Patwa constructions that were otherwise rare in her speech. She called it "*modi*" (bad/brazen) and used a Patwa verb: "I must *bawé* it" (I must <u>block</u> it). She even whispered softly, "*Manjé'y dyab*" (<u>Eat her, devil</u>). At the time I only heard "*dyab*" and did not ask her if she was referring to me, and if so, why! Her siblings had used these constructions in other recordings, suggesting their impact on her socialization to use Patwa. When older children talk about fearful supernatural creatures and the activities and places related to them in Patwa, they highlight its affective saliency and link it to the expression of strong emotions such as fear and excitement.

Children's Use of Ga *('to look at')*

By far the most frequently used Patwa marker in children's speech is one of the shortest at just one syllable: the imperative *ga*, a short form of the verb *gadé* (to look at). An analysis of children's use of *ga* offers insights into their agency in organizing social action. *Ga* was so pervasive in children's speech that villagers described it as "rampant" and heard "everywhere" among children. "All the children like to say that," said one mother. "Every single one of them saying *ga*." Another mother explained: "The children say *ga* because they learn it from adults, but they abuse it anytime something wows them. They say it constantly." All adults that I questioned told me that *ga* is a Patwa term, and most use *ga* almost strictly within Patwa utterances to direct the attention of others toward something in particular. It appears as an imperative in commonly heard, very formulaic phrases that negatively evaluate someone, such as "*ga djèl li*," "*ga fidji'y*," or "*ga kalité'y*," translated as "look at his or her mouth," "face," or "mannerisms," respectively.[6] These are usually spoken fast in a harsh tone of voice and typically refer to someone—often a child—who is acting rude, greedy, or otherwise disagreeable. Adults rarely say *gadé* in place of *ga* in these phrases even though *gadé* is regularly used as an imperative or main verb, such as "*i ka gadé sa*" (he is looking at that). *Ga* is restricted to second-person imperative usage only, but additionally functions in adult speech as an interjection indicating intense shock, surprise, and emphasis. Its usage is so salient that young children pick up on this function as soon as they begin to talk.

Adults were terribly bothered by children's use of *ga*, yet no one claimed they were using it in grammatically incorrect ways. Many were perplexed that children chose to use *that* Patwa word to such a greater extent than any other. Even though it appears so frequently in their English speech, children's use of *ga* follows the same syntactic constraints as adults and does not appear randomly. Like adults children use it as an imperative with additional pragmatic functions, particularly for emphasis and marking affective intensity. For children, though, the social meanings of *ga* extend well beyond telling someone to "look at" something, as they will often do the latter before switching to *ga*. A fifteen-year-old secondary school student once defined it for me as, "Wow, look at that!" As I began recording the focal group, all six children were using *ga* regularly to point out objects, people, and events. They also used the more unmarked English "look" encouraged by their caregivers at least twice as much as *ga* on average. However, *ga* seemed to carry strong affective meaning that was appropriate in particular situations and they were attentive to the pragmatic saliency of their switch. This was visible not only in the frequency with which they used it, but also in its positioning within discourse sequences in relation to English alternatives such as "look," "watch," or "see." For example, when Alisia (two years and seven months) tried to show her brother Tedison (five years) a barrette, she told him to "come," "come see," and "look" three times to no avail before using *ga*. The situation had escalated and *ga* acted as an intensifier to help her successfully gain the floor.

Caregivers occasionally respond to children's use of *ga* with short corrections such as "Is not *ga*. Is look at that." Most simply let it pass. Like other Patwa usage, many caregivers blame children's use of *ga* on peers. In fact, children do tend to use *ga* more often in peer interaction than other contexts. Alisia's use of *ga* increased an average of four times as much when her siblings were present compared to when she was alone with her mother. Alisia's mother was concerned that her children learn to speak a more standard variety of English and often tried to stop her children from saying it, typically with little success. Yet none of the other family members corrected her use of *ga* and once Alisia (two years and two months) said it nineteen times to her father without correction before her mother entered the room and told her, "Not *ga*. Daddy look at that." The following example demonstrates another attempt to curb her children's use of *ga*. Alisia (two years and three months) initiates a common game she and Tedison (four years) play, where they point at something outside and claim it to be their "own":

Example 5.3

1 Alisia: ((pointing at a stick on the ground)) *Ga* my motorbike!
           (Look at my motorbike!)
2 Mother: Not *ga*. LOOK at my motorbike.
3 Alisia: No! Is not your motorbike. [misunderstands Mother's correction]
4 (3)
5 Alisia: ((pointing at the sky) *Ga ga ga* my bird!
6 Alisia: *Ga*   [my bird!
7 Tedison: [*Ga*
8 Tedison: ((pointing at the sky)) *Ga* my bird!
9 Tedison: [*Ga* my bird!
10 Mother: [Not *ga!*

11 Mother: LOOK   [at my bird.]
12 Alisia: [*Ga ga ga*   ] my bird!
13 Alisia: My – my bird my bird!
14 Tedison: ((chanting)) Plenty bird, plenty bird, [plenty bird, plenty
                                                                bird.
15 Alisia: [My bird, my bird.

Alisia's use of *ga* signals that she is calling attention to new information and structuring the interactional frame. Her mother tries to correct her (line 2), but like other caregivers, does not provide an explanation of why *ga* should not be used. Further, her repair does not fit the play frame and Alisia misinterprets the correction as a claim to ownership of the motorbike (line 3). Once Tedison joins in, their mother's attempts at correction are futile. The children say *ga* eleven times between them (eight by Alisia and three by Tedison).

Children's use of *ga* to signal affective intensity illustrates their emergent understanding of language as a form of social action. Further, children are transforming *ga* into a much more agentive and potent multifunctional grammatical marker. It is a means by which children can shape and reshape interactions by emphatically calling attention to something *they* regard as relevant or important. Adults appear to find this threatening, and not just to children's acquisition of English. It is threatening to adult authority and control, particularly when used in such an innovative, ubiquitous, and agentive way.

Revoicing Adult Language

Similar to their use of *ga*, children employ affectively marked Patwa forms in a revoicing of adult speech, or a "double-voicing" in Bakhtin's terms, whereby a speaker uses someone else's discourse for their own purposes so that "in one discourse, two semantic intentions appear, two voices" (Bakhtin 1984: 189; also Hill and Hill 1986; Rampton 1995; Watson-Gegeo 2001). Jonah, the most English dominant of the focal group, recycled salient Patwa utterances by the adults who shared his yard. At age two years and eight months he repeatedly proclaimed "I *las*" (I'm tired) when he did not want to walk although he was using English "tired" regularly prior to this. Here his mother has told him to "come" but he acts too exhausted to move:

Example 5.4
 1 Jonah: ((speaking slowly)) But I *las*.
                (But I'm <u>tired</u>.)
 2 AP: You *las?*
 3 Jonah: Yeah.
 4 Mother: ((to Jonah)) What you do you *las?*

(What did you do that made you <u>tired?</u>)
5   Jonah: But I *las*.
6   Mother: ((in a mock serious tone)) You - you don't do no work. You
              – you *las?*
7   Jonah: Mm.

Work is not the only way a person gets tired, but that is what *las* evokes as a particularly adult usage and Jonah's mother explains that for him (lines 4 and 6). Jonah has undoubtedly heard *las* used many times by the adults in his family, particularly by his grandmother who frequently complains of being tired after a hard day working in the garden. Jonah's repeated use of the Patwa term could have been due to the novelty of using a word for the first time once its meaning is understood. But it appears to be a revoicing of adult speech and is recognized as such by Jonah's mother. When he again claims to be *las* and refuses to come a short while later, she reiterates this connection, laughing, "Not when people working they does be *las?*" Her gentle teasing reconfirms it as an adult utterance while explaining the semantics of the word for Jonah— that people become *las* when they work, something that Jonah is too young to do (though it is acceptable for him to claim to be "tired" in English).

Particularly common among children are negatively evaluative adjectives that caregivers frequently call them when they misbehave, such as *malpwòp* (nasty), *mal élivé* (badly brought up), and *sòt* (stupid) (see chapter 4). Older children regularly issue these negative assessments when younger children fail to comply with their directives. Similarly, both boys and girls employ Patwa verbs and nouns that act as intensifiers when used in English utterances. Common examples include verbs referring to destruction or injury that are used in threats or rebukes issued by adults to children, as in these recorded examples:

I going *kwévé* you.	(I'm going to <u>beat you badly.</u>)
I going *fouté* him one lick of that.	(I'm going to <u>hit</u> him with that.)
You *dékatyé* it!	(You <u>broke</u> it!)
You *blésé* my *bobo*.	(You <u>hurt</u> my <u>sore/injury.</u>)
Bawé her!	(<u>Block</u> her!)

These appear in children's interactions with peers and in otherwise English stories about particularly emotional experiences. As children co-construct narratives of their adventures or other noteworthy events in English, they frequently employ Patwa lexemes and report adult speech in Patwa, highlighting salient experiences, details, and affective stances (Koven 2006).

In the following narrative Marcel (eleven years) describes a physical altercation between his cousins, Junior (nine years) and Julius (ten years), that morning. The narrative emerges twice and Reiston (three years and five months) listens attentively even though he does not appear to be a primary addressee. Marcel recalls the event for Kenneth when he hears Junior yell to Julius on the road. He refers to two adults—Junior and Julius's grandmother Paula and Junior's mother Nerice—in the story:

Example 5.5

1	Marcel:	((looks up)) *Ga. Bondyé.* Look him there. He - he - he had fighting with Julius.
2	Kenneth:	Junior?
3	Marcel:	Uh huh. ((points toward the road)) He make Julius cry!
4	Kenneth:	((looking up, somewhat incredulous)) Junior making Julius cry?
5	Marcel:	Uh huh. In front their yard *wi.* (.5) In front their yard *wi* Junior take cutlass to cut Julius.
6	Kenneth:	((looking back down at bamboo he is playing with)) Boy! He *fèb* boy.
		(He is <u>weak</u> boy.)
7	Marcel:	Who?
8	Kenneth:	Julius.
9	(3)	
10	Marcel:	((speaking fast)) But Julius seeing Nerice the:re. He seeing Paula the:re.
11	Kenneth:	And what they had telling Junior?
12	Marcel:	*Paula menm ka di Junior* ((speaking loud and fast)) *"Junior - um - um - pa fouté zanfan la kou."*
		(<u>Paula is telling Junior,</u> "Junior - um - um - don't hit the child.")
13	Marcel:	Nerice hold the cutlass. Nerice had going to cut Junior in TWO.
14	Marcel:	((swinging arms up and down)) She JUMP on him like a *mama poul. "Pa goumé èvè Julius!"*
		(She jumped on him like a <u>mother chicken.</u> "<u>Don't fight with Julius!</u>")
15	Marcel:	Julius say is then he know to do something.
16	(2)	
17	Kenneth:	That Julius say?
18	Marcel:	I tell him if you know now Nerice is (xxx).
19	Reiston:	Bo::y.
20	Kenneth:	When they had going school this morning?
21	Marcel:	No. They did not bathe yet.

Marcel contextualizes the story by calling attention to Junior with *ga*, the interjection "*Bondyé*," and declarative, "Look him there." He then launches the narrative: "He - he - he had fighting with Julius" (line 1). Kenneth indicates interest, "Junior?" (line 2). Marcel confirms this and offers a story preface that grabs Kenneth's attention: "He make Julius cry!" (line 3). Kenneth questions this incredulously (line 4), as Julius is older and bigger than Junior. He then offers a negative evaluation of Julius as *fèb*, a Patwa adjective that is strongly negatively marked for males as a critique of their masculinity (line 6). Marcel challenges this evaluation, suggesting that Julius did not act for fear of reproach from the adults (line 10). He then recounts the scene excitedly using present tense and rapid speech. He switches to Patwa to report the adults' speech, which is appropriate since both are Patwa dominant. He also uses Patwa rather than English to introduce Paula's speech, "*Paula menm ka di Junior*" (line 12). He switches to English to describe the next series of actions (line 13). He then colorfully describes Nerice as acting like a "*mama poul*" and reports her speech in Patwa (line 14). He switches back to English to indirectly report the *child's* speech (line 15). Marcel's use of contrasting languages, emphasis, fast-paced speech, and present tense increases rhetorical effect and adds authenticity, making it seem like he was actually there although Julius reported this to him later. Kenneth probes this by asking, "When they had going school this morning?" (line 20), since Marcel would have been able to witness the fight at that time. Marcel's response (line 21) suggests that he was not there since he also would have been preparing for school.

Ten minutes later Kenneth and Marcel are arguing over responsibility for feeding their rabbits when Junior and Julius enter the yard. Marcel asserts that Julius told him that Kenneth fed his rabbit *zèb gwa*, a vine that is harmful to rabbits. Kenneth denies it, and Marcel reproaches Julius. This launches a retelling of the narrative in front of the boys' grandmother who appears to have overheard the first telling from the outdoor kitchen:

Example 5.6

1	Marcel:	((looks at Julius)) I glad Junior burst your skin.
2	Kenneth:	((speaking fast)) I'll never give it [food] again. [to Marcel's rabbit]
3	Marcel:	((to Julius)) *Haché* for him to had *haché* you. (<u>Chop</u> for him to have <u>chopped</u> you.)
4	Marcel:	Lucky Theresa take the cutlass in his hand. [from Junior]
5	Grandmother:	*I sé an tèbè pou'y wèsté la kité Junior fouté'y an koul koutla.* (<u>He's an idiot for staying there and letting Junior hit him with a cutlass.</u>)
6	Marcel:	But he stay there (.5) and Junior going to *haché* mister to cry:

7	Reiston:	((makes noises))
8	Grandmother:	He's a *tèbè* then.
		(He's an <u>idiot</u> then.)
9	Marcel:	((nodding toward Junior)) Junior. Nerice had going to *haché* him lick of the cutlass.
10	Reiston:	((to Grandmother)) Granny. You going and boil it? [re: green bananas]
11	Marcel:	((to Julius)) Not that you say?
12	Kenneth:	((speaking loud and gruff)) You was there?! Mm hmm!
13	Marcel:	((yelling)) Julius tell me that!
14	Kenneth:	((yelling)) You saying that as though you was there!
15	Marcel:	Boy!
16	Grandmother:	((speaking fast)) Finish with that conversation in the yard.

Marcel refers back to the morning's events as he rebukes Julius on lines 1 and 3. His use of the Patwa verb *haché* adds rhetorical impact. He then supplies an evaluation of the narrative events: "Lucky Theresa take the cutlass in his hand" (line 4). This prompts a moral evaluation from the boys' grandmother who, similar to Kenneth, criticizes Julius's inaction by calling him a *tèbè* (idiot) (lines 5 and 8). Marcel agrees with this assessment (line 6) unlike his defense of Julius during the first telling to Kenneth (Example 5.5, line 10). His alignment with the negative assessment distances him from Julius and his powerless behavior. Marcel then recounts a detail from the story (line 9) and requests confirmation from Julius, "Not that you say?" (line 11). Kenneth seizes on this fact check to challenge Marcel's authoritative depiction of the event, "You was there?! Mm hmm!" (line 12). Kenneth then says what he appears to have suspected from the first telling, "You saying that as though you was there!" (line 14). The boys' grandmother then implicitly censors their talk as inappropriate, "Finish with that conversation in the yard" (line 16). It is unclear what she finds unsavory: the narrative events, the language used to describe them, the argument brewing between Marcel and Kenneth, or all of the above. However, she effectively silences the narrative, illustrating how adults maintain ultimate authority over children's speech in adult-controlled settings like "the yard."

Navigating Inclusion, Exclusion, and Morality with Peers

Even when children try to cooperate to achieve a common goal, such as hanging a swing, their interactions are punctuated by directives, insults, and evaluations of the behavior and character of those involved. Directive-response sequences are "a means through which children can enact positions of dominance and subordination" (M. Goodwin and Kyratzis 2007: 283). Code and/or register choice is an important resource in navigating inclusion and exclusion. Children, especially older ones, can evoke an adult-like authority to control other children by using Patwa directives and disparaging remarks, as in these commonly heard examples:

Pa fè sa.	(Don't do that.)
Sòti la.	(Come out of there.)
Annou ay.	(Let's go.)
Ba mwen sa.	(Give me that.)
Ou pa ka tann?	(You're not hearing?)
Ou ka sanm (an vyé) …	(You look like/resemble (an old) …)

These speech forms are considered more commanding than their English equivalents and mark negative affect. As in adult speech to children a switch to Patwa can indicate an escalation in the situation and may be accompanied by a threat or use of embodied aggression. Such Patwa usages evoke a taste of the adult world and are highly effective in structuring children's social organization and relationships. The following are three examples drawn from my recordings of four focal children and their peer groups, all ranging in degrees of Patwa proficiency.

Ga Soukwiyan!: Shifting Power Dynamics in Tamika and Kenrick's Peer Group

Tamika and Kenrick play in a large mixed-gender group of siblings and cousins ranging in age from two to nine years (Figure 5.3). In this group alliances shift regularly and the children frequently engage in verbal dueling and critiquing of one another's behavior.

In the following example Tamika (three years and seven months) and Glenda, Vanessa, and Samuel (all six years) are playing in the bedroom of Tamika's house while her mother cooks in the outdoor kitchen. The conversation is predominantly in English until Glenda and Vanessa have an altercation in the bedroom. Glenda was born just minutes before her twin sister yet she considers herself in charge and tries to keep the other children in check. Enacting an authoritative stance, Glenda scolds the children for playing on her parents' bed and takes Tamika's crayons. In response Vanessa, who is attributed the role of Tamika's *dada* (elder caregiving female), tries to take Glenda's coloring book. Glenda then revoices an earlier reprimand from their mother, "You doesn't hear behave yourself?" Vanessa retorts by calling her a *soukwiyan* (witch) and driving her from the house:

Figure 5.3 Kenrick and Tamika's large peer group of siblings and cousins

Example 5.7

1   Glenda: ((punches Vanessa's head)) I hitting you a tump *wi* girl. I hitting you.

2   Vanessa: ((pointing at Glenda)) *Ga::: ga: ga:* a *soukwiyan zò. Ga::: ga:* ((laughing)) *Ga soukwiyan zò!* ((laughs))
     (Look at that, look at that, look at a <u>witch</u> (exclamation). Look at that, look at that. Look at a witch (exclamation)!')

3   Glenda: ((grabs a broom and hits Vanessa with the handle)) Girl you doesn't hear?!

4   Vanessa: *Tèt papa'w!* ((grabs broom))
     (Your father's head.)

5   Glenda: ((punches Vanessa on the head and walks away with a scowl))

6   Samuel: *Tèt papa'w wi* she say there ((laughs)).

7   Glenda: ((stomps out of the house))

8   Vanessa: *Ga:: ga ga ga* a *soukwiyan. O li? O li? Soukwiya::n. O li?*
     (Look at that, look at that, look at that, look at a <u>witch</u>. Where is she? Where is she? Witch. Where is she?)

9   AP: *I alé.*
     (She went.)

10   Vanessa: ((climbs off the bed with the broom, looks under the bed))
     Ola MODI la fè?

(Where did the BAD/BRAZEN ONE go?)
11 Simon: ((laughs))
12 Vanessa: ((walks out the front door, looking for Glenda))
13 Tamika: ((follows Vanessa outside))

Vanessa undermines Glenda's claim to authority by calling her an insulting name, using exaggerated intonation, and hunting an imaginary witch. Tamika, Samuel, and I are her audience, prompted to look at the "witch" with ten uses of *ga*. Her language choice plays a key role as the Patwa terms *soukwiyan* and *modi* are more negatively affectively marked than their English equivalents. The use of Patwa is appropriate for the function, teasing and excluding Glenda, and the topic, as adults and children alike use Patwa to refer to fearful witches that enter people's bedrooms at night to suck their blood. Glenda employs physical force (lines 1, 3, and 5) to counter Vanessa's attack, but it is ineffective. Vanessa levels a Patwa curse at her, "*tèt papa'w*" (line 4), to which Samuel calls attention with a laugh (line 6), aligning with Vanessa. Vanessa continues taunting Glenda in Patwa (lines 8 and 10) until she drives her out of the house. Tamika attentively observes the shifting power dynamics and her sister's use of Patwa to create an imaginary play frame that morally evaluates another child. In fact, Tamika became fond of calling children who offended her *soukwiyan* at this time, suggesting Vanessa's influence on her growing repertoire of options for defending herself and criticizing the moral comportment of others.

You're Not at Your House: Playing with Reiston and His Cousins

The use of Patwa to control and structure play activities is particularly salient among Reiston's peer community, which includes a core group of nine siblings and cousins, six boys and three girls, ranging in age from three to thirteen years. They have the least adult supervision of the focal children and take advantage of this during play. Marcel in particular often assumes an authoritative role and speaks Patwa to announce the type of play, who controls what aspect, what each person can do and say, and in which language. While primarily speaking English he uses Patwa to direct and critique the other children's actions, often calling them *sal* (dirty), *ochan* (busy/impatient), and *tèbè* (idiot) (like his grandmother called Julius in Example 5.6). Conversely, Marcel occasionally uses Patwa to describe very positive personal attributes, such as when he highlighted Reiston's braveness for riding a new swing: "Reiston don't *kapon!*" (Reiston is not <u>cowardly</u>!). Despite Marcel's frequent harshness, his closest friends typically ratify his bids for leadership of the group and go along with his games and schemes.

Like other older children Marcel plays an important role in the language socialization of younger children. He usually tries to persuade Reiston to be on his side during games and competitions and directs him what to tell the other children. In the following example Marcel (eleven), Reiston (three years and two months), and their cousins Junior (nine years), Alex (five years), and Sherona (three years) are on Reiston and Marcel's veranda. I have just begun videotaping and Marcel is prompting the children to sing songs, while monitoring their every move. When Sherona hides behind Junior, Marcel presses his index finger against her forehead and says, "Stay good. Stay good. *Sé pa an kaz Boyd ou yé*" (You are not at Boyd's (her father's) house). Marcel uses Patwa to invoke "a larger social framework of rights over property" (M. Goodwin 1990: 89), implying that Sherona (and Junior and Alex by implication) is subject to the rules at Marcel's home. Further, it is disparaging by suggesting that her father would allow her to misbehave at his home. Marcel then positions himself on the veranda wall so that he is above the children in a dominant position—spread out with one leg hanging down and the other straight out behind his cousin's heads so he can kick them periodically while telling them to "behave." Reiston is playing with a toy car on the floor. Suddenly Alex snorts:

Example 5.8

1   Alex: ((snorts loudly, seemingly by accident))
2   Marcel: ((kicks his foot against Alex's head)) *Pa di* honk *ou la. Ou pa kochon.*
           (Don't say honk you there. You are not a pig.)
3   Alex: ((snorts again))
4   Marcel: *Ou pa bèf.*
           (You are not a cow.)
5   Alex: ((snorts again))
6   Reiston: ((repeating Marcel)) *Ou - ou pa bèf.*
           (You are not a cow.)
7   Marcel: Reiston.
8   Reiston: Break - break that. [re: toy car]
9   Marcel: ((to Reiston)) *Di Alex ou pa bèf, ou pa chyen, ou pa kabwit.*
           (Tell Alex you are not a cow, you are not a dog, you are not a goat.)
10 Reiston: I break that.
11 Marcel: I'll take the car if you don't say it.

Marcel critiques Alex's behavior with adult-like authority through his use of a Patwa directive, "*Pa di* honk *ou la,*" and moral commentary comparing Alex to farm animals (lines 2 and 4). When Alex snorts again Reiston repeats Marcel's reprimand without prompting (line 6). Marcel seems to read this as alignment with his evaluative stance and tries to prompt Reiston to say an expanded Patwa utterance through a "tell" routine (line 9). This could be interpreted as an attempt to socialize use of Patwa as moral critique or as a petition for Reiston to ratify Marcel's claims to authority. Reiston usually does what Marcel tells him but he does not respond here, perhaps indicating a refusal to play Marcel's power game or a lack of interest. The subject is dropped when Reiston ignores Marcel's threat (line 11).

That is Your *Place: Exclusion in Jonah's Social Group*

An example from Jonah's family further demonstrates how children utilize multiple semiotic resources to engage in conflict talk including embodied action, gestures, directives, threats, and linguistic varieties. Jonah regularly plays with his sister Theodora (five years), fostered cousin Roma (eleven years), and cousin Claudette (thirteen years). The children often cooperate in collaborative play; however, tensions frequently arise as Roma and Theodora unite to exclude and make fun of Claudette (see the joke pulled on her in Example 5.1), drawing Jonah to their side through "tell" routines. Claudette, however, is the most proficient in Patwa and employs it for self-defense and to gain inclusion by making the other children laugh. She frequently plays with language to create hybrid constructions, such as when she did not understand something Jonah said and replied with a laugh, "I was too un*kopwann*" (English prefix *un* with the Patwa verb *kopwann* "to understand," meaning she did not understand). However, her use of this power code rarely is enough to prevent the girls from excluding her. In this example, Roma has taken Claudette's hair clip and is teasing her with it. Claudette calls outside to her Aunt Marlena for aid. From outside Marlena scolds Roma but the girls continue. Jonah (two years and one month) observes the interaction:

Example 5.9

1	Claudette:	((chases Roma around the table))
2	Theodora:	((loudly)) Roma mommy tell her - you to give her - her clip.
3	Claudette:	((to Roma, speaking in low voice)) *Kw'a sanm an vyé sketel.*
		(You look like an old slut/promiscuous female.)
4	Roma:	Sketel like you!
5	Claudette:	((laughs slightly))
6	Roma:	[(xxx)]
7	Theodora:	[I'll tell mommy] that for you yeah Claudette! [re: her comment to Roma]
8	Roma:	((runs to couch and sits by Theodora, putting her leg across the remaining space))
9	Roma:	((to Claudette)) You not sitting there! [re: on the couch]

10	Claudette:	((runs to the couch))
11	Roma:	((sucks teeth in annoyance))
12	Claudette:	((sits next to Roma)) Settee *la sé sa'w?*
		(<u>The</u> settee/couch <u>is yours?</u>)
13	Roma:	((pushes Claudette off the couch with her foot))
14	Claudette:	((grunts as falls to floor))
15	Roma:	Don't call me sketel next time.
16	Claudette:	((laughs)) I'll TELL auntie Monica that for you. You don't want me to sit? I'll tell auntie Monica you don't want me to sit =
17	Claudette:	[= down on the settee.]
18	Roma:	[I'll go and tell mommy] you call me sketel and then ask you what ske- sketel means.
19	Claudette:	((whines))
20	Roma:	((pointing at another chair)) Look there. That is YOUR place.
21	(2)	
22	Claudette:	((stands up from the floor and flops down on the chair))

Roma sparks the conflict by taking Claudette's hair clip and taunting her with it. When Claudette's appeals to a higher authority (Roma's foster mother) are unsuccessful, she chases Roma (line 1). Theodora appears to align with Claudette by trying to enforce her mother's directive for Roma to stop (line 2), though this could be interpreted as an attempt to protect Roma from punishment rather than to aid Claudette. In the next turn Claudette insults Roma with the potent, "*Kw'a sanm an vyé* sketel" (line 3). As noted above, children frequently employ the "*kw'a sanm an vyé ...*" frame to evaluate and scold one another. Claudette's use of *sketel*, a Jamaican English word meaning "promiscuous woman" (Kempadoo 2004: 49, 168–169), illustrates how children creatively draw on the multiple resources available in their verbal environments. It is unclear where she may have learned it as her Aunt Marlena was not aware of this meaning.[7] However, Roma and Theodora interpret it as a particularly derogatory insult and hold Claudette accountable for violating their peer group norms. Roma responds by recycling the insult (line 4) and barring Claudette from the seat she shares with Theodora both verbally, "You not sitting there!", and nonverbally, blocking the remaining space with her leg and sucking her teeth in annoyance/disgust. Theodora aligns with Roma, threatening to tell on Claudette (line 7). Claudette retorts with another use of Patwa challenging Roma's claims to control of the furniture (line 12). Roma nevertheless continues her negative sanctioning and exclusion of Claudette by physically pushing her off the couch and issuing the directive, "Don't call me sketel next time" (line 15). Claudette again challenges Roma by threatening to tell on her (lines 16–17). However, Claudette concedes when Roma threatens to make her explain the meaning of sketel to the adult (line 18). She whines while in a subordinate position on the floor below the girls (line 19). Roma points to another chair and effectively exiles her: "That is YOUR place" (line 20). Claudette complies by sitting there.

These examples illustrate how older children use Patwa with and around younger children, transmitting assertive verbal skills and demeanors while reinforcing associations between Patwa and authority. They employ their (often limited) knowledge of Patwa to negotiate local social hierarchies, alliances, and exclusion of some participants over others. Yet such claims are always open to contention and rejection, and for a child to wield power in this way they must be able to speak and stand up for themselves in English as well. The next section examines how these very same children in other contexts monitor younger children's isolated Patwa uses and try to ensure that they know the English equivalents, hence transmitting ambivalent language ideologies.

English as Symbolic Resource: Children's Corrections of Other Children's Patwa

Children rarely discuss their attitudes toward English and Patwa. However, their commentary on other children's speech and corrections of Patwa to English provide clues into their otherwise unarticulated language ideologies. Older children frequently encourage younger children to "say the English names" for things in everyday interactions and when playing school. They employ a metalanguage about English being the "correct," "right," or "real" alternative to Patwa, which by implication is "wrong" or not real. Sometimes this carries over into negative assessments of a child's intelligence as "stupid" for not knowing an English translation. Employing a strategy used by teachers, older children point out when a child uses Patwa and provide the English equivalent. Further, they typically explain why they are correcting it, unlike adult caregivers who rarely offer an explanation. Sometimes they simply repeat a Patwa utterance in a high-pitched whiny or discordant tone, which is a common means of poking fun at other children, such as when they threaten to tell on one another. Drawing on school discourses, children depict other children's use of Patwa and lack of English fluency as signs of verbal or intellectual weakness. This provides another means for asserting power through claims to greater knowledge and possession of linguistic capital.

Marcel again provides an example of this monitoring and innovation. Though he frequently uses Patwa during play, he also patrols other children's Patwa usage. He sometimes plays school in the yard or simply begins quizzing the children on English lexicon, as in the following examples. The group of children includes Marcel, Junior, Alex, Sherona, and Reiston. Marcel had initiated a "what is that?" routine common with caregivers, but heavily influenced by the school, in the outdoor kitchen. There is no indication that he is playing school, yet the younger children willingly submit themselves to his testing and evaluation of their language skills. There also is no negotiation about what language is required. The following are three sequential examples of Marcel's corrections when the children answer in Patwa:

Example 5.10

1 Marcel: ((holding a jar of instant coffee)) And that?
2 Alex: Huh? U:::m.
3 Marcel: ((puts hands to face)) Not to say - Alex! Not to say -
4 Alex: *Kafé.*
           (Coffee.)
5 Marcel: I - ((stops short in disapproval)).
6 (1)
7 Reiston: ((repeating Alex)) *Kafé.*
8 ((laughter))
9 Marcel: (Better known as/The Patwa name is) *kafé.* What is it REAL
           name? Granny make it for you - Papa make it for you this
           morning. What is that?
10 Reiston: *Kafé.*
11 Alex: [((laughs))
12 Sherona: [((laughs))
13 Marcel: ((loud and impatiently)) COFFEE boy!
14 Reiston: Coffee.
15 Alex: I WELL know.
16 Sherona: I know, I know, I WELL know!

Marcel's preemptive directive "not to say" and embodied action (line 3) indicate that he anticipates an "incorrect" answer from Alex. He expresses annoyance at Alex's Patwa response (line 4) and Reiston's repetition of it (lines 7 and 10), and asks for the "REAL name" of the item (line 9), implying that Patwa is not a "real" language like English. He impatiently corrects them (line 13). Alex and Sherona concede to Marcel's authority and claim they knew the "correct" answer all along (lines 15 and 16).

Marcel leads the children into the house and continues quizzing them. He picks up a candle and asks, "What is that Reiston? When light go, Granny lighting it." When Reiston fails to answer, Marcel tests the others. No one knows the name in English or Patwa except for Junior:

Example 5.11

1 Marcel: ((tossing the candle up and down)) Junior?
2 Junior: ((softly)) A *bouji.*
   (A <u>candle.</u>)
3 Marcel: ((stops tossing the candle)) English speaking I want now. English!
4 Junior: A line. A line.
5 Marcel: ((tossing the candle up and down impatiently)) What is that in English?
6 Junior: A line.
7 Marcel: ((walks away)) Make Amy tell all you.
8 Alex: A line.
9 Marcel: ((impatiently)) Make Amy tell all you. I not telling all you.

When Junior hesitatingly offers the Patwa word for candle (line 2), Marcel explicitly directs the children to speak English (line 3). When the children still do not answer correctly, Marcel directs them to ask me for the name (lines 7 and 9). He does not tell them the English word but continues his game by showing them a rosary. When only Junior knows the name—in Patwa—Marcel prompts the English version but quits the game by calling them "*sòt*" (stupid):

Example 5.12

1 Marcel: ((holding the rosary in front of Junior's face)) What is that Junior?
2 Junior: Huh? A:: (.5) a chain and papa holding it.
3 Marcel: ((speaking fast and impatiently)) Boy that not a - no chain! (1) ((calmly)) Just now there you had going to say it. ((prompting the Patwa version)) Cha::
4 Sherona: Cha::
5 Junior: *Chaplé.*
6 Marcel: What is the ENGLISH word for it?
7 Alex: *Chaplé*
8 Marcel: No::
9 Sherona: *Chaplé.*
10 Marcel: ((prompting the English version)) Ro:-
11 Sherona: Ro:-
12 (1)
13 Alex: Rose *chaplé.*
14 Marcel: ((louder)) Ro:s-
15 Sherona: Ro:s-
16 Marcel: -ry.
17 Junior: -ry.

18 Marcel: A rosary! ((under his breath)) *Sòt.*
          (Stupid.)
19 Alex: Rosary!
20 Marcel: ((loudly)) *Sòt!* I not playing with you.
21 Junior: You that *sòt.*

Marcel prompts Junior for the Patwa name when it is apparent that no one will provide the English one (line 3). After Junior says *chaplé* (line 5), Marcel demands that the children speak English (line 6). The children seem unable to provide the answer, even when he sounds it out for them—leading to Alex's inventive "rose *chaplé*" (line 13). In the end Marcel supplies the English word and evaluates the children as 'stupid,' ironically in Patwa despite his demand for English (lines 18 and 20). Marcel demonstrates his own language proficiency as he knows the terms in Patwa and English, while contrasting his intelligence with their lack thereof. In fact, his tone throughout the activity is impatient and condescending as if he *expects* them to answer incorrectly. Critically, I have never heard a child call another *sòt* or anything derogatory for knowing only the English term for something—nor did a child ask another what an English word means in Patwa—highlighting the position of English as the normative and unmarked code. The activity ends with Junior recycling Marcel's insult against him (line 21). This example illustrates how older children wield power over younger ones by utilizing pedagogical practices and claims to superior knowledge of both English and Patwa. Similar patterns of correction implying the superiority of English were found across the other families.

Discussion: Children's Agency and Language Choice in Play

These examples demonstrate how peer groups create a rich verbal environment in which children are socialized through and to use a diverse linguistic repertoire, including a language they are restricted from speaking in adult-controlled settings. In their local speech economy a child's ability to use Patwa strategically can give them an upper hand in organizing play and the actions of other children. Children must be proficient in both English and Patwa to maintain such a position, however, as a child who only knows how to say something in Patwa may face correction or ridicule by peers. Children blend affectively marked aspects of Patwa with their local English vernacular in particular contexts (peer play), for particular genres or speech acts (teasing, shaming, cursing, argument, negative assessment, role play), and for indexing powerful subject positions (adults). Their peer groups create a protected space for such exploration since adults negatively sanction children's use of Patwa and other speech forms when they are judged to threaten adult authority and/or English acquisition (as in Examples 5.1, 5.3, and 5.6). Children's peer interactions are a critical site of language socialization and a key resource for language maintenance, yet are overlooked in language revitalization efforts that focus only on school settings, formal performances, and adult–child transmission.

Children play with this forbidden language in child-controlled settings, thus illustrating their agency and creativity. They are not simply the passive recipients of culture or merely doing what adults tell them to do; according to adult expectations they should speak only English. Rather, they are attentive to the affective and pragmatic functions of Patwa in adult speech and employ it themselves for such purposes and for establishing their own peer group identities that are distinct from other age cohorts. Children use Patwa to mark affective intensity and create dramatic effects as they try to outdo, tease, control, and include/exclude one another. It is a linguistic strategy and form of symbolic capital used to shape social relations, assert their will and dominance over other children, and affect the world by calling attention to things that are important to them—and in a way that is hard for even adults to ignore, as in their innovative use of *ga*. By code-switching into Patwa children can craft more intense and cutting insults, directives, curses, and narratives as they tease, shame, and challenge one another's authority to describe and direct play. Children's understandings of how the languages index places, categories of persons, and social characteristics such as gender, class, and education become even more evident in their imaginary role play, to be explored in the next chapter.

Notes

1. In addition to these studies, see Butler (2008), Butler and Weatherall (2006), Cromdal (2001, 2004), Cromdal and Aronsson (2000), Evaldsson (2007), García-Sánchez (2010), Garrett (2005), M. Goodwin (1990), Hewitt (1986), Howard (2007, 2009), Jørgensen (1998), Kyratzis and Guo (2001), Kyratzis et al. (2001), Minks (2010), Paugh (2005a, 2005b), Rampton (1995), Reynolds (2007, 2008), Schieffelin (1994), Sheldon (1996), and Zentella (1997).

2. Children's use of multiple language varieties as resources in the negotiation of power has been documented in some multilingual settings. Jørgensen (1998) finds that bilingual Turkish-Danish immigrant teenagers in Denmark code-switch for "power-wielding" by drawing on both global (attitudes toward Turkish in the dominant society) and local (controlling the conversation) factors. Also considering how language ideologies impact code choice, Meek (2007) shows that children in an Athapascan community in the Yukon Territory, Canada, employ Kaska, a language they associate with elders and are shifting away from, to direct one another in peer contexts where its use does not challenge expectations of respect toward elders. Children even compete to be peer group leader by producing Kaska words/phrases until a child says an utterance that the others cannot comprehend and thus wins the competition (Meek 2007: 34).

3. E.g., Hewitt (1986), Jørgensen (1998), Lytra (2007), Rampton (1995), Zentella (1997).

4. Adults do not approve of any child roaming the village, but it is more common to see boys walking around than girls. Girls are expected to return promptly home from school or other activities.

5. I must admit that I sometimes felt that way as well. It was not until I systematically reviewed the videos that I began to see patterns in children's play and came to appreciate their creativity and co-constructed exploration of the world.

6. *Djèl* refers to the jaws of an animal and is considered more pejorative than *bouch* (mouth).

7. Marlena told me that sketel is a type of hair clip from Martinique. I remained puzzled, however, about why Claudette calling Roma "an old barrette" would warrant Roma threatening to tell on her and prompt Claudette to give in. Later, I asked Roma and she told me that it referred to a "bad girl." I did not discuss this with Marlena for fear of getting the girls in trouble.

CHAPTER 6

Acting Adult: Children's Language Use in Imaginary Play

It is a warm sunny day and the adults have left Reiston (three years and nine months), Junior (nine years), Alex (five years), and Sherona (four years) under Marcel's (eleven years) supervision while they are at work. After playing school the children begin a new game in which Marcel becomes a *kochon* (pig) and the boys are hunters trying to catch and butcher it. Sherona, however, is excluded for not assuming the role of "mommy" the boys assign to her and instead trying to enact the high status position of head teacher.[1] This is one segment from their imaginary play:

Example 6.1

1　Junior:　　*Mwen ka haché'y. Tèt li gou!*
　　　　　　　(I'm cutting it. Its head tastes [good]!)

2　Junior:　　((to the pretend hunters)) *Zò pa ka koupé tèt li.*
　　　　　　　(You are not cutting its head.)

3　Reiston:　　((looks up at Sherona)) Mommy! Go for - mommy go for yam!

4　Junior:　　[*I pa mò. I pa mò.*
　　　　　　　(It isn't dead. It isn't dead.) [re: pretend pig]

5　Reiston:　　[((to Sherona)) Mommy go for yam!

6　Sherona:　　((makes a throwing gesture with hands)) Look all you food. Cook your food.

7　((the three boys pretend to chop Marcel))

8　Sherona:　　I NOT a mommy. (1) And I is a - a head teacher though. ((shaking head)) I is NOT a mommy.

9　Junior:　　Well *nou ka koupé'y.*
　　　　　　　(Well we are cutting it.)

10　Sherona:　　((sits and watches the boys wrestle with Marcel))

This is a prime illustration of how children can activate their Patwa competence to alternate between languages in the creation of vivid imaginary play. Junior uses a great deal of Patwa in his construction of the event (lines 1, 2, 4, and 9), employing the language associated with the predominantly male rural activity of hunting and the outside places where such activity occurs. Reiston uses English in an effort to include Sherona, who has been excluded from the rough-and-tumble play, by addressing her as "mommy" and directing her to harvest root crops to cook to accompany the pork dinner (lines 3 and 5). This is the third time one of the boys has tried to assign the motherhood role to her (see Examples 6.8–6.11 below). This four-year-old desires a professional job, however, and rejects the role with the dismissive gesture of throwing the imaginary food while verbally asserting herself (line 6). She declares, "I NOT a mommy" (line 8). However, by rejecting a role that complements the hunters and pig, and trying to claim one (that of head teacher) outside the current play frame, she is ignored. In peer-controlled settings children negotiate their own social organization and compete over skills, roles, and levels of authority not always available to them. Further, group play illustrates that children are sensitive to gendered and class-inflected roles and exercise some control over which ones they will enact. Significantly, the children use Patwa for the role of hunter and to refer to the animal being hunted while they use English to address the nominated "mommy" and to negotiate about the roles themselves.

I analyze in this chapter how children draw on their verbal resources to create complex imaginary play spaces, roles, and scenarios. Pretend play offers children a prime context for cultural and linguistic exploration and socialization of one another.[2] They can experiment and play with various social identities or "voices" that are otherwise restricted from them. Children's pretense displays their burgeoning understandings of local, national, and global power hierarchies, including those related to gender, class, status, and familial roles.[3] In this exploration and reflection of social norms children create alternative social realities in which *they* hold positions of authority, power, and control, and in doing so, may also challenge and transform them (M. Goodwin and Kyratzis 2012; Reynolds 2002, 2007). What is striking is that while their everyday conversations and other forms of object play (such as tossing a ball or playing with a crayfish or bug) consist primarily of English with occasional code-switches into Patwa, in role playing their Patwa speech often spans several turns and consists of complete Patwa sentences. As will be explored, children who can use either Patwa or English often choose Patwa to represent particular adult roles. The examination of pretend activities as children construct them thus offers a window into their emergent understandings of adult cultural and linguistic practices—and how they shape them in turn. This sheds light on children's roles in processes of language shift and maintenance, and suggests that children's pretend play is an untapped resource in language revitalization efforts.[4]

Children's Imaginary Role Play

Role playing is a common activity when Dominican children play in groups. They pretend to engage in activities that they observe adults doing regularly but normally are excluded from or can only participate in marginally, such as cooking, farming, or driving. Children use household furniture or materials they find, such as garbage, kitchen knives, cardboard boxes, pets, and insects to construct imaginary places and props for their play. As children tend to play outside the home and apart from adults (see chapter 5), they are able to structure and perform such activities without adult evaluation. Examination of such play demonstrates "the salience and importance of these activities and the child's ability to understand the details and sequences that constitute them" (Schieffelin 1990: 225). Key details include the languages used, the places where the activities occur, what kinds of people do them, and the affective stances associated with them. Children's code-switching practices demonstrate their emerging sensitivities to how both languages index social identities, places, and activities (Paugh 2005a).

Talk is very important in creating and sustaining play frames since children usually do not own many toys to act as props. In fantasy sequences that involve performance of adult roles, older children often describe the activity and direct younger children in what to do or say. Small children rarely are excluded and often become lead characters. Yet children's politics become visible as they dispute participation frameworks including who gets which role and who will direct the activity. As M. Goodwin and Kyratzis (2012: 373) state, "Enacting stratified roles in pretend play provides children with resources for constituting hierarchical relationships among themselves and constructing the local social order of the peer group." Language proficiency is an important tool for accessing powerful roles.

There are differences between children's negotiations *about* role play and their language use *within* role-playing frames. As has been documented for bilingual children in some settings (e.g., Halmari and Smith 1994; Kwan-Terry 1992), alternation between two languages creates contrasts between the negotiation of the roles and activities, and the imaginary play itself.[5] Children generally use English for interactions about the play, including directing one another's actions. Sometimes they use Patwa for local interactional functions like affective marking and intensifying directives as in regular peer interaction (see chapter 5). Within the play frame itself, however, children switch languages according to the activities and roles. In other words children use both languages, but they tend to employ more Patwa for enacting certain personas than they do in any other kind of social interaction. Therefore, their performance of adult roles matches the activities undertaken and languages used by adults. Children's understandings of the interrelations between language and place, and the meanings and appropriateness of using particular linguistic varieties in context, become especially evident (see Schieffelin 2003).

Studies of children's imaginative play have shown that they distinguish and depict roles using language features that index salient characteristics of the ways individuals speak. Preschool children collaboratively key (Goffman 1974) pretend play through story-appropriate register shifts and a range of devices such as pre-positional discourse markers ("let's say that"), use of past tense verbs to mark modality (the imaginary past), and "rich modes of in-character voicing" (Blum-Kulka et al. 2004: 313–314). Anglo-American children have been shown to employ registers associated with adult roles and activities, and to switch actively between registers to negotiate imaginary and real identities (Andersen 1996; Hoyle 1998; Kyratzis et al. 2001; also Agha 2005). Goldman (1998: 155–156) found that Huli children in Papua New Guinea occasionally use Tok Pisin lexemes along with changes in intonation and voice quality in their Huli speech to add "role authenticity and integrity" to their portrayals of post-colonial roles like administrators and hospital personnel who speak Tok Pisin. In Dominica a child's use of Patwa can trigger an imaginary play scene and invite other children without specific metacommunicative framing such as "let's play farmers." This evokes Gumperz's description of "situational switching" (as distinct from "metaphorical switching"):

> In situational switching, where a code or speech style is regularly associated with a certain class of activities, it comes to signify or connote them, so that its very use can signal the enactment of these activities even in the absence of other clear contextual cues. Component messages are then interpreted in terms of the norms and symbolic associations that apply to the signalled activity. (Gumperz 1982: 98)

Code-switching acts as a contextualization cue that indexes multiple aspects of the activity at hand and can serve as a means to change the nature or definition of the speech event. Agha (2004: 26) highlights this in terms of register switching:

> If the current scenario of use is already recognizable as an instance of the social practice the utterance appears appropriate to that occasion; conversely, switching to the register may itself reconfigure the sense of the occasion, indexically entailing or creating the perception that the social practice is now under way.

This is particularly applicable to how children employ Patwa as an adult register. Patwa appears to be so strongly associated with certain adult activities that the switch into Patwa signals the enactment of the role, similar to how children switch into a school-like register for playing teachers. By switching codes and manipulating other features of their speech, children use language as a vital resource to signal social roles in play.

English-Speaking Roles and Activities

From soon after they begin to talk children are able to identify which language varieties to employ and what activities are entailed in enacting roles. For certain activities children tend to employ English with little or no use of Patwa, often accompanied by neutral or calm affective stances. Patwa is used when children pretend to enact predominantly male adult roles—such as farmers, bus drivers, and pig hunters—but rarely as mothers, teachers, and doctors, which in the village are more female dominated and/or educated occupations. The following sections explore common English roles and activities and how they are performed by children in my corpus of recorded peer interaction.

Playing School

Playing school is one of the most common pretend activities among village children. The structuring of the play frame, participant roles of teacher and students, and activities are carried out almost strictly in English. As teachers children strive to speak a more standard variety of English with careful articulation and an authoritative tone of voice. They try to wield control over their pretend pupils by issuing directives and assessments. Though rare, they occasionally switch to Patwa within the role to issue an intensified command such as "*Sizé!*" (Sit down!) or negative evaluation such as "You *mal élivé*" (You are badly brought up/badly behaved), like teachers themselves admit to doing when school children are unruly. This again points to children's understandings of Patwa as part of a register linked to authority and control. But more typically children employ English, the only accepted language of the education system. As teachers they instruct their students to sing songs learned at school or church, to tell about themselves, to spell their names or other words, and to identify objects or answer questions about things they have seen or done. They employ physical props such as old lesson books and pretend chalkboards made from cardboard or old metal roofing. Children demonstrate an understanding of the unequal positions of authority in the teacher–student relationship, particularly ways in which teachers can control their students.

For example, pretend teachers frequently find a "whip," such as a twig, and threaten to "give licks" if students disobey or answer questions incorrectly.

Such themes are illustrated in the following segment from Marissa's peer group. Sonia (six years) initiates playing school with six other children including Marissa (three years and eight months), Nicholas (eleven years), Oscar (seven months), and neighbors Henrietta (seven years) and twin brothers Aaron and Albert (nine years). Sonia's mother has placed three chairs on the veranda while she mops the kitchen floor. The children arrange the chairs in a line facing out from the veranda, which becomes the classroom.[6] Sonia retrieves a school workbook entitled *Practice Reading* from inside and stands in front while Marissa and Henrietta (holding Oscar) sit on the chairs and the boys sit on the veranda wall. She commands her students to stand up, which is how teachers obtain children's attention to begin the school day: "All stand." The children stand and face her, indicating their agreement to participate in the play frame. Sonia then assumes a deeper, more authoritative tone of voice as she leads them through activities common to a school day: morning prayer and songs, stretching exercises, picture book study, days of the week, months of the year, ABCs, counting, and reading exercises. In this segment she requires each student to stand and tell the class about themselves. She is holding a "whip" (a branch) for threatening unruly students:

Example 6.2

1 Sonia: Marissa come at the front. Ta::lk. Say about your ho::me. Say where you living.
2 Marissa: ((stands and turns toward the class))
3 Albert: ((jumps down from the wall and stands in front of the chairs)) I am living -
4 Sonia: ((to Albert, waving her "whip")) No!
5 Sonia: [((grabs Marissa's sleeve and pulls her in front))
6 Albert: [I am living ((laughing)) *Lod Bò*. [Patwa name for Lower Penville]
7 ((Nicholas, Aaron, and Albert laugh hysterically then quiet down))
8 Marissa: ((standing in front)) I am living Lower Penville.
9 Sonia: ((to Marissa)) Very good.
10 Sonia: ((to all)) Give her a big hand clap ((claps hands)).
11 ((children clap))
12 Sonia: Albert.
13 Albert: I - I living to ((puts chin out)) bobo ((laughs)).
14 Sonia: BoBO?!
15 ((Nicholas and Aaron laugh))
16 Sonia: ((clapping hands)) Give him a big hand clap.
17 ((children clap))

18 Sonia: Nicholas.
19 Nicholas: U::m what you say again?
20 Sonia: Say where you li::ving. Say what - what you doing at your
            ho::me.
21 Nicholas: Ok.
22 Marissa: [((points one finger in the air, yelling)) I am sleeping at my
            home!
23 Sonia: [Say about your schoo::l.
24 Nicholas: My mother? My mother? She giving me plenty work. I
            sleeping in Lower Penville in a white house.
25 ((Albert and Aaron laugh loudly))
26 Nicholas: The teacher's always hitting me at school but ((nods head))
            I give them - ((waves one hand)) I had - I show them how
            I was doing good at school? I get a bursary ((waving hands
            in the air)) and so on and so on and so on.
27 Sonia: ((clapping hands)) Give him a big hand clap.
28 ((children clap))

Sonia initiates the activity by calling on Marissa (line 1), but before she can begin Albert jumps to the front and answers, laughing as he says "*Lod Bò.*" (line 6). This utterance prompts intense laughter from the other boys (line 7), presumably because he uses the Patwa name for Lower Penville in this pretend school setting since the boys did not laugh when he initially jumped down and tried speak out of turn (line 3). Sonia tries to stop him and pulls Marissa to the front (lines 4 and 5). Marissa answers as directed using the English name for their hamlet (line 8). Sonia praises her and prompts the other children to clap for her as they do in school (lines 9 and 10). She then gives Albert his turn (line 12), to which he responds by playfully making up sounds for the place name "to bobo" and laughing (line 13). Sonia does not scold him but repeats his answer as a rhetorical question, "BoBO?!" The other boys laugh (line 15), but she nonetheless tells everyone to clap for Albert (line 16).

Sonia then calls on Nicholas, who acts the part of an inattentive student (line 19). She repeats her question but adds, "Say what - what you doing at your ho::me" (line 20). Marissa, who did not have the opportunity to answer this question, then shouts, "I am sleeping at my home!" (line 22). Sonia continues talking and does not respond to this outburst (line 23). Nicholas then provides the most elaborate and comical response so far. He elicits loud laughter from the other boys by claiming that his mother gives him "plenty work" and by recycling Marissa's utterance (line 22) by stating, "I sleeping in Lower Penville in a white house" (line 24). He then blends reality with play as he describes his performance in school. He claims that the teacher is "always hitting" him, seemingly referring to Sonia's actions in the play frame since

Nicholas is well known as a polite and accomplished student who would not be subjected to corporal punishment in school. He references this by citing the real bursary he earned from scoring high on the Common Entrance Exam for secondary school (line 26). The children clap for him at Sonia's prompting (lines 27–28). After this the boys become increasingly rowdy as if trying to provoke the teacher to discipline them. Sonia becomes impatient and smacks them with her whip, but does not switch to Patwa to scold them. All roles and activities in this sixteen-minute bout of play are performed in English. The children then disperse into gender-segregated groups, with the girls going inside to play house. Playing school in English, as well as dressing up and enacting religious rituals from the Pentecostal Church, were common among Marissa's siblings (Figure 6.1).

Playing Mommies and Daddies

When pretending to be parents or playing house children carry out routine tasks like cooking, cleaning, and feeding their offspring, who typically are younger siblings, pets, or dolls if they have them. Children enacting these roles tell their pretend charges in English to "come and bathe," "eat your food," and "sleep, baby, sleep." Many do, however, employ Patwa lexicon and terms of endearment that characterize the baby talk register used by adults and older children with young children (see chapter 4). These appear in their

Figure 6.1 Marissa (front left) and her siblings sing and clap to songs from the Pentecostal Church, while their mother helps baby Oscar dance behind them

English speech and frequently are spoken in a higher-pitched voice. When I began recording Alisia (one year and eleven months), she played "mommy" with her baby brother. She lifted her shirt, pulled her brother toward her, and said, "Baby, look *tété* (breast)." Even Jonah (two years and nine months) once called to his puppy and then asked it if it wanted to breastfeed:

Example 6.3

1	Jonah:	Puppy: puppy: you want *tété?* You want *tété?* You want *tété?* You want *tété?*
2	Mother:	Where you taking *tété* to give it?
3	Claudette:	((laughs))
4	Jonah:	Huh?
5	Mother:	Where you have *tété* to give it?
6	Jonah:	There.
7	Mother:	Where?
8	Jonah:	((points to left side of his chest)) There.
9	Claudette:	((laughs quietly))
10	Jonah:	((points to right side of his chest)) And there.

Jonah indicates a keen awareness of how caregivers speak to infants. He talks to the puppy as if it can understand yet does not wait for a response. As a pretend parent his speech is in English with use of Patwa baby talk lexicon (*tété*) and simple repetitive questions (line 1). His mother playfully questions how he will breastfeed (lines 2 and 5) and Jonah shows her by pointing at his chest (lines 8 and 10). His cousin Claudette (13 years) laughs quietly at his exploration of this female domain, but no one overtly tells him that as a male he would not be able to nurse a baby.

Other English Roles and Activities

There are other adult roles that children tend to enact in English, such as when they pretend to perform religious and official activities. Children as young as two years demonstrate awareness of ritualized speech and behavior, for example, when Jonah (two years and one month) spontaneously began blessing Theodora (five years), and Roma (eleven years) like a Catholic priest:

Example 6.4

1	Jonah:	((begins to pray)) Father.
2	Jonah:	((putting hand on Theodora's head)) Father the son holy spirit /mamum/ [Amen].
3	Jonah:	((putting hand on Roma's head)) Father the son holy spirit /mamum/.
4	Roma:	((laughs)) Make in the name. [re: pray]

5 Jonah: ((putting hand on Roma's head)) Father the son.
6 Jonah: ((putting hand on Theodora's head)) Father the son.
7 Jonah: Holy Spirit /mamem/.
8 Jonah: ((putting hand on top of his own head)) Father the son.
9 Roma: Jonah say father son holy spirit /mamem/. [mimicking
            Jonah's pronunciation]
10 Jonah: ((repeating Roma)) /Mamum/.

Jonah demonstrates his understanding of the verbal and embodied steps of the religious ritual, reciting a prayer while touching the heads of his playmates. Roma, the eldest, laughs at first but encourages Jonah's play sequence and provides scaffolding by naming the speech act, "Make in the name" (line 4), which is a common way to refer to the prayer "In the name of the Lord." She also, however, subtly pokes fun at his babyish pronunciation of Amen in her prompt for him to say the prayer (line 9).

Children use English to re-create official rituals, speeches, and performances observed at school, during cultural events, and on television. For example, Reiston's cousin Marcel was a member of the Dominica Boy Scouts and often apprenticed his peers in common scout activities. On several occasions he led Reiston and the other young children in scout marches on the road near their homes. He always claimed the powerful role of troupe leader and used a series of English commands specific to a formal register used in the scouts and by the police force: "stand up," "at ease," "attention," "mark time," "quick march," "right turn," and "left" and "right" as imperatives. Sometimes other neighborhood children joined in and one day Marcel attracted a group of nine children who acquired the routine and then marched back and forth while he called out orders in this official English register.

In general, even when they have some Patwa proficiency, children choose English to depict authoritative high-status adult positions such as the teacher, priest, and scout leader examples above. Such roles require special training and are associated with formal education and institutional authority. Children are attentive to the linguistic, affective, and physical forms associated with these ritualized events including choice of language, key, and non-verbal action.

Patwa-Speaking Roles and Activities

In contrast to English roles and activities, which typically take place in home, school, and other formal settings (including ones children create to resemble these settings), children employ Patwa for roles and activities that occur in places outside the built environment. These include predominantly male uneducated occupations that take place in the garden, road, or bush, where adults regularly speak Patwa with one another. These constitute the most extensive uses of Patwa that I heard among children and help to sustain lengthy stretches of imaginary play when apart from adults. Three recurring pretend activities that were observed in the families are analyzed here: "playing transport," hunting, and farming.

Playing Transport

Penville children are fascinated by automobiles, which are commonly called "transports" and are few in number in the village. Favorite pastimes include calling out when vehicles pass by and pretending to be drivers and passengers. Caregivers and children recognize this common childhood activity and refer to it as "playing transport." Boys tend to assume the role of driver and operate vehicles including buses, cars, trucks, and motorbikes. This reflects the gendered nature of driving, as few female villagers had learned to drive or sought their driver's licenses. Girls are less likely to initiate a driving game but often join an ongoing one. Boys build trucks out of materials they find or turn household furniture, the natural environment, or an anthropologist's car into their play vehicle. Reiston (three years), for example, held the steering wheel of my Jeep one day and exclaimed that he would *fouté* (hit) speed on it:

Example 6.5
I - I go by - when I go by - when I go by Shero ... I - I - I *FOUTÉ* speed on - on that *wi*. When I - when I hold that - when I hold that and I *FOUTÉ*ing speed on it. When when - when it going (1) I *fouté*ing speed on it.

Reiston's speech is full of false starts, hesitations, and repetition as it excitedly builds to *fouté*, which is emphasized and punctuated over the rest. This helps him claim a particular kind of voice and social identity—"*fouté*ing speed" indexes a more mature (male) adult identity of driver and being able to move fast. During transcription his grandfather commented, "*I nonm wi*" (He's mannish yeah), highlighting the adult character of his voice and the activity.

While many instances of role play unfold in the actual places where such adult activities occur, such as a vehicle or banana field, children also verbally and physically create places both associated with and acceptable for Patwa use.[7] In the following example three very young children employ Patwa to construct an evocative playing transport scene. The bus is a prime context for the use of Patwa for adult gossip and bus drivers typically speak Patwa rather than English to passengers, especially in rural areas. Tamika (two years and seven months), Kenrick (two years and one month), and their cousin Henry (three years) co-produce a shared imaginative frame that enacts the roles of bus driver and two passengers in appropriate social spaces—the bus and a bus stop on the road—constructed within the living room of Tamika's house. The children are alone aside from me, while Tamika's mother Lorna cooks lunch in the kitchen located five feet from the house. First, Kenrick and Tamika close the front door and windows, making it impossible for anyone to see inside. The "closing up" of the house is significant as people are expected to leave the front door and windows open when home during the day or risk being considered antisocial. Further, it is considered rude for children to shut out adults and implies inappropriate behavior. In this case it facilitates the children's private display of competence.

Without any prompts Henry transforms the couch into a bus driving on the road. He becomes the driver, positioning himself at one end of the couch with his feet dangling through the railing and pretending to hold a steering wheel. Imitating real-life bus drivers Henry then advises his passengers when to embark/disembark by excitedly calling out two commands in Patwa: "*Batjé!*" (Get on board!') and "*Atè!*" (On the ground! i.e., disembark). He does not provide metacommunicative framing, such as "we are playing bus," but Tamika and Kenrick take his cue from these simple commands and non-verbal actions, and climb on like passengers. Tamika echoes Henry by calling out "*batjé:*" as she climbs aboard, and adds to the joint construction of the play by exclaiming "*Nou alé!*" (We go!), a common expression among adults at a bus stop. Kenrick excitedly repeats her (see Paugh 2005a: 74).

The children get on and off for several minutes as Henry exclaims "*Batjé!*" until Tamika decides to move the couch for better access. The negotiation of the move takes place entirely in English, mainly consisting of Tamika issuing directives to the others:

Example 6.6

1	Tamika:	Just now.
		(Wait.)
2	Henry:	((makes driving noises))
3	Tamika:	((to Henry)) Henry move on that. [re: the couch]
4	Henry:	((stops making driving noises and slides back on the couch))
5	Tamika:	((to Henry)) Move on that. Move you on that. Move on that. Move!
6	Henry:	What you going do?
7	Tamika:	((touching bottom of couch)) There. There.
8	Kenrick:	((repeating Tamika)) There. There.
9	Tamika:	Henry!
10	Henry:	Hm?
11	Tamika:	Come push there. Push it.
12	Kenrick:	(xxx)
13		((the children slide the couch to the center of the room; Henry is hesitant, but helps))

14 Henry: ((climbing on the couch)) *Bondyé! Annou batjé!*
            (God! Let's get on board!)
15 Kenrick: *Bondyé!*
16 Henry: *Annou batjé::! Annou batjé::!*
17 Kenrick: Yeah!

While it appears that Henry is in control of the play, Tamika plays an important part in co-constructing it as passenger and director of the play space (it is, after all, her house). She issues numerous English directives (lines 1, 3, 5, 7, and 11) until Henry consents to moving the couch. When they finish he happily resumes the play with a new Patwa construction (line 14). Soon after, however, Henry tries to persuade Tamika to return the couch because of the potentially negative consequences of reorganizing her mother's furniture. He repeatedly tells her, "Lorna hit us" (Lorna will hit us). Again, negotiations about the play space are conducted in English not Patwa. After playing for a few more minutes Henry finally convinces Tamika but the children cannot maneuver the couch back in place. They give up and begin jumping off the couch, loudly thumping on the floor when they land. Lorna hears this and quickly enters the house; she stops abruptly when she sees the furniture:

Example 6.7

1 Lorna: ((loudly)) Tamika WHO tell all you to pull that right there?
2 Tamika: Not me. Henry.
3 Lorna: ((disapprovingly)) Mm! ((stomps back outside))
4 Henry: ((jumps down and inspects the couch))
5 Kenrick: Eh. Beep bee::::p. Beep bee::p.
6 Henry: Let me see it. ((trying to push the couch)) That CANNOT
           go more!
7 Tamika: ((speaking fast)) Leave it, leave it, leave it.
8 Henry: ((trying to push the couch)) It cannot go::!
9 Kenrick: It good.
10 Lorna: ((reenters the house, speaking fast)) Leave that! Leave that
           all you before all you - all you break my thing eh? *Pa sizé yo
           di zò sizé pou zò palé?* ((pushing through the children to get
           to the couch)) *Ba mwen lè.*
           (Didn't they tell you (plural) to sit and talk? Give me space
           [to move the furniture].)
11 ((Lorna puts back the couch; the children watch silently))
12 Lorna: ((speaking fast)) *Ng'a ni fè zò ay lakay zò si sé wété zò pa ka
           wété byen. Zò mal élivé kon sé ti zanfan kochon.*
           (I'll make you (plural) go home if you don't stay well. You
           (plural) are badly brought up like little pig children.)

As predicted by Henry, Lorna scolds the children for moving her couch. Amusingly, when confronted by her mother Tamika blames Henry for being the initiator (line 2). This displaces the blame from herself since she would face a harsher punishment from her mother. Lorna berates the children in both English and Patwa as she fixes the couch and sits down, utilizing Patwa to highlight a threat to send Henry and Kenrick home and a negative evaluation of the group (line 12). Her Patwa comment on line 10, translatable as "Didn't they tell you all to sit and talk?", suggests an underestimation of the children's communicative competence and complexity of their play, assuming they are misbehaving and not providing me with linguistic data. She dismantles the imaginary play space by rearranging the furniture and reopening the door and windows. Further, she guides the ensuing talk, with Henry and Kenrick remaining practically silent and only speaking English when they do talk for as long as she is in the house. During transcription Lorna expressed surprise at how much Henry spoke, claiming that he rarely talks because he is "too afraid" of people. But with no adult evaluating their speech and behavior, Henry and his cousins talked extensively, creatively employing their linguistic resources to construct an imaginary sequence of a kind that I never witnessed when adults were present.

These examples illustrate the awareness of children as young as two or three years of role-appropriate language and how to creatively and pragmatically use it for make-believe. But where did such young children learn about riding buses and the use of Patwa by bus drivers and passengers? Their primary caregivers rarely take the bus to Roseau because of the cost and lengthy ride. When adults do go, they typically leave children with relatives or friends as they have many errands to accomplish before the once-daily bus returns to Penville. However, children frequently are present as people wait for rides and they overhear interactions as adults get on board. As small children silently trail their adult caregivers, they observe what is going on around them and are socialized to how speech indexes people, practices, and places. But importantly, older children also expose young children to such ways of playing and portraying adult activities during peer play. Kenrick and Tamika's older siblings and cousins frequently give each other (and pets, insects, etc.) rides on objects they find around the house, such as old plastic bags and cardboard boxes. On several occasions I heard them say *batjé* to their "passengers," although not in the same sequence created by Henry, Tamika, and Kenrick. During a recording session two months prior to the above, Kenrick received an explicit lesson on the meaning of *batjé*. He and three cousins were taking turns "riding" a box down a hill in Tamika's yard, pretending it was a truck. At one point Kenrick began whining. His cousin Robert (eight years), who was in the box, asked him, "You want a ride? To *batjé*? To go up?" Despite Robert's offer Kenrick became interested in a flap of the box that had fallen off and began sliding on it down the hill. Nevertheless, Robert's questions had implications beyond ascertaining if Kenrick wanted a turn in the box. They also defined and socialized the use of the Patwa verb *batjé*, offering insights into the activity and multiple ways to talk about it (to get "a ride" and "to go up" into a vehicle). Similar examples occurred in other families.[8] Children learn not only from their observations of and participation in the adult world, but also from how they reconstruct and portray that world in their interactions with other children.

Hunting and Preparing Food

As children co-construct and socialize one another through imaginary play, they simultaneously negotiate their own local politics. Each move made by a participant creates the opportunity for a response from another that may take the action in new directions. It is in this way that children create extended and elaborate role-play sequences, but also dispute what will happen next. The following transcript excerpts are from twenty minutes of pretend play in Reiston's peer group that revolves around an imaginary animal hunt, part of which was described in Example 6.1. As mentioned, there were no adults present other than myself during most of the recording session, which included Marcel, Reiston, Junior, Alex, and Sherona (Figure 6.2).

When I arrived the children were playing school. Marcel was the teacher, using broken chalk and metal roofing as his chalkboard. The younger children were sitting on two large pieces of cardboard serving as a classroom. They played for seventeen minutes until they became fed up with Marcel's authoritative demeanor and use of corporal punishment for incorrect responses. They were speaking English but as the play frame changed the children began switching to Patwa. The transition from school (in English) to hunting an animal (in Patwa) appears to happen through two shifts triggered by the sequential actions of participants in relation to the cardboard used as a prop for school. The first occurs when Reiston removes the cardboard, thus dismantling the classroom. Marcel struggles to grab it back and Reiston begins hitting him with it. Marcel then flops face down on the ground as if he has given up. Reiston seizes the opportunity to change the play by pretending that Marcel is sleeping and needs to be covered as if the cardboard is a blanket. The others join in until Sherona tries to initiate school again (with her in charge):

Example 6.8

1 Reiston: ((putting the cardboard over Marcel)) Let's cover - cover Marcel. Let's cover Marcel. He sleeping.

2 Junior: ((pushes cardboard on Marcel)) *Annou ay. Annou ay.*
(Let's go. Let's go [cover Marcel].)

3 Sherona: ((repeating Junior and pushing the cardboard on Marcel)) *Annou ay, annou ay, annou ay, annou ay.*

4 Reiston: ((shoves Sherona off Marcel)) Mm! He sleeping.

5 Sherona: ((stands back)) *Annou ay.*

6 Reiston: ((pulling another piece of cardboard from under Alex, whispering fast)) Let's cover him. Let's cover him. Let's cover him.

7 Alex: ((stands up))

8 Reiston: ((takes the cardboard)) Cover him. He sleeping. Cover him. Cover him.

9 Reiston: [((pulls the cardboard over Marcel's head))

10 Junior: [((helps Reiston cover Marcel)) *Annou* cover him, *annou* cover him.
(<u>Let's</u> cover him, <u>let's</u> cover him.)

11 Reiston: *Annou* cover him aye!

12 ((the children laugh, except for Marcel under the cardboard))

Figure 6.2 Marcel stands over the members of his peer group with his hands on Alex's (left) and Junior's (right) heads and Reiston (left) and Sherona (right) crouching below

13 Junior: ((stepping back)) We cover him. We cover him. We cover him.
14 Sherona: I going. ((walks to the pretend chalkboard))
15 Reiston: ((climbs on Marcel, bounces up and down, laughing))
16 Sherona: ((banging on the chalkboard, loudly punctuating each syllable)) WHAT IS THAT EVERYBODY?
17 ((the boys play and laugh while Sherona bangs on the chalkboard))

On line 1 Reiston launches a new game through embodied action (covering Marcel with the cardboard), verbally enlisting the help of the others ("Let's cover Marcel"), and defining Marcel's activity ("He sleeping"). Junior helps push the cardboard over Marcel and partially recycles Reiston's command, but in Patwa: "*Annou ay*" (line 2). At the time it is unclear what prompts his change in language; however, it appears to be the beginning of the second shift in the play, discussed below. Sherona repeats Junior's imperative four times (line 3), illustrating how younger children imitate or "shadow" (Björk-Willén 2007) older children's verbal and non-verbal actions as they acquire and display competence and show willingness to be part of the activity. Reiston, however, pushes Sherona back, rejecting her attempt to join by implying she will wake Marcel (line 4). Junior begins to takes over narration of the play, again with a code-switch to Patwa (line 10). When Marcel is covered, Junior steps back and announces that the task is finished (line 13). Sherona appears to interpret this as a transitional moment and thus an opportunity to change the play. She attempts to gain the floor by returning the activity to playing school with her as head teacher (lines 14 and 16). The boys are now engrossed in the new play frame and ignore her. The children laugh and talk all at once for a few minutes with the boys pushing the cardboard on Marcel. Sherona gives up her bid to play school and begins looking at a book alone.

Junior then accomplishes the second shift in the play frame: the boys become hunters who have caught an animal played by Marcel. Key to understanding this new direction is that when hunting men typically cover the carcass with cardboard, a tarp, or banana leaves to keep flies off until the meat can be taken away. It is likely that Junior's earlier shift to Patwa on line 2 was prompted by Reiston covering Marcel with the cardboard in the first place. In turn, his use of Patwa for narrating sets the context for this masculine outdoor activity. The play continues with Reiston sitting on Marcel and Alex watching:

Example 6.9
1 Junior: ((urgently)) *Annou koupé'y. Pa sizé anlè'y! Pa sizé anlè'y!*
((pulling the cardboard from underneath Reiston)) *Bouden i ké waché.*

(Let's cut it. Don't sit on top of it! Don't sit on top of it! Its belly will come out.)

2   Reiston: ((gets up, laughs))

3   Junior: ((putting the cardboard on Marcel)) *Nou kay kouvĕy non. Annou kouvĕy. Annou kouvĕy. I mò.*
(We're going to cover it (tag). Let's cover it. Let's cover it. It's dead.)

4   Reiston: ((repeating Junior)) *I mò.*
(It's dead.)

5   Junior: *I mò! Wé!*

6   Reiston: ((repeating Junior)) *Wé!*

7   Junior: *Dé pat li.*
(Its two paws.)

8   Reiston: ((repeating Junior)) *Dé pat li.*

9   Junior: ((grabbing Marcel's feet, counting)) *Dé pat li, yon.*
(Its two paws, one.)

Junior does not tell the others that they are pretending to hunt an animal. This becomes clear, however, through his embodied action and language use. He covers Marcel and grabs his feet while calling them paws (*pat*) rather than feet (*pyé*) (lines 7 and 9). He uses Patwa to issue imperatives to cut and cover it and to describe the object as dead.[9] He also uses the same inclusive imperative used by Reiston in English in Example 6.8 line 6, "Let's cover him," but in Patwa: "*Annou kouvĕy*" (line 3). Reiston shadows Junior by repeating his Patwa utterances (lines 4, 6, and 8).

The boys continue laughing, screaming, and wrestling for three minutes. During this time Sherona makes another attempt to initiate playing school by walking up to the boys with a stick in her hand and ordering "Now everybody stay well" like teachers say when they want students to behave. She strikes Junior on the buttocks with the stick and walks back to the pretend chalkboard. The boys ignore her, however, systematically switching between Patwa and English as they alternate between constructing the imaginary play in Patwa and planning to hide Marcel's book, a prop from playing school, in English. Marcel is getting pummeled at this point and begins demanding his book. They ignore him until he throws off the cardboard and sits up:

Example 6.10

1   Marcel: ((sitting up, impatiently)) Go for my book for me.

2   Junior: We don't hide no book! We don't hide NO book. ((grabbing books from the ground)) Look book!

3 Marcel: ((crawls toward Junior))
4 Reiston: ((runs to the cardboard)) Me first all you! Me first!
5 Junior: ((to Reiston)) A game we playing?!
6 Marcel: ((quickly crawls back to the cardboard))
7 Reiston: ((puts cardboard on his head))
8 Junior: *Wé! Wé! Wé!*
9 Marcel: ((to Reiston)) No! ((lies down on the cardboard)) Me!
10 Junior: *Annou kouvèy!* [re: Marcel]
           (Let's cover it!)
11 Reiston: ((stands up, holding a piece of cardboard))
12 Junior: *Wé! I mò. I mò. I mò.*
           (Yeah! It's dead. It's dead. It's dead.)
13 ((Reiston and Junior cover Marcel with cardboard))
14 Junior: *Wé! Wé! Alex! Wé!*
15 Reiston: *Annou kouvèy:. Wé! Wé! Annou kouvèy.*
16 Sherona: *Annou kouvèy.* ((grabbing Marcel's foot)) *Patat.* *Patat.**
           (Let's cover it. Potato/vagina.* Potato/vagina.*)

Marcel exits the play frame by knocking off the main prop, sitting up, and issuing an impatient directive in English (line 1). In addition to obtaining his book, this off-stage demand may be an attempt to curb the rough play. Junior reacts to Marcel's verbal and non-verbal actions as indicating an escalation in seriousness, shifting dramatically from his previously playful tone and extensive Patwa use to absolute seriousness. He defends the children in English (line 2), possibly affiliating with Marcel's language choice or simply speaking in the "normal" child code. His use of Patwa only for constructing the imaginary scenario highlights associations between the language and the activities involved in hunting an animal in the bush versus other roles, such as playing a teacher, and for regular conversation.

Meanwhile Reiston seems to interpret Marcel's physical move as him vacating the animal role. Reiston quickly runs to the unoccupied cardboard and claims it "Me first all you! Me first!" (line 4). Both Junior and Marcel reject his claim. Junior's metapragmatic rhetorical question, "A game we playing?!" (line 5), dismisses him as incompetently assuming it is a formal game with turns and rules. Marcel denies him verbally and non-verbally: he quickly crawls back to the play space (line 6) and exclaims, "No! Me!" (line 9). Junior aligns with Marcel by ignoring Reiston's actions and returning to the earlier frame with Marcel as the object, "*Annou kouvèy!*" (line 10). Reiston relinquishes his claim, thus ratifying the older children's authority to direct the play and control the roles. Again, the negotiation of the role and out-of-play talk, like the discussion about the book, takes place in English, while the in-character play is predominantly in Patwa. As the boys cover Marcel again,

Junior tries to draw in Alex by calling his name (line 14). He does not summon Sherona. However, she attempts to become a hunter, calling out "*Annou kouvèy*" like the boys. She also pulls on Marcel's foot like Junior, but instead of *pat* mistakenly calls it *patat* ("potato" or "vagina"). The boys do not acknowledge her error; however, it could be one reason why this young child is not attributed a leading role in the play.

The children spend the next two minutes forty-five seconds covering and uncovering Marcel and wrestling on top of him. The talk mainly consists of grunting noises and overlapped speech until Alex changes the play by specifying the type of animal and embodying Junior's earlier directive to cut it. This launches a more formal negotiation of roles:

Example 6.11

1	Alex:	*Kochon* ((pretends to slice Junior's back with his outstretched hand)). *I kochon.*
		(Pig. It's a pig.)
2	Alex:	((moves to Marcel, slicing with his hand)) *I kochon.*
3	Reiston:	((banging his hand hard on Marcel's back)) *Hachup hachup hachup hachup!*
4	Sherona:	((banging her hand hard on Junior's back)) *Hachup hachup hachup!*
5	Reiston:	((turns to Junior and bangs his hand on his back)) *Hachup!*
6	Marcel:	((looking up at Junior and Sherona, laughing)) Mommy and daddy.
7	Reiston:	Yes.
8	Marcel:	((nodding toward Junior and Sherona, laughing)) Mommy and daddy.
9	Alex:	((steps back))
10	Reiston:	((flops on Marcel's back and hugs his neck))
11	Junior:	WHAT all you saying? Me and - mommy and daddy? Shero is mommy and I is daddy.
12	Junior:	((pointing at Alex and Reiston)) And two brothers.
13	Reiston:	And two brothers.
14	Alex:	((pointing at Marcel)) *I kochon.*
		(It's a pig.)
15	Sherona:	I not a mommy though.
16	Marcel:	((softly)) I not a pig.
17	Sherona:	I not a mommy! ((walks to the veranda step and sits))

Despite his earlier silence Alex now contributes significantly to the play: he defines the animal as a pig and augments the non-verbal action by using his hand as a knife to cut the meat (line 1). Reiston follows him but alters the action by chopping rather than cutting, making a sound that villagers use to represent the noise made by a cutlass, "*hachup*" (line 3). Sherona imitates him (line 4). Marcel notices that Sherona is participating and attributes her and Junior new roles as mommy and daddy (lines 6 and 8). Reiston and Junior ratify this attribution (lines 7 and 11) and Junior adds to it by designating Alex and Reiston as brothers, thus creating an imaginary family (line 12). Reiston agrees (line 13) and Alex reiterates Marcel's role as pig (line 14). Marcel appears to reject the pig role on line 16, but quickly accepts it as the play continues. Sherona, however, strongly rejects the female role assigned to her (lines 15 and 17). While she plays "mommy" in other contexts, this is a less desirable and more passive role in the current play frame with its heightened focus on masculine agency. She embodies her rejection by leaving the play space for the veranda step.

The boys climb on Marcel and talk over one another again until Marcel scolds them for pulling on his clothing. He then tries to regulate the play by redirecting their actions in an off-stage mitigated directive, "All you can *cut* me, like play I'm a pig." He designates what they will use as knives, nodding toward sticks on the ground, "Look all you knife. Look a knife there." The boys find pretend knives and resume play with Junior describing Alex's knife as "*an gwo kouto*" (a big knife). Marcel then tries again, in English, to assign Sherona a female role and activity—cooking food for men/boys—in contrast to the male roles of hunting and butchering the pig: "Shero you is the mommy. You have to cook the food." Sherona quickly refuses the motherhood role, sucking her teeth and exclaiming, "I not cooking *no* food!" She stomps over to the boys and acts as a hunter chopping Marcel's leg. A few minutes later, however, Reiston tries to attribute the role of mommy to Sherona (shown in Example 6.1), which prompts her to leave the game. Despite her many attempts to join as a hunter or redirect the play as a teacher, Sherona is unable to fully participate. Her rejection of the gendered role, and the boys' failure to negotiate another one for her, effectively excludes her. Significantly, while the pig role is described in Patwa, negotiation over the roles of mommy, daddy, and brothers—all related to the English-dominant home environment—occurs in English. The boys' use of Patwa themselves helps to construct a male domain, and their use of English for Sherona a female one.

Junior continues his elaborate discursive construction of the play in Patwa over his next six turns, producing a number of complete utterances like "*Mwen pa ka tjwé kochon pou i mòdé mwen*" (I'm not killing the pig for it to bite me) and "*Eh, i pòkò mò ou sav. I pòkò mò*" (Eh, it isn't dead yet you know. It isn't dead yet). This excites the children even more and Marcel appears to be getting hurt by stones and metal the boys are now using to "cut" him. After four more minutes Marcel changes the play by chasing the children and trying to "eat" them. As they are negotiating the new game, however, Marcel's grandfather returns and scolds him in Patwa for not completing his chores. The extended play is over: Marcel fills pails of water for the kitchen and the other children wander off to play by themselves.

This lengthy and complex example, only partially reproduced here, illustrates how children can activate a level of Patwa competence during imaginary play that may be unrecognized by adults and even their own peers. This became clear when I transcribed the recording with Marcel with help from Junior and Kenneth. When reviewing the stretch of play in Example 6.9, Marcel stopped, turned to Junior, and questioned him: "Junior *where* there you getting this Patwa *there?*" Junior requested clarification, "Huh?", but Marcel simply shook his head. Even though Marcel and Junior have grown up together and play nearly every day, Marcel was surprised at how much Patwa Junior could produce to construct this scenario in which the roles and activities related to a particular category of persons: male, rural, and outdoor-oriented. Further, Junior exerted considerable control over the animal hunt through his Patwa narration, constructing an exciting pretend activity that drew in the other children and created, however inadvertently, a context for the transmission and practice of Patwa. He produced 40 percent of the total intelligible utterances concerning the play frame, with 73 percent of those in Patwa. Reiston, a hunter, produced 25 percent of the total, with 32 percent in Patwa. All but two of Reiston's Patwa utterances were repeated or recycled from Junior and Alex, illustrating the impact of older children on younger children's socialization through and to use language.[10]

Going to the Garden: Farming Roles and Activities

Imaginary play is often sparked by the finding of an object, such as a tool or pair of work boots, or by moving into a particular setting, such as a garden, where adult activities take place. For children between two and four years these episodes are brief but telling (see Paugh 2005a: 72–74). They demonstrate links between affect and code choice, as children tend to use Patwa to depict characters that are excited, frustrated, or non-human and wild. Reiston often adopted a troubled demeanor when pretending to work in the garden. One afternoon, for example, Reiston (three and a half) and Sherona were digging the ground with a stick and pretending to "plant" under Reiston's house. Suddenly Reiston became agitated, complaining of an imaginary "they" who were giving him problems about his land or crops:

Example 6.12

I going plant flour you know. ((speaking fast and angrily)) I going FUCKing plant flour there. They *ACHÉ*ing me *twèn*. ((stomps around under the house)) They - they thinking they are - ((xxx, trails off as he stomps away)).

(I'm going to plant flour you know. I'm going to FUCKing plant flour there. They are <u>GIV</u>ing me <u>trouble.</u> They - they are thinking there are -)

Reiston displays his understanding of how to enact affective stances associated with frustrated farmers. He speaks fast in an angry tone, curses in English ("fucking"), and uses the Patwa phrase *ache twèn* (to trouble/to give trouble). The farmer Reiston portrays sounds a lot like his grandfather when he complains about problems with other adults.

Children use the language varieties and affective stances available to them to create realistic imaginary activities, characters, and scenes. Language functions to produce an imaginary place where it is safe, or at least more appropriate, to use Patwa, namely in outside spaces. Children's language choice helps to establish the context (C. Goodwin and Duranti 1992) and to create the role and activity, and is as important as the use of physical props such as tools to play garden or a couch for a pretend bus. However, the constraints on children's Patwa usage become clear when imaginary play enters the "real" world. For example, Marcel once directed Reiston (three years and eight months), Alex, and Junior in a play frame structured around the routine practice of going to the garden to tend one's crops. The boys were playing on their concrete-paved yard while their grandmother was sitting on the veranda, out of the children's view. Prompted by the discovery of work boots under the house, Marcel begins:

Example 6.13

1 Marcel: ((putting on the boots)) Let's put our boots yeah? We going *jaden*.
   (Let's put on our boots yeah? We're going to the <u>garden.</u>)
2 Reiston: ((putting on another pair of boots)) Yes.
3 Marcel: We going *sèklé* our *patat*. ((comes out from under the house)) Let's go and *sèklé* the *patat*.
   (We're going to <u>weed</u> our <u>potatoes.</u> Let's go and <u>weed</u> the <u>potatoes.</u>)
4 Reiston: ((tries to follow Marcel, but walks slowly in the large boots))
5 Marcel: ((loud and impatiently)) Let's go Reiston!
6 Marcel: ((stops just outside the yard and looks at some grass on the ground))

7   Marcel: *Patat sala ka fè zèb déja wi zò.* ((sucks teeth, then bends down and pretends to weed a potato patch))
(The potato patch is making grass already yeah (exclamation).)

8   Marcel: Reiston go and cut the *patat* with me:. *I ka fè zèb.*
(Reiston go and cut the <u>potatoes</u> with me. <u>It [the potato patch] is making grass.</u>)

Prior to this event Marcel was speaking English with the children. The finding of the work boots appears to trigger the enactment of the Patwa-speaking farmer role. At first, he uses English to direct Reiston to join him but frames the place (*jaden*) in Patwa (line 1). He further defines the activity by describing the act of weeding a potato patch in Patwa (line 3). Then, as he moves from the yard to just outside its boundaries and becomes involved in his role as farmer examining his garden, his Patwa usage increases. Once he is off the concrete paved yard and in the garden behind the house—a place associated with adult male activity and Patwa—he produces a completely Patwa utterance: "*Patat sala ka fè zèb déja wi zò*" (line 7). In addition, he draws air through his clenched teeth to make a sharp sucking sound, employing the common adult gesture known as "suck teeth" to indicate his annoyance that weeds are growing so soon. He switches to English to direct Reiston to cut the potatoes, but uses Patwa to refer to the object, "*patat,*" and to provide narrative description, "*I ka fè zèb*" (line 8).

After approximately ten minutes of play, Marcel ends the play frame and leads the boys out of the garden and back into the English-speaking domain of the yard:

Example 6.14

1   Marcel: *Annou ay. Nou sòti an jaden.*
(<u>Let's go. We're leaving the garden.</u>)

2   Junior: ((stumbles as he walks))

3   Reiston: ((laughs at Junior))

4   Marcel: *Nou sòti an jaden. Nou sòti an jaden.*
(<u>We're leaving the garden. We're leaving the garden.</u>)

5   Reiston: ((tries to step up where the concrete begins, but falls forward onto it))

6   Alex: *Ga!* ((laughs))
(<u>Look at that!</u>)

7   Alex: [Reiston cannot even going* up.

8   Marcel: [*Ga! Nonm la fèb. I pa sa mouté bik la.*
(<u>Look at that! The man is weak. He cannot climb the hill.</u>)

9	Marcel:	((walks back to Reiston to help him stand up and walk))
10	Marcel:	((to Reiston)) *Nonm ou fèb* yeah. *Ou ni GWO* boot *la, ou la.*
		(<u>Man you are weak</u> yeah. <u>You have the BIG</u> boot, <u>you there.</u>)
11	Grandmother:	((to Marcel, speaking fast)) Stop the Patwa in the yard *mouché Marcel.*
		(Stop speaking Patwa in the yard <u>mister Marcel.</u>)

Marcel employs Patwa to issue an imperative and to define the act of leaving the garden (line 1). When Reiston falls (line 5), both Alex and Marcel call attention to it by exclaiming "*Ga!*" (lines 6 and 8; see chapter 5 for more on *ga*). Alex then exits the play frame, referring to Reiston by name rather than as a farmer and speaking in English (line 7). This could be interpreted as Alex orienting himself to leaving the garden and re-entering the adult-controlled yard where children are prohibited from speaking Patwa. In contrast, Marcel includes the fall as part of the play action by pretending that Reiston is a farmer having trouble climbing a hill on his way out of the garden (line 8). Marcel helps Reiston up and continues narrating in Patwa (line 10). He is now within earshot of his grandmother, however, who quickly scolds him for his language choice, "Stop the Patwa in the yard *mouché Marcel*" (line 11).

With very few props Marcel's use of Patwa helps to create the adult role of farmer. He draws on the distinction between the home area and the garden, which in the village is viewed as a more Patwa-speaking domain, to create an imaginary space where it is more acceptable to use Patwa, according to local language ideologies. By incorporating Reiston's fall into the original play frame, however, Marcel continues to structure the activity in Patwa even though he is now inside the boundaries of the yard and within hearing range of his grandmother. This violates the usually unspoken rule of no Patwa in the home or yard for children, and she negatively sanctions Marcel with a place-related admonishment, "in the yard." This is significant in that she does not tell him to stop speaking Patwa completely—this suggests that there may be places where children are permitted to speak the language thus implicitly (yet inadvertently) condoning his earlier use of Patwa in the garden away from adults. Further, she uses the Patwa address term "*mouché*" ('mister'), which is often employed by caregivers when scolding children and implies that a child is acting too adult-like. This calls attention to adult–child status differences. When children use Patwa they come across as acting too grown-up for their age, challenging adult control. Her word choice was successful in reinstating the social hierarchy as Marcel returned to speaking mostly English for the rest of the afternoon.

Discussion: Children's Imaginary Play and the Maintenance of Patwa

Children's peer play affords a glimpse into their acquisition of Patwa without active use with adults, the presumed "experts." Peer groups create a safe context in which children can try out language varieties and social identities without negative consequences from adults. This allows them to experiment with roles, positions of authority, and languages that are otherwise restricted from them. Further, it illustrates their agency in using an otherwise forbidden language to explore adult voices and creatively structure their play. Children tend to use English with occasional code-switching into Patwa for most social interactions and for negotiating play frames, but in role play they actively choose between languages according to the role, activity, and place they are depicting. They also enact demeanors and affective stances that they associate with those personas. Children who assume the roles of teacher, priest, or scout leader tend to speak in a relatively affect-neutral tone that is calm yet authoritative and firm. When enacting farmers or drivers, children's use of Patwa signals intensified affect, indexing an excited and sometimes agitated stance. The pig hunt among Reiston's peers is frenzied as the children try to capture, cover, and chop the animal. Even pretend mommies and daddies use Patwa baby talk lexicon to index intensified positive affect. Thus while the children in this study could very well have enacted all their imaginary roles in English, they nonetheless employed Patwa in ways that indexed particular adult activities and actively embellished their imaginative play.

Gender and class associations with language also become visible in these examples, which represent patterns observed in other families. Children may perform certain roles and activities such as farming or bus driving in either English or Patwa; however, authoritative, educated roles like teacher, nurse, or priest are carried out almost strictly in English. Role play initiated and controlled by boys often imitates rural adult male activities and, related to this, tends to entail more use of Patwa than role play initiated by girls. This is evident in the male-dominated roles discursively constructed in Patwa in several examples: Henry as bus driver, Junior and his male cousins as pig hunters, and Reiston and Marcel as farmers. Both boys and girls enact the English-dominant role of teacher, a high status role that young children like Sherona struggle to acquire. However, the associations of this career with women occasionally emerge when children call out "Miss! Miss!" to a male pretend teacher to get his attention. Playing "mommy," a common activity for girls, is less desirable in mixed-gender play then when girls play together, as seen in Sherona's rejection of the role (perhaps as lower status) during the pig hunt with the boys. The type of imaginary play often depends on the power dynamics, sex and age ratio, and linguistic abilities of participants in the local interactive context. Through such play children may challenge and transform dominant ideologies, such as stereotypical gender roles and expectations, and negative attitudes toward Patwa.

Children's differential language use when enacting adult roles reproduces more broadly held ideologies about the languages, the people who use them, and appropriate social spaces for their use. Yet, while Patwa speakers are associated with lack of education and social mobility in wider Dominican society, children do not use Patwa to portray submissive, unintelligent, or unskilled roles. Rather, their use of Patwa provides access to practices, identities, and positions of autonomy or authority, which in turn enable them to become leaders of play activities and hence direct and shape the actions and speech of other children (see also Cromdal 2004; Jørgensen 1998; Meek 2007). Children draw on local language ideologies in innovative ways, creating imaginary play spaces where Patwa in theory is allowed rather than merely submitting themselves to such ideologies. Sometimes even the highly coveted role of head teacher becomes marginalized when someone initiates a Patwa-speaking role. In other words, children explore and comment on existing power structures, but in ways that do not belittle the people or activities they are depicting and in fact can empower children who have the linguistic resources to perform a range of roles. Children play with the age-graded language ideologies of their community—Patwa for adults and English for children—in ways that could create enduring positive associations between Patwa and power, status, and autonomy. This dynamic may prove critical in regulating the language shift if children transform local language ideologies in ways that may motivate them to continue to play with Patwa with their peers as adults.

Notes

1. A head teacher is the school's principal and thus in a position of authority.
2. As Blum-Kulka et al. (2004: 323) explain, "Pretend play powerfully displays the interaction of the socio-cultural and developmental realms." Pretend play has long been a focus in developmental psychology in terms of children's psychosocial and linguistic development (see, for example, Bretherton 1984; Göncü et al. 1999; Piaget 1962; Vygotsky 1967).
3. Notable studies include Aronsson and Thorell (1999), Ervin-Tripp (1996), García-Sánchez (2010), Goldman (1998), M. Goodwin (1990, 2006), M. Goodwin and Kyratzis (2012), Kyratzis (2000, 2004), Kyratzis et al. (2001), Lancy (1996), Minks (2006, 2010), Paugh (2005a, 2005b), Reynolds (2002, 2007), Rindstedt (2001), Rindstedt and Aronsson (2002), Schieffelin (1990), Schwartzman (2001), Thorne (1993), and Watson-Gegeo (2001).
4. A point of contrast to children's multilingual role play in Dominica is described by Rindstedt and Aronsson (2002; also Rindstedt 2001) regarding Quichua Indian

children's play in San Antonio, Ecuador. Bilingual adults speak Spanish and Quichua, while children under age ten are monolingual in Spanish. Sibling caregiving and pretend play reinforces this dynamic, with children only using Spanish, the school language, rather than Quichua. Children's play, then, is advancing the shift to Spanish, despite an ongoing ethnic revitalization movement. This case further highlights the need to attend to child-structured play in language shift situations.

5. Even studies that do not find systematic language alternation in role enactment suggest that children's code choice does important interactional work. Guldal (1997), examining three pre-arranged Norwegian–English bilingual play triads (ages four to six years) in Norway, found that children used contrasting code selection to mark different "reality levels" (real life, directing, and fictional) but that norms for language choice varied according to group preference rather than for particular roles. Similarly, Cromdal and Aronsson (2000) attributed children's code-switching during recess in a bilingual English–Swedish school (forty children ages six to eight years) to individual language choice, accommodation to monolingual children, or for displaying shifting orientations toward play activities rather than for specific roles. Minks (2006) illustrated how indigenous Miskitu children on Corn Island, Nicaragua, playfully exploit their heteroglossic repertoires when playing school, utilizing the Spanish of the classroom and vernacular languages Miskitu and Creole English in their exploration of unsanctioned behavior.

6. See Paugh (2005a: 71–72) for more examples from this play episode.

7. Research highlights the importance of attending to the physical spaces and objects children employ when constructing imaginary play (M. Goodwin 2006; Griswold 2007; Paugh 2005a; Schieffelin 2003).

8. Reiston's peer group frequently played transport and used the Patwa terms *batjé* (to get on board) and *débatjé* (to disembark). One day when the children were playing in the back of my Jeep, Marcel employed four alternatives to tell them to get down from the vehicle, in this order: *débatjé*, go down, down, and *désann* (go down).

9. I translate the third-person Patwa pronoun *y* here as "it" (it also can refer to "he" and "she") because this is how Marcel interpreted it, since Junior was treating him as an animal.

10. In total, 42 percent of the intelligible utterances in this play frame were in Patwa, with 58 percent in English. This includes talk about and in the play, including repetitions. Sherona produced 14 percent of the total turns, with 14 percent of those in Patwa. Marcel produced 16 percent of the turns, with 10 percent in Patwa. Alex spoke the least with just 5 percent of the turns, yet 30 percent of those were in Patwa.

Conclusion

Nou ké vwè, si Bondyé vlé.

(We will see, God willing.)

The above quotation is a common Dominican expression for taking leave from an interaction and when discussing the future. It is also what comes to mind concerning the ongoing language shift from Patwa to varieties of English in rural villages. As in many Caribbean post-colonial societies language purism in schools and historically negative attitudes toward creole languages spilled over into Dominican homes, resulting in a community-wide English only policy with children and displacement of Patwa from many settings. The course and outcomes of language shift are known, however, to be difficult to predict. Social, political, and economic factors may come into play to halt or speed up such processes. Even when a code is maintained, what is expressed by that code may change.[1] Further, research may not shed light on contexts of use that may facilitate maintenance of a language, such as those involving children.

In Dominica various groups ranging from language planners to cultural activists to national developers play with the island's languages as they make efforts to keep Patwa alive, if only for special performances, special audiences, and in specific forms. Yet rural caregivers purposefully speak English to their children and require them to do the same in hopes of increasing their future socioeconomic success. Children find ways to navigate this complex political and cultural landscape by creating "safe" spaces among peers in which they can speak and maintain Patwa as they negotiate their identities, power dynamics, and play. Further, attention to everyday language socialization practices reveals the subtle ways in which their parents implicitly encourage Patwa transmission despite overtly negative ideologies and statements, though not within the adult-controlled spaces of the home and school. A key finding of this research is that all of these forms of play impact language vitality, but sometimes in incongruous and even contradictory ways. Critically, children play an active though often invisible role in processes of language maintenance and shift.

This book has explored these complex language ideologies and interactional practices across multiple interrelated spheres and linguistic marketplaces: the home, school, village, and nation. The study of both theory and practice—in other words, ideologies of language and beliefs about child rearing in conjunction with actual language use and socialization practices—reveals that contrary to the starkly anti-Patwa and English-only ideologies expressed by teachers and parents, speakers hold more complex views toward the languages as being complementary in everyday life. Parents provide enough exposure to Patwa for children to employ language choice as a way of indexing valued aspects of being a person and being a Dominican, such as showing respect in some contexts (through English), but being bold and "good for oneself" in others (largely through Patwa). The languages fulfill different functions and in doing so make a whole person. English may be instrumental for certain, not insignificant, goals, like succeeding in school and obtaining a white-collar job, but Patwa is an important emblem of village identity and means of affective expression.

Attention to children's language use with peers yields critical insights into on-the-ground processes of linguistic reproduction and change as children actively construct their social worlds within the constraints imposed upon them. Children's play is a critical site of Patwa transmission and maintenance in Dominica, but it is not accorded symbolic value in language revitalization efforts, which focus on the creation of written materials, formal pedagogical settings, and heritage culture performances. Nor is it symbolically valued by caregivers and other adults, who describe children's play as "nonsense" and disruptive to the orderliness of the household and classroom. However, I suggest that a space for child-directed play and child-valued forms of verbal expression needs to be further carved out to foster attempts at reversing language shift.

The Process of Language Shift: Generation, Gender, and Education

Seeming to lack native child speakers and rural community support, Patwa could be considered "endangered" (Fishman 1991; Grenoble and Whaley 2006; Hinton 2001a; Krauss 1998; Wurm 1998). Proficiency in Patwa varies by age or generation, although other salient differences include socioeconomic class, education, gender, and religion. In Penville there remain only a few elderly monolingual Patwa speakers, typically over the age of seventy. Most speakers over forty claim they are more comfortable speaking Patwa, but command at least some variety of English. Adults between the ages of twenty and forty tend to speak varieties of English much more fluently than their parents, though many say they are less fluent in speaking Patwa. These young to middle-aged adults are bilingual to varying degrees but now attempt to speak only varieties of English to children and require them to respond in

English. The extent to which they accomplish this varies but most children speak English as their first and primary language. Adults recognize this, as one middle-aged villager explained:

> Because remember these children coming up, they're not going to speak Patwa. Eh? And then afterwards, the others coming up, they're not going to speak Patwa. And the reason why our parents was speaking so much Patwa [was that] they did not go to school. ... So they did not get the education to change the Patwa into English. And then these grandparents, they died. They've been going one by one. They're not there again.

As this resident highlights, schools have provided a valued domain for English acquisition, making it possible for rural children "to change the Patwa into English." Today schools continue to promote purist language ideologies that devalue Patwa use and code-mixing. Now Patwa-speaking elders are "going one by one," further restricting Patwa transmission.

In addition, villagers say that a main reason children are now proficient in English is that there is a "younger" generation of parents. They claim that parents are now more educated, "enlightened," and exposed to the outside world through travel and television, and they realize the importance of education and English for social mobility. The fourth-grade teacher explained:

> To be a young parent growing up now, I mean seeing the importance of education with everything. Even to - to cut your bananas you need to be well educated. You need to fill in on your tally sheets and so. The parents go out and they seeing how hard it is when you cannot read and write. And they know *for sure* the Patwa is keeping back the children, and to have your children now speaking the Patwa, growing up the way you yourself was raised? I mean no young parent would want that.

Patwa was "keeping back" the children, and this is blamed on older villagers (those "going one by one"). As was explored in chapters 2 and 3, the "old" is frequently contrasted with the "new" in village discourse. According to one resident, "it's a new era in the village." Yet the grandparents fostering young grandchildren were just as adamant that the children speak English as the "younger" parents.

But while children now have more limited productive competence in Patwa, my video recordings of children's interactions demonstrate that their comprehension may far exceed this. Many are exposed to a full Patwa grammar in the daily social interaction between adults around them, and often in speech directed to or at them as shown in chapter 4. Their productive abilities become more visible during peer play when there are no teachers or caregivers to monitor their speech and actions, as chapters 5 and 6 demonstrate. Yet there is variation across families that is largely related to caregivers' socioeconomic resources and aspirations for their children's futures, and hence their linguistic strategies with them, as none were highly educated themselves. Other factors that shaped children's language development included how much adult supervision they were subject to, the languages used by regular playmates, and characteristics of their social networks, including religious affiliations.

Among the focal children gender was not a defining variable in distinguishing who spoke more Patwa and who spoke less. Among the six young focal children in the language socialization study, two boys were at either end of the spectrum: Reiston spoke the most Patwa while Jonah spoke the least. It appears, however, that there may be an incipient gendering of linguistic practices in the community that may become more apparent as the current generation of children matures. At present women are responsible for childcare for the majority of the day and while many use Patwa to speak to other adults, they concentrate on creating English environments for their infant and school-age children. Men, who spend much of their days working with other men in the garden or in construction, and spend their evenings playing dominoes with other men in the rum shop (with older women present), tend to speak more Patwa, although they usually speak English with children at home. This relates to the roles of men and women in Caribbean societies generally, where women are expected to be the keepers of the family and household (also see Sidnell 2005 on gendered spaces and linguistic practices in an Indo-Guyanese community).

English is associated with the built environment and female-dominated domains, such as the school, home, and church, while Patwa is associated with the outdoors and male-dominated domains, including the road, bush, and garden. This becomes strikingly apparent in terms of children's imaginary play, as chapter 6 illustrates. When I first told villagers that I wanted to learn Patwa, I was told repeatedly that I should speak to older men in rum shops where Patwa is used far more than English. But I was also told that a respectable woman should not spend time at the rum shop; I heeded this advice in order to remain welcome in families' homes and at the school without reservation.[2] Many women in their twenties and thirties claimed that their boyfriends or husbands knew more Patwa than them. "It is their language," one woman told me. In practice, however, both men and women speak Patwa with variations in proficiency and frequency in both sexes, especially by generation. Adult conversation and domestic arguments are often carried out in Patwa with code-switching into English for rhetorical effect. Yet one would be more likely to hear Patwa spoken by men in the garden or rum shop, and English among women and children at home and school where teachers traditionally are women (although there are also male teachers). Further, while both men and women have played a part in the language and cultural heritage movement, there has been significant male participation in Patwa revitalization efforts, including such key figures as Gregory Rabess, Marcel Fontaine, and Felix Henderson. As Cavanaugh (2006: 195) points out, such "gendering may influence the viability of such languages in the long run." It seems that in the course of the language shift, code differentiation may become increasingly important in the production and indexing of gendered identities and stances.

The Power of English and Patwa

Villagers say that Patwa is disempowering in the national and global speech economies. It indexes and reproduces inequality. English, in contrast, is perceived as offering access to jobs, money, education, and high-status roles such as government employee, political candidate, and socially mobile individual. It is the language of international communication. Both women and men who attend newer Evangelical churches in the village tend to speak more English; these residents are associated with higher socioeconomic status and aspirations. English thus appears to afford symbolic and material resources in institutional and formal contexts, while Patwa is largely, and sometimes strictly, excluded from such domains. But investigation of everyday speech and local ideologies indicates that Patwa is perceived as being very powerful in the village context; it carries significant symbolic value as a means of control, emotional expression, verbal creativity, joking, and evaluation of peoples' morality, actions, and characteristics. These verbal skills are critical aspects of being a communicatively competent social actor. This is usually contingent, however, on an individual having *both* languages, as English is increasingly powerful in all contexts whether one speaks Patwa or not. Monolingual Patwa-speaking elders are disempowered both in and outside the village for not "having" English and are excluded from formal positions of power. The repercussions for only knowing English are not as extreme and may be mitigated by even the most limited use of Patwa; this is reminiscent of the Gaelic "semi-speakers" and "near-passive bilinguals" in East Sutherland, Scotland, described by Dorian (1982). This begs the question of whether or not younger generations will continue to acquire this important piece of social capital as they shift to English.

According to adults, Patwa is so powerful that it can "kill" English and hence must be suppressed among children until their English becomes "strong." Notions of Patwa interference in English speech and writing permeate language ideologies in schools and homes. But through attention to social interaction between children and adults my research indicates that this is not the whole story. Adults' use of Patwa, while not allowing children to speak it, is related to more than the instrumental goal of helping them succeed at English mastery—it is a continual assertion of their own power to control children's lives. Adults maintain this status largely through talk backed by threat and occasional use of physical force. They speak Patwa to direct and criticize children's actions, scold them, and issue moral evaluations, while English is chosen for most other purposes. At the same time a fundamental tension in language socialization is finding a balance between socializing obedience and respect while simultaneously encouraging children to become independent and "bold," all important parts of a larger constellation of sociability and local ideas about the self.[3] This is largely accomplished through the division of labor between Patwa and English, and is contributing not just to language shift but also to language retention. As active participants and observers children pick up on these functions of Patwa in the direct and indirect input they receive and begin to use them in such ways themselves. The language socialization methodology made it possible to tap into the changing meanings of the languages for speakers, including how in the course of the shift ideologies of language have meshed with theories of child rearing. Through their use of Patwa adults reaffirm their rights as more mature culturally knowledgeable members to control children's lives and actions in the home, yard, and school. Such usage marks Patwa as an "adult" language and English as a "child" language. Ethnographic research was thus critical for getting at otherwise unspoken and unseen socialization processes and beliefs.

For children Patwa gains its affective saliency in part because it is associated with adults and becomes subversive as they are not permitted to speak it. When children do use Patwa around caregivers, they are interpreted as trying to act too grown-up and become a threat to adult control. The repercussions for using Patwa are similar to those children face for other forms of insubordination, such as refusing a directive. While adults move fluidly between Patwa and English in conversation, they regularly distinguish the languages as distinct codes by speaking predominantly English to children and negatively sanctioning children for using Patwa. Further, adults employ Patwa for affective marking, particularly to indicate an escalation when children disobey (negative affect) and through Patwa baby talk lexicon and lullabies (positive affect). These practices forge indexical links between the language and the people who speak it—those in a position of authority over children's lives. Children learn early on that they are expected to speak English but they also learn to use Patwa in ways that evoke this adult power in peer interactions. Drawing on Silverstein's work, Woolard (2004: 88) suggests that:

> The indexical value of a linguistic form can be transferred ideologically not just from context to context, but from context to speaker, or vice versa,

and can be transformed in the process. Individuals who use the kind of language now perceived as authoritative can project themselves as authoritative kinds of people.

In the course of the shift to English children have come to interpret Patwa as an index of adult authority and they exploit this association in their talk. Thus, while adults consciously try to minimize children's exposure to and use of Patwa, they nevertheless render the contrast between languages meaningful through their language socialization practices.

The admonishments children hear from adults when they use this "transgressive" language confirm this interpretation and suggest socialization toward using it in other contexts. When adults catch children speaking Patwa, for example, they evoke ideas about place and context, telling them "not in the home" or to "go in the road," but rarely not to speak it at all. We see this in action in the place-related admonishments issued by adults in several examples in this book: the first-grade teacher as she corrected a child's use of *vòlè* during picture study (Example 3.3.a: "And when we are in school we spea::k?"); Jonah's mother as she scolded Claudette for speaking Patwa in the kitchen (Example 5.1: "*Ou déwò?!*" (Are you outside?!)); and Marcel's grandmother as she rebuked him for using Patwa for role playing in the yard (Example 6.14: "Stop the Patwa in the yard *mouché Marcel*"). Though infrequent, since children tend to speak English near adults, these examples offer critical insights into local ideologies of language and child rearing. The comments indicate that there are place- and age-related constraints on Patwa usage, suggesting some recognition that Patwa has become an adult-associated register in participation frameworks involving children. In their place-related reprimands, adults implicitly allow or even encourage children to use Patwa when away from adults.

Children must defer to adults but also stand up for themselves and be bold—qualities that are strongly associated with the use of Patwa. Adults highlight Patwa as affectively marked and powerful in its own right when they use it in conversation with each other and to scold and command children, despite associations of English with "official" power. They also condone children's use of Patwa for particular functions, like when Alisia and Tamika's brief uses of Patwa were interpreted as positive expressions of their burgeoning boldness in Examples 4.1 and 4.11. This transmits to children that they can use Patwa for similar ends outside of adult-controlled settings, such as with their peers. In a sense, caregivers are already undertaking a major step in retaining their language. By implicitly encouraging children to speak Patwa in peer contexts they are "counter-balancing the forces which have caused or are causing the language shift" (Grenoble and Whaley 2006: 21), including their own efforts at banning children from speaking it. Whether consciously or not adults are facilitating the development of age-graded bilingual subjectivities among their children. This age-grading of communicative practice is relatively new in the village, made possible once the parents of today's generation of children began gaining sustained access to English through the school.

Children's Agency in Linguistic and Cultural Reproduction and Change

This book demonstrates that the study of children's peer and sibling interaction, situated within its broader ethnographic and cultural context, is essential to elucidating processes of linguistic reproduction and change. This is particularly relevant in societies where older children assume significant roles in the caretaking and socialization of other children, as in other Caribbean islands and Latin America. Younger children are often supervised by older children and spend a significant amount of time playing in mixed-age groups. Older children are entrusted with the care of younger children and with a wide range of chores and responsibilities; one of those responsibilities may be the maintenance of a threatened language. Older children draw on wider symbolic frameworks to employ Patwa creatively in asserting their own wills and social identities among siblings and peers, and in turn socializing younger children. Code-switching into Patwa is a multifunctional linguistic strategy used, amongst other things, to assert dominance and claim adult-like roles and status through the revoicing of adult commands, evaluations, and characteristic speech. Their play with Patwa generally occurs outside the adult-monitored home and school, in participation frameworks solely involving children, and for particular functions, such as acting adult.

For children it is not simply the contrast created by a switch to another language that matters like in adult–adult speech; rather, it is a switch from English to Patwa that creates rhetorical effect, indexes affective stance, indicates an escalation in seriousness, and fashions an assertive and authoritative persona. Children's Patwa usage highlights its salience as an emblem of adult subject positions and as a potent means to influence and control others.[4] Children employ Patwa as symbolic capital (Bourdieu 1977, 1991) and as a means for exploring alternative identities in their peer interactions. It is akin to what Rampton describes as "crossing," or "the use of language varieties associated with social and ethnic groups that the speaker does not normally 'belong' to" (1995: 14). In this case it is not ethnic but rather age and status boundaries that children cross when they speak Patwa. The language carries subaltern prestige as a "non-standard" language opposing that required at home and at school (Howard 2008: 194). Further, as the interactions in chapters 5 and 6 illustrate, using Patwa is an enjoyable form of play in itself.

It is a way to have fun with language. Attention to children's private social worlds indicates that children are picking up on the functional distribution of the languages in adult speech and employing Patwa as a symbolic, pragmatic, and playful resource in interaction with peers.

Children's unmonitored peer interaction offers the most extensive and elaborate Patwa usages that I observed among them. Their imaginary play demonstrates an understanding of local ideologies that link Patwa with roles and activities related to particular occupations, places, and people, especially men (see chapter 6). When they depict these roles children tend to produce appropriate affective stances that are related to their choice of language, keying calmer, lower affect for English-speaking roles such as teachers, parents, and religious officials, and higher, sometimes frantic affect for Patwa-speaking roles such as agitated farmers, hurried bus drivers, and exited pig hunters. This again highlights associations between Patwa and intensified affect. Most strikingly children employ their verbal resources to create imaginary play spaces both organized by and appropriate for Patwa. Their use of Patwa often increases as they wander away from the house and yard, and it is also used to verbally create pretend gardens, vehicles, and other outdoor places.

Critically, children's linguistic practices during peer play show how they socialize Patwa use amongst one another without active participation with adults, the presumed experts. Children's peer groups provide a protected space in which they can try out language varieties and social identities without negative consequences from adults. Children encourage one another in these performance genres of play, opening up a creative space that may better represent their heteroglossic world as they experience it. They are active agents in using the otherwise prohibited language to creatively explore and play with multiple voices and identities, and to construct their own social organization. The children who can enact such roles using appropriate linguistic varieties and demeanors assume considerable power in their peer groups in terms of directing and negotiating play, perhaps attributing greater prestige to occupations and roles that might otherwise not carry so much value in adult culture. Their role play is not simply a process of imitating others or passively developing into some predisposed adult end state; rather, it offers a context within which children can actively explore power dynamics, social rules, and positions of authority not accessible to them when they are subordinate to adults. Children's peer groups—at least in rural areas—offer a critical context for language maintenance in which they can try out Patwa without evaluation or ridicule from adults.

At the same time, children's recognition of English as the ultimate standard also becomes visible in their corrections of one another's Patwa and non-standard English usage. Children witness the symbolic value accorded to English in institutions such as government, schools, businesses, and the media, and in their own homes. They are socialized to favor English by being addressed in English, portrayed as speaking English in reported speech, and chastised for speaking Patwa by adults. Their metalinguistic comments when evaluating one another suggest that they in some ways do not view Patwa as "real" or "right" as compared to English, hence reinforcing English-dominant ideologies (see chapter 5). This further enables them to assert power in their own social hierarchies on the basis of possessing greater linguistic capital, often by criticizing another child's Patwa or non-standard English speech as indicating verbal or intellectual weakness. Children hold one another accountable to the pervasive ideology that one must possess adequate knowledge of both languages in order to wield power with Patwa.

Although they generally do not talk about them, children's complex and often ambivalent ideologies become evident in school-related activities and in their prescriptive comments. For example, Alisia's sister Josette (twelve years) attended secondary school where she was instructed to make posters for the school hallways to celebrate "English Week." She created two that stated, "English is fantastic and romantic" and "I speak English!" Her third poster was the most elaborate:

> "Alas!! Look here young people! If the nobles, queens, kings, prime ministers and princesses can speak English, why don't we the local people speak English as properly as they! [drawing of a heart with a face] English!"

This theatrical poster does more than encourage appreciation of English. It contrasts "the local people" with foreign people in power as Dominica has a prime minister but no resident nobles (although it is part of the British Commonwealth). This aristocracy speaks English "properly" while the local people categorically do not. The use of the interjection "Alas!!" evokes sorrow or pity, but also the formality of the royals. This contrasts with the "young people" to whom the poster is addressed and who are included in the collective "local people" who do not speak proper English. Addressing her message to young people fits the educational context, but also reflects contemporary national discourses targeting youth for the development and modernization of the nation. English is the language associated with that process.

When asked directly, many school-age children told me that they "don't like" speaking Patwa, that it is "not a nice language," or that they do not care to learn more, usually without elaboration. One nine-year-old boy who was raised in a Patwa-speaking household explained to me why he had problems when he started school: "When I was talking Patwa, I was stupid. Now I speaking English, I smart." He proudly claimed that his school work improved dramatically when he began speaking English and that he even won a prize in science. Teachers report that children now laugh at students who speak Patwa in the classroom. The third-grade teacher describes it:

The other children will tell them not to talk Patwa. Okay? As if they see Patwa as something for them to talk somewhere else, not in school. That's how I see it. Or if the children speak and they use a word in Patwa - half English, half Patwa, the others would laugh. Those who know the word, they would laugh.

Children who speak Patwa are subject to censure from their classmates through laughter and prescriptive comments. Yet as this teacher points out, children's comments indicate awareness that Patwa is "something for them to talk somewhere else." Children recognize that Patwa may be acceptable outside of institutional settings, but that English indexes education, intelligence, and the ability to succeed in formal contexts.

During my final day of recording Reiston's family I had an unusually long conversation about language with his peer group. I asked if the children like to speak Patwa. To my surprise, Marcel replied that he did *not* like to speak it. Marcel was in my opinion the most proficient Patwa speaker of the group, so I asked why. Referencing the fact that he was born in Guadeloupe (to Dominican parents), he answered, "I'm a French boy but I don't like to speak it. Since I born is English I speaking." He explained that although he does not like Patwa, he has to speak it sometimes to communicate with the elderly like his cousins' grandmother who lives next door. When I asked if he liked Patwa or French, Marcel replied firmly, "None. English alone." I then asked, "So to your friends you only speak English?" To my surprise, and despite his use of Patwa with his playgroup throughout the day's recording, Marcel nodded yes. Finally, I asked if he thought he might speak Patwa when he got older, such as with his own children. He looked at me and replied confidently, "I'd like to hear my child speaking English instead than Patwa." "Not at all?" I asked. "No," replied Marcel, ending the discussion. Marcel's claims to not speak Patwa with his peers despite his extensive Patwa usage with them may suggest ambivalence toward the language, or a recognition of the cultural prescription that children should not speak Patwa. Or perhaps Marcel envisions his present and future self as having no use for the language.

On the one hand, then, children contribute to the ongoing language shift by learning and speaking English as their primary language and through their own linguistic prescriptivism. But on the other hand, they also contribute to the maintenance of Patwa for certain culturally valued pragmatic functions. Children's communities of practice with peers create a rich verbal environment in which they are socialized through and to use a diverse linguistic repertoire, including a language they are forbidden to speak in adult-controlled settings. Children employ Patwa as a strategic tool for organizing play frames and the actions and demeanors of others; it takes on considerable value in their local speech economies. Children's peer interactions are a critical site of Patwa language socialization, yet often are overlooked in national language planning efforts that focus on cultural performances and elder-child interaction. An examination of interaction in child-controlled settings suggests that they continue to assign value to Patwa and thus there is still the groundwork for keeping the language in use. But this is increasingly restricted to certain contexts such as the road, bush, and other parts of the non-built environment that are less monitored by adults and more open to children's linguistic creativity and agency. Compared to their everyday use of English varieties in all contexts, children's use of Patwa was much more restricted.

Language Revitalization at the National Level

In the national arena Patwa is extolled as a symbol of a distinctly Dominican identity, a marker of creole culture and authenticity, a link to other Francophone areas, and a "heritage culture product" (see chapter 1). The documentation and revitalization efforts of KEK, the main language-planning organization, have helped legitimize Patwa in many ways. KEK's accomplishments are in line with what is suggested in current research on reversing language shift (e.g., Batibo 2009; Crystal 2000; Fishman 1991, 2001; Grenoble and Whaley 2006; Hinton and Hale 2001), including: increasing the language's prestige and legitimacy in official settings such as radio; developing an orthography and literacy materials; providing training workshops (such as for Peace Corps volunteers), with the goal of teaching Patwa in the formal education system; and facilitating celebrations such as cultural shows and the World Creole Music Festival (WCMF). Yet KEK struggles to maintain active membership and funding, particularly for implementing Patwa curriculum in schools. Such pragmatic constraints are significant issues for language revitalization efforts (Hinton 2001a).

According to language planners in Dominica's English-Creole dictionary, "losing one's 'mother tongue' is like losing one's soul" (Fontaine 2003; Fontaine and Roberts 1992). In one sense this statement highlights the commitment of language activists to halting the loss of a heritage language. In another sense it gets at the ideological heart of Patwa language maintenance. According to many villagers, Patwa does in fact better represent their "soul" and express their emotions than English. The language remains so salient that English-speaking children learn to use it for affective marking during play. At the same time, however, this statement paradoxically obscures the complexities of the island's linguistic ecology and speech economies. Inclusively hailing Patwa as the "mother tongue" of the entire population erases key differences in power and access between urban/rural peoples that have persisted for centuries. It similarly erases other varieties, such as Kokoy and the Kalinago language. Not all the population would consider Patwa to be their "mother tongue," such as many Roseau residents, while some stake claims to it but did not learn it as their first language. This reminds us that language revitalization movements are political and prescriptive in nature despite desires simply to represent "the masses" or "ancestral practices" (Cameron 1995; Duchêne and Heller 2007; Jaffe 2007a, 2007b). Creating a unitary language policy for all Dominicans obscures the varied interests of different groups, particularly across rural/urban lines.

The focus on promoting Patwa as a form of performance seems to be contributing to the shift in subtle ways rather than slowing it down, despite the intentions of those who support Patwa maintenance. Within the contexts of the cultural/linguistic preservation and revitalization movement and developing tourism industry, the everyday practices of the rural population are re-imagined, re-invented, and consciously formalized—moved from the ordinary to the "exotic," "ethnic," or "uniquely Dominican." During cultural shows and Independence celebrations Patwa and other aspects of "traditional" culture are separated out from regular life and performed to audiences. English, meanwhile, remains the sole official language of the nation. *Jounen Kwéyòl* is but one day a year when Patwa is in theory to be spoken in all places. It is doubtful, however, that this single day could be enough to encourage its maintenance and break down historically deep-rooted boundaries, assuming that people did in reality speak Patwa everywhere on that day, which does not seem to be happening. Nor does revalorizing the language alone fundamentally change the structural position of rural Dominicans.[5]

In addition to other functions, language and culture are becoming objects of exchange in the local and global economy. Such visions are not lost on villagers or cultural group members, many of whom have hopes of starting careers and being paid for the "talents" they are being encouraged to cultivate. While the commodification of culture may offer alternative means of economic survival, it further aids the separation of Patwa and other aspects of "traditional" culture from modern life, marking them as "special" activities for "special" days and shows, such as the Cultural Gala, Creole Day, the WCMF, and displays for cruise ship tourists. The commodification and championing of Patwa in national discourses reflects changing attitudes and conceptions of the language. Such rhetoric does not necessarily represent reality, however, even for language activists and national planners who do not use Patwa in their daily lives. While efforts to accord Patwa value through its commodification may offer rural peoples the socioeconomic means they need and desire— though if it will is debatable—it is impossible to say whether that will be enough to stop or slow the shift to English.

Language planners face an even deeper ideological obstacle in terms of community acceptance of their plans to teach Patwa in schools, particularly rural ones (see chapters 3 and 4). With English the language of politics, education, international communication, and the most desired occupations, urban-based efforts to accord Patwa more official institutional status are rejected by rural villagers who maintain that allowing it into such domains could very well jeopardize their children's learning of English and thus their futures. As one teacher questioned, "But if on the job you reject it, and in the office you reject it, [and] in the exam room, why would you put it into the classroom?" Such debates are not unique to Dominica or the Caribbean. In the U.S. African American community, for example, many have been suspicious of and resistant toward efforts to recognize African American English (AAE) as a distinct language variety in schools (Morgan 1994). They assert multiple and competing ideologies including viewing AAE as a symbol of Africanness, as a counterlanguage, and as an indicator of slave mentality. Some view any use of AAE in schools, even as a means to teach "standard" English, as continuing mis-education of African American youth. The sentiments among rural Dominicans are strikingly similar. Most villagers do not view the introduction of Patwa in schools as empowering, but rather as disempowering by (once again) holding them back from obtaining ideal proficiency in English. The school empowered them by providing a strictly English domain; introducing Patwa into it threatens that protected space. Further, their rejection of Patwa in schools may be a form of resistance to authoritative language-planning discourses and "the experience of linguistic and cultural domination" (Jaffe 1999: 272). Introducing Patwa in schools may undermine rural communities' self-determination as they have set up their own informal English-only policies relative to local social dynamics, with an expectation that children will speak it with one another and later as adult members. Other forms of linguistic alienation could emerge as some regional varieties of Patwa are privileged in a school-based curriculum and literacy materials (Jaffe 1999).

The continuing functional distribution of the languages—and exclusion of Patwa from formal settings such as Parliament, business, and education—says a lot about societal views toward the language. Villagers who are aware of the orthography and publications by KEK say that Patwa literacy has helped to legitimize its usage in the eyes of urban residents, yet few say they want their own children to learn to read and write it. They say that it would be fine to teach Patwa to children in Roseau or other communities where it is not spoken but not in their community, despite dramatically improved school performance. While long-established negative attitudes toward Patwa and its speakers surely play a part, this also relates to local theories of childhood and child rearing that promote age-graded language use related to adult–child status differences. Patwa can be hindering in some contexts but empowering in others—and for teachers and parents concerned with losing control of their children, even threatening. Children's use of Patwa, then, is not only a threat to their developing competence in English, but is interpreted by adults as a threat to their power, highlighting the language's salience in this regard. These critical underpinnings of village life and Dominican culture would be challenged, at least at this moment in time, by authorizing Patwa use in school. At the same time, without some sort of intervention, it seems that Patwa may be increasingly restricted to particular domains and very likely lost (as a distinct code) over the next few generations.

Implications for Understanding and Reversing Language Shift

With recent predictions that half of the world's languages will disappear within the century, efforts to reverse language loss have taken on growing relevance. Yet the majority of such efforts meet with limited success and researchers have found that there is no single model that can be applied across societies (Grenoble and Whaley 2006). In most approaches language preservation and revitalization are perceived as resting in the hands of community elders, educated intellectuals, and policy makers.[6] Children are important but are portrayed as passive recipients (or not) of traditional culture and language, not the active, dynamic culture makers shown in this book. While researchers increasingly take into account the ideologies behind language shift and maintenance, adults and elders continue to be privileged in terms of transmission and action. Despite being one small Caribbean island nation, the case of Dominica has implications for language shift and revitalization efforts worldwide.

An important concern among scholars and practitioners of language revitalization and "reversing language shift" (RLS; see Fishman 1991, 2001) is the process of transmission of an endangered language across generations. As Grenoble and Whaley (2006: 6) suggest, "The dynamics of intergenerational transmission are perhaps more important to understand than any other relevant factor in assessing the need for language revitalization." In practice this process has been addressed largely through efforts to use endangered languages in schools, with some programs more successful than others. For example, Māori (New Zealand) and Hawaiian language revitalization efforts cultivated full immersion "language nests" in preschools, where fluent elders teach the languages to young children. These have been characterized as very effective (King 2001 and Spolsky 2003 on Māori; Warner 2001 and Wilson and Kamana 2001 on Hawaiian), although their specific circumstances may be difficult to replicate. In both locations the endangered language has been accorded official status and has strong community and institutional support, along with other historical factors. Notably, as Friedman (2012: 640) points out, these programs take the language socialization practices of the home into account to some degree within the school context. Other methods focus on the transmission of endangered languages from elders to young adults as in the

Master–Apprentice Language Learning Program for Native American languages in California in the U.S. (see Hinton 2001b). These young adults are charged with the task of transmitting the language to others, for example children.

Beyond language instruction in formal education programs, researchers highlight the importance of the home environment in providing input in and positive attitudes toward the endangered language to ensure its continued transmission. This process of transmission is often described as all or nothing, rather than a complex interaction of multiple ideologies, practices, social forces, and human agency. Hinton (2001a: 12–13), for example, describes various strategies for "family-based programs at home" to raise children to speak an endangered language. The languages should be kept separate with either the endangered language as the sole language of the home (with the dominant one spoken outside) or through creation of a bilingual home setting according to a strict "one parent, one language" format. In this and other models, widespread heteroglossic multilingual practices like code-switching are considered detrimental to transmission. Further, children's agency and the complexities involved in language acquisition are downplayed, as in this statement:

> In fact, in most situations where a language is truly endangered, meaning that it is not spoken as the main language of the community anymore, if parents focus on using the endangered language in the home, the child will "automatically" learn the main language of the general environment anyway. (Hinton 2001a: 13)

Here children are portrayed as "automatically" acquiring the dominant language regardless of home input. As this book has illustrated, however, an attention to language ideologies and on-the-ground practice shows that this process is far more complicated and nuanced.

More relevant to the argument of this study is Meek's (2007, 2010) research on language shift in a northern Athapascan community in the Yukon Territory, Canada. Meek explicitly seeks to reframe "language endangerment and revitalization as a language socialization issue" (2007: 24) and in doing so calls attention to children's own language ideologies and their transformative role in the course of a language shift from Kaska to English. In the Liard River First Nation community cultural and linguistic revitalization efforts and pedagogical practices are contributing to the increasing association of elders with traditional practices and expertise, including knowledge and fluent use of Kaska. Further, elders are associated with the socialization of respect, a core value in this community. In the process of the shift Kaska and English varieties have come to index generational differences, as might be expected, but also status differences related to the authoritative social positions occupied by elders. Because children have re-conceptualized Kaska as the language of elders, they engage passively rather than actively with Kaska-speaking elders in order to display respect. Therefore, they do not take advantage of the opportunity to speak the language during traditional Kaska activities when elders could help them learn. Language revitalization efforts, then, have paradoxically reinforced the language shift. As in Dominica the shift is naturalized through age-graded language ideologies linking differential language use to notions of respect, authority, and status.

Children's vital roles in the process of language shift and attempts to reverse it are thus grossly underestimated when they are portrayed simply as receptacles of adult language transmission or lack thereof. If we assume that Patwa will disappear because parents are no longer speaking it directly to their children for conversation, we underestimate the role of indirect input in language acquisition, especially when there is strong affective saliency attributed to Patwa. Further, we underestimate the impact of local theories of child rearing and language ideologies that assume a model of bilingual language development throughout the life cycle. And perhaps most critically we underestimate the agency of children and their capacity to make active choices as they construct their own cultures, play frames, power relations, and social identities while socializing one another through and to use language. This highlights the need for long-term ethnographic fieldwork to investigate the process of transmission in depth and across multiple settings when children interact with and apart from adults (including but also beyond the school playground). More research is needed into how children do or do not play with endangered languages in other societies. How does children's language play impact local processes of reproduction and change in cultural and linguistic practices and ideologies?

An understanding of cultural and linguistic reproduction in the village illuminates both the process of language shift and the tensions between rural speakers and the urban-based language movement. English was chosen to represent the state when it became independent from England, but Patwa—a non-official "common heritage" language—has been chosen to represent the "true" identity of the nation and the people, at least in nationalist discourses and on the coat of arms. Yet children are forbidden from speaking Patwa in the adult-controlled social spaces of the home and school. This then contributes to the language shift by effectively eliminating children's use of Patwa from the majority of their daily lives in the presence of adults. Adults do not seem concerned that Patwa is not being passed on as many assume that today's children eventually will speak it with their peers as adults and for particular functions with their own children when they enter that culturally significant stage. An important implication of this study is that nationalist movements to preserve and promote Patwa do not recognize many of these links between ideology and practice, and that these links need to be taken into account when developing and implementing programs to preserve and revitalize Patwa. This is particularly critical in terms of introducing it into such strongly English-dominated domains as the school, thus suggesting the need for more cultural sensitivity to local language ideologies.

In efforts to understand intergenerational and intragenerational transmission, speakers of all ages must be taken into account as cultural and linguistic producers. The ethnographic study of language socialization and language ideologies offers a critical means of investigating these processes. A one-size-fits-all scale for assessing intergenerational transmission may be skewed if a society has developed age-graded models of language use whereby children are not expected or supposed to speak the language until they reach a certain age or have children of their own. An assessment of Dominican children's Patwa usage would be difficult and partial at best without observing their everyday language use with peers in naturalistic contexts. Many children who I asked to speak Patwa were unsure what I meant, yet they could activate their knowledge of the language in situated social interactions within their age cohort. This indicates the difficulties in assessing children's competence in a potentially threatened language as they may not speak it to or around adults or out of social context. The study of language socialization in tandem with the study of language ideologies provides an ideal method for such investigation, shedding light on inter- and intra-generational transmission. Attention to children's peer interactions offers insights into the mechanisms behind both shift and maintenance, including the minute details of why a language might be considered valuable enough for children to maintain.

A critical resource for revitalization research and implementation, then, is children's peer play. It is possible that an expansion of children's imaginary role-playing activities through drama classes, language arts, and after-school activities could offer a productive context for introducing Patwa in a less threatening manner. It might also keep Patwa speaking fun—an enjoyable activity that children look forward to rather than view as additional schoolwork. It would be essential, however, to look to the ways in which children themselves structure and experience their play, rather than relying solely on traditional forms (such as ring games). Recent studies in the anthropology of children and childhood seek to augment children's participation in the research process through use of participatory methods, such as giving children the tools to document and explain their own experiences through photography and audio-recording (see Montgomery 2009: 43–48 for a discussion of these methods). Children can become active contributors in the research and revitalization process, guiding language planners toward what is important to and workable for them.[7] Understanding children's play with multiple languages and registers through ethnographic research can serve an important role in formulating pedagogical activities to promote their use of Patwa, provided that parents decide to accept and pursue this as well.

Empowering Speakers

Gaining an understanding of the local political economy within which language shift and revitalization occur is perhaps as pressing as understanding patterns of intergenerational and peer transmission. As Heller and Duchêne (2007: 11) point out, "Rather than assuming we must save languages, perhaps we should be asking instead who benefits and who loses from understanding languages the way we do, what is at stake for whom, and how and why language serves as a terrain for competition" (see also Mufwene 2008). We must ask fundamental questions about why particular groups are trying to retain a language, what impact this may have on other communities, and what benefits or disadvantages language planning, such as introducing a language into schools, might bring across a population. In other words whose interests are served by revitalizing a language? In Dominica Patwa speakers remain marginalized in official contexts. Rural peoples speak of Patwa revitalization and potential use in schools as a luxury for those who can afford the time and effort and do not have anything else to lose. If villagers do not want to save the language, why should they be made to do so?

At the same time, taking a hands-off approach to cultural and linguistic loss leaves unattended the unequal power relations that Dominicans and others experience throughout their daily lives. Those who advocate a non-interventionist approach to language endangerment suggest that since languages are always changing to suit the needs of their speakers, linguists should document the remaining languages while letting nature—or speakers who wish to adopt a more economically viable language—proceed. But this perspective neglects the fact that language shift is not a neutral process. It is embedded in a larger context of social inequality and symbolic domination. As linguist Suzanne Romaine (2008: 9) puts it, "Language death does not happen in privileged communities; it happens to the dispossessed and disempowered." Often language death occurs within a backdrop of collective shame about native languages and cultures, cultivated through years of disparagement and political subjugation based partly on language ability. Recording endangered languages provides a record of linguistic diversity and can form a basis for historical memory and even future revitalization. But attending to the political, socioeconomic, and ideological contexts of language loss can provide a more nuanced perspective on local and global power inequalities in a way that might facilitate change. As Garrett (2006: 187–188) poignantly states:

A final, special consideration for those who study contact languages [like creoles], and who care about the people who speak them, is that to allow their endangerment to go unnoticed and unremarked is to be tacitly complicit in perpetuating the kinds of structural and symbolic violence that were key factors in the emergence of so many of these languages—and that in all too many cases continue to confront their speakers, in one form or another, on a daily basis.

Indeed, language shift is a symptom, an effect, and a producer of social inequality. Crystal (2000: 127–166) proposes six factors that may help a community maintain an endangered language. All have to do with increasing the social, economic, and political status of speakers: 1) increasing their prestige in the dominant community; 2) increasing their wealth; 3) increasing their power; 4) giving their language a strong presence in the education system; 5) developing a written form of the language; and 6) making use of electronic technology. Ultimately it is the speakers that need to be empowered so they do not feel it is necessary to give up one of their languages—or be forced to acquire another—due to pervasive inequalities. Despite potentially permanent loss, abandoning a language is a short-term solution that does nothing to solve the underlying problems that have contributed to such abandonment.

The Future of Patwa

Recent discourses valorizing Patwa as a symbol of national identity and as a commodity may affect the course of language shift to English varieties, helping to reverse or slow it. Or they may continue to emerge only around Independence Day, in tourism discourses, and in other specific contexts that hardly impact daily life. Attitudes toward Patwa have changed since Dominica's 1978 independence from colonial rule. But will Patwa become merely something for performances at the national level and for outsiders like tourists? Or material for archives rather than the living entity most villagers and language activists currently describe it as? Rural Dominicans do not exhibit the same degree of motivation toward Patwa language planning as many Māori or Hawaiian communities do. The Penville nurse's statement that "Creole Day is every day" articulates the paradox at the heart of the language shift—rural adults view their villages as being saturated with Patwa to the point that it interferes with their children's English and puts them at a disadvantage. Yet for urban residents and those who already have "good English," as many Dominicans pointed out to me, what good does one day of speaking Patwa do when people are no longer using it in daily practice? This gets at a fundamental disjuncture between language revitalization efforts and everyday experience.

We also are left with the significant question of what will happen as this generation of children, those on the cusp of dramatic linguistic and social change, matures and begins having their own children. Will parental strategies of speaking Patwa around and to children for some functions, and encouraging English explicitly in adult-controlled settings and Patwa implicitly in child-controlled settings ensure transmission? What linguistic varieties will these children use to socialize their own children into communicative competence and community membership? What will their children speak, both in their presence and when interacting with members of their own age cohort? Will a combination of age-graded language ideologies and increasingly positive attitudes at a national level create a continued cultural need for the use of Patwa? Will pro-creole movements in other Caribbean societies further influence the Dominican population? Some readers of this book may perceive children's use of Patwa for expressing intensified affect and negotiating play, rather than for everyday speech and conversational functions, as indicative of the impending loss of a once vibrant creole. Or perhaps it can be viewed as the emergence of Patwa competence over developmental time in an age-graded society. It is likely a blending of both possibilities. Language revitalization efforts would do well to understand this dynamic and nurture local strategies of language socialization through culturally sensitive approaches to age-related expectations and responsibilities.

At the point that I encountered the shift in Penville, much of what Christie (1982: 48) had described still rang true:

> [T]he English and the French-lexicon Creole in Dominica are still viewed as separate codes by the speakers themselves and they still evoke different emotional responses. As long as this remains the case, Dominican [French-lexicon] Creole will survive even if its actual form becomes more influenced by local varieties of English and vice versa. Its death will come about only if the majority of speakers are no longer conscious of a difference between the two or if they deliberately abandon the one for the other.

The people with whom I spoke continued to distinguish between the two languages, despite use of heteroglossic language practices including extensive code-switching, calquing, and other forms of bilingual simultaneity. The languages also continued to "evoke different emotional responses" in speakers, which was being transmitted to children. Villagers were, however, deliberately attempting to shift languages. Most did not want to abandon Patwa completely but were willing to give it up in order to provide their children with English.[8]

If the functional distribution and complementarity between the languages continue and Patwa remains to some degree a positive marker of village social identity, it may persist along with varieties of English. But as farming is increasingly devalued and adults seek employment outside their villages and outside Dominica, English garners considerable importance. Today's children are learning to associate Patwa with certain kinds of adults, such as farmers, fisherman, bus drivers, and elderly people. Many Penville children express hopes of becoming office workers, government employees, travel agents, and business people, or continuing their education—all pursuits that require English and exclude Patwa. But careful attention to language ideologies and language socialization practices show that it is not a wholesale abandoning of one language for another, nor that language shift is fueled solely by a desire for socioeconomic mobility. Villagers are shifting languages because of a deeper shift in how they view themselves, their identities, and what it means to be a person, a child, and a Dominican today. This must be addressed by urban language activists in order for their efforts to positively impact the lives and linguistic practices of rural peoples.

At this stage of the shift—at the particular moment in time when I happened upon it—Patwa and English are both still necessary for being a whole person in Penville. Villagers are straddling both identities, maintaining aspects of Patwa while trying to "bring in" English. They do not want Patwa to "die out," but are contributing to language shift through their socialization practices. But while it may appear from an examination of communicative patterns with children at home and at school that the community is quickly shifting languages, analysis of children's peer interactions when not subject to adult monitoring suggests that the roots of language maintenance are in the voices of children. How language socialization practices and children's play will affect the future of Patwa and varieties of English remains to be seen. *Nou ké vwè, si Bondyé vlé.*

Notes

1. Jaffe (1999: 285) highlights this point regarding language revitalization in Corsica.
2. Sidnell (2005) describes the production of male exclusivity in rum shops in a Caribbean Indo-Guyanese village.
3. This is similar to what Kulick (1992) reports in Gapun, Papua New Guinea, where the local conception of self, represented by the duality of *hed* and *save*, has become split along linguistic lines and is directly contributing to the language shift from the vernacular, Taiap, to Tok Pisin through child-rearing practices. Kulick's study beautifully illustrates how language ideologies and local interpretations of a changing world can impact the longevity of a language.
4. Garrett (2007) similarly suggests that children in St. Lucia develop distinct "age-inflected" bilingual subjectivities (including a sense of belonging to an age cohort) through socialization to use, or not use, linguistic resources as they interact and contrast with other age groups.

5. Thomas (2004: 5) makes a similar point regarding the revalorizing of rural Afro-creole cultural practices and performances in Jamaica.
6. For example, see cases described in Grenoble and Whaley (2006) and Hinton and Hale (2001).
7. This may entail use of new technologies, such as the Internet or language-learning software, although these require funding that might not be available.
8. One outcome of this could be speakers using Patwa in new syncretic ways. See Christie (1990, 1994) on the restructuring of varieties of Dominican English.

Bibliography

Abrahams, Roger. 1970. "Patterns of Performance in the British West Indies." In *Afro-American Anthropology: Contemporary Perspectives*, eds. Norman Whitten and John Szwed, 163–179. New York: The Free Press.

Agha, Asif. 2004. "Registers of Language." In *A Companion to Linguistic Anthropology*, ed. Alessandro Duranti, 23–45. Malden, MA: Blackwell.

———. 2005. "Voice, Footing, Enregisterment." *Journal of Linguistic Anthropology* 15(1): 38–59.

Ahearn, Laura M. 2001. "Language and Agency." *Annual Review of Anthropology* 30: 109–137

Alleyne, Mervyn C. 1985. "A Linguistic Perspective on the Caribbean." In *Caribbean Contours*, eds. Sidney Mintz and Sally Price, 155–175. Baltimore, MD: Johns Hopkins University Press.

Amastae, Jon. 1979a. "Dominican Creole Phonology, I." *Georgetown University Papers on Languages and Linguistics* 15(Spring): 83–122.

———. 1979b. "Dominican Creole Phonology, II." *Georgetown University Papers on Languages and Linguistics* 16(Fall): 1–32.

———. 1979c. "Dominican English Creole Phonology: An Initial Sketch." *Anthropological Linguistics* 21(4): 182–204.

———. 1983. "Agentless Constructions in Dominican Creole." *Lingua* 59(1): 47–75.

Andersen, Elaine S. 1996. "A Cross-Cultural Study of Children's Register Knowledge." In *Social Interaction, Social Context, and Language: Essays in Honor of Susan Ervin-Tripp*, eds. Dan Slobin, J. Gerhardt, Amy Kyratzis, and J. Guo, 125–142. Mahwah, NJ: Lawrence Erlbaum.

Anderson, Benedict. 1991[1983]. *Imagined Communities: Reflections on the Origin and Spread of Nationalism*. London: Verso.

Appel, René, and Ludo Verhoeven. 1994. "Decolonization, Language Planning, and Education." In *Pidgins and Creoles*, eds. Jacques Arends, Pieter Muysken, and Norval Smith, 65–74. Philadelphia: John Benjamins.

Aronsson, Karin, and Mia Thorell. 1999. "Family Politics in Children's Play Directives." *Journal of Pragmatics* 31(1): 25–48.

Arteaga, Alfred, ed. 1994. *An Other Tongue: Nation and Ethnicity in the Linguistic Borderlands*. Durham, NC: Duke University Press.

Bailey, Benjamin. 2007. "Heteroglossia and Boundaries." In *Bilingualism: A Social Approach*, ed. Monica Heller, 257–274. New York: Palgrave Macmillan.

Baker, Patrick L. 1994. *Centring the Periphery: Chaos, Order, and the Ethnohistory of Dominica*. Buffalo, NY: McGill-Queen's University Press.

Bakhtin, Mikhail M. 1981. *The Dialogic Imagination: Four Essays*, ed. Michael Holquist, trans. Caryl Emerson and Michael Holquist. Austin: University of Texas Press.

———. 1984. *Problems in Dostoevsky's Poetics*. Minneapolis: University of Minnesota Press.

Batibo, Herman M. 2009. "Poverty as a Crucial Factor in Language Maintenance and Language Death: Case Studies from Africa." In *Language and Poverty*, ed. Wayne Harbert, 23–36. Tonawanda, NY: Multilingual Matters.

Baud, Michiel, and Annelou Ypeij, eds. 2009. *Cultural Tourism in Latin America: The Politics of Space and Imagery*. Boston, MA: Brill.

Bebel-Gisler, Dany. 1976. *La Langue Créole, Force Jugulée: Étude Socio-linguistique des Rapports de Force entre le Créole et le Francais aux Antilles*. Paris: Editions L'Harmattan.

Ben-Rafael, Eliezer. 1994. *Language, Identity, and Social Division: The Case of Israel*. Oxford: Clarendon Press.

Besnier, Niko. 1990. "Language and Affect." *Annual Review of Anthropology* 19: 419–451.

Biber, Douglas, and Edward Finegan, eds. 1994. *Sociolinguistic Perspectives on Register*. New York: Oxford University Press.

Björk-Willén, Polly. 2007. "Participation in Multilingual Preschool Play: Shadowing and Crossing as Interactional Resources." *Journal of Pragmatics* 39(12): 2133–2158.

Blank, Sharla. 2005. "Women Don't Want to Stoop Too Low: Help-Seeking Among Female Household Heads in Dominica, West Indies," Ph.D. dissertation, California: University of California, San Diego.

Blom, Jan-Peter, and John Gumperz. 1972. "Social Meaning in Linguistic Structures: Codeswitching in Norway." In *Directions in Sociolinguistics*, eds. John Gumperz and Dell Hymes, 407–434. New York: Holt, Rinehard and Winston.

Blommaert, Jan. 1994. "The Metaphors of Development and Modernization in Tanzanian Language Policy and Research." In *African Languages, Development and the State*, eds. R. Fardon and G. Furniss, 213–226. London: Routledge.

Blommaert, Jan, and Jef Verschueren. 1992. "The Role of Language in European Nationalist Ideologies." *Pragmatics* 2(3): 355–375.

Bluebond-Langner, Myra, and Jill Korbin. 2007. "Challenges and Opportunities in the Anthropology of Childhoods." *American Anthropologist* 109(2): 241–246.

Blum-Kulka, Shoshana, Deborah Huck-Taglicht, and Hanna Avni. 2004. "The Social and Discursive Spectrum of Peer Talk." *Discourse Studies* 6(3): 307–328.

Blum-Kulka, Shoshana, and Catherine E. Snow. 2004. "Introduction: The Potential of Peer Talk." *Discourse Studies* 6(3): 291–306.

Bolonyai, Agnes. 2005. "'Who was the Best?': Power, Knowledge and Rationality in Bilingual Girls' Code Choices." *Journal of Sociolinguistics* 9(1): 3–27.

Bonner, Donna M. 2001. "Garifuna Children's Language Shame: Ethnic Stereotypes, National Affiliation, and Transnational Immigration as Factors in Language Choice in Southern Belize." *Language in Society* 30(1): 81–96.

Boromé, Joseph. 1969. "Dominica during French Occupation." *English Historical Review* 84(330): 36–58.

Bourdieu, Pierre. 1977. *Outline of a Theory of Practice*, trans. Richard Nice. Cambridge: Cambridge University Press.

———. 1984. *Distinction: A Social Critique of the Judgment of Taste*, trans. Richard Nice. Cambridge: Harvard University Press.

———. 1985. "The Genesis of the Concepts of Habitus and Field." *Sociocentrum* 2(2): 11–24.

———. 1991. *Language and Symbolic Power*, ed. John B. Thompson, trans. Gino Raymond and Matthew Adamson. Cambridge, MA: Harvard University Press.

Bourdieu, Pierre, and Jean-Claude Passeron. 1990[1970]. *Reproduction in Education, Society, and Culture*. London: Sage.

Bretherton, Inge. 1984. "Representing the Social World in Symbolic Play: Reality and Fantasy." In *Symbolic Play: The Development of Social Understanding*, ed. Inge Bretherton, 3–41. Orlando: Academic Press.

Bucholtz, Mary, and Kira Hall. 2004. "Language and Identity." In *A Companion to Linguistic Anthropology*, ed. Alessandro Duranti, 369–394. Malden, MA: Blackwell.

Bully, Alwin. 2003. "Culture, Tourism and Development: The Essential Trio." *Fifth CTO Annual Caribbean Conference on Sustainable Tourism Development, September 9, 2003.* St. Kitts. (Retrieved 11/15/2009 from http://da-academy.org/essentrio.html)

Burton, Richard D.E. 1997. *Afro-Creole: Power, Opposition, and Play in the Caribbean*. Ithaca, NY: Cornell University Press.

Butler, Carly W. 2008. *Talk and Social Interaction in the Playground*. Burlington, VT: Ashgate.

Butler, Carly, and Ann Weatherall. 2006. "'No, We're Not Playing Families': Membership Categorization in Children's Play." *Research on Language and Social Interaction* 39(4): 441–470.

Byres, John. 1776. *Map of Dominica*. London: S. Hooper.

Cameron, Deborah. 1995. *Verbal Hygiene*. New York: Routledge.

Carrington, Lawrence D. 1996. "Ambient Language and Learner Output in a Creole Environment." In *Creole Languages and Language Acquisition*, ed. Herman Wekker, 51–64. New York: Mouton de Gruyter.

Cavanaugh, Jillian R. 2006. "Little Women and Vital Champions: Gendered Language Shift in a Northern Italian Town." *Journal of Linguistic Anthropology* 16(2): 194–210.

Christie, Pauline G. 1969. "A Sociolinguistic Study of Some Dominican Creole Speakers," Ph.D. dissertation, York: University of York.

———. 1982. "Language Maintenance and Language Shift in Dominica." *Caribbean Quarterly* 28(4): 41–51.

———. 1983. "In Search of the Boundaries of Caribbean Creoles." In *Studies in Caribbean Language*, ed. Lawrence Carrington, 13–22. St. Augustine: Society for Caribbean Linguistics.

———. 1990. "Language as Expression of Identity in Dominica." *International Journal of the Sociology of Language* 85: 61–69.

———. 1994. "Language Preference in Two Communities in Dominica, West Indies." *La Linguistique* 30(2): 7–16.

Clifford, James. 1988. *The Predicament of Culture*. Cambridge, MA: Harvard University Press.

Commonwealth of Dominica. 2001. "Population and Housing Census." Roseau, Dominica.

Corsaro, William A. 2005. *The Sociology of Childhood*, 2nd ed. Thousand Oaks, CA: Pine Forge Press.

Craig, Dennis R. 2008. "Pidgins/Creoles and Education." In *The Handbook of Pidgin and Creole Studies*, eds. Silvia Kouwenberg and John Victor Singler, 593–614. Malden, MA: Wiley-Blackwell.

Cromdal, Jakob. 2001. "Overlap in Bilingual Play: Some Implications of Code-Switching for Overlap Resolution." *Research on Language and Social Interaction* 34(4): 421–451.

———. 2004. "Building Bilingual Oppositions: Code-switching in Children's Disputes." *Language in Society* 33(1): 33–58.

Cromdal, Jakob, and Karin Aronsson. 2000. "Footing in Bilingual Play." *Journal of Sociolinguistics* 4(3): 435–457.

Crystal, David. 2000. *Language Death*. New York: Cambridge University Press.

Cultural Division, Government of Dominica. 1993. "A Directory of Cultural Activities, Artists and Major Cultural Groups and Institutions in Dominica." Roseau, Dominica.

da Silva, Emanuel, Mireille McLaughlin, and Mary Richards. 2007. "Bilingualism and the Globalized New Economy: The Commodification of Language and Identity." In *Bilingualism: A Social Approach*, ed. Monica Heller, 183–206. New York: Palgrave Macmillan.

de León, Lourdes. 1998. "The Emergent Participant: Interactive Patterns in the Socialization of Tzotzil (Mayan) Infants." *Journal of Linguistic Anthropology* 8(2): 131–161.

———. 2005. *La Llegada del Alma: Lenguaje, Infancia y Socializacion entre los Mayas de Zinacantan* (*The Advent of the Soul: Language, Childhood and Socialization among the Mayans of Zinacantan*). Mexico: CIESAS, INAH.

Devonish, Hubert. 1986. *Language Liberation: Creole Language Politics in the Caribbean*. London: Karia Press.

Dorian, Nancy C. 1982. "Defining the Speech Community to Include its Working Margins." In *Sociolinguistic Variation in Speech Communities*, ed. Suzanne Romaine, 25–33. London: Edward Arnold.

Duchêne, Alexandre, and Monica Heller, eds. 2007. *Discourses of Endangerment*. New York: Continuum.

Duff, Patricia A., and Nancy H. Hornberger, eds. 2008. *Encyclopedia of Language and Education*, Volume 8: Language Socialization, 2nd ed. New York: Springer.

Duranti, Alessandro. 2004. "Agency in Language." In *A Companion to Linguistic Anthropology*, ed. Alessandro Duranti, 451–473. Malden, MA: Blackwell.

Duranti, Alessandro, Elinor Ochs, and Bambi B. Schieffelin, eds. 2012. *The Handbook of Language Socialization*. Malden, MA: Wiley-Blackwell.

Durbrow, Eric H. 1999. "Cultural Processes in Child Competence: How Rural Caribbean Parents Evaluate their Children." In *Cultural Processes in Child Development: The Minnesota Symposia on Child Psychology*, Volume 29, ed. Ann S. Masten, 97–121. Mahwah, NJ: Lawrence Erlbaum Associates.

Errington, J. Joseph. 1988. *Structure and Style in Javanese: A Semiotic View of Linguistic Etiquette*. Philadelphia: University of Pennsylvania Press.

———. 1998. *Shifting Languages: Interaction and Identity in Javanese Indonesia*. Cambridge: Cambridge University Press.

Ervin-Tripp, Susan M. 1996. "Context in Language." In *Social Interaction, Social Context, and Language: Essays in Honor of Susan Ervin-Tripp*, eds. Dan I. Slobin, Julie Gerhardt, Amy Kyratzis, and Jiansheng Guo, 21–36. Mahwah, NJ: Lawrence Erlbaum.

Evaldsson, Ann-Carita. 2007. "Accounting for Friendship: Moral Ordering and Category Membership in Preadolescent Girls' Relational Talk." *Research on Language and Social Interaction* 40(4): 377–404.

Evans, Nicholas. 2010. *Dying Words: Endangered Languages and What They Have to Tell Us*. Malden, MA: Wiley-Blackwell.

Fader, Ayala. 2009. *Mitzvah Girls: Bringing Up the Next Generation of Hasidic Jews in Brooklyn*. Princeton, NJ: Princeton University Press.

Farris, Catherine S. 1992. "Chinese Preschool Codeswitching: Mandarin Babytalk and the Voice of Authority." *Journal of Multilingual and Multicultural Development* 13(1–2): 187–214.

Field, Margaret. 2001. "Triadic Directives in Navajo Language Socialization." *Language in Society* 30(2): 249–263.

Fierman, William. 1991. *Language Planning and National Development: The Uzbek Experience*. New York: Mouton de Gruyter.

Fishman, Joshua A. 1991. *Reversing Language Shift: Theoretical and Empirical Foundations of Assistance to Threatened Languages*. Clevedon, UK: Multilingual Matters.

———. 2001. *Can Threatened Languages Be Saved? Reversing Language Shift, Revisited: A 21st Century Perspective*. New York: Multilingual Matters.

Flinn, Mark V. 2008. "Why Words Can Hurt Us: Social Relationships, Stress, and Health." In *Evolutionary Medicine and Health*, eds. Wenda Trevathan, E.O. Smith, and James McKenna, 247–258. Oxford: Oxford University Press.

Fontaine, Marcel. 2003. *Dominica's English-Creole Dictionary*, 2nd ed. Roseau, Dominica: Paramount Printers.

Fontaine, Marcel, and Jonathan Leather. 1992. *Kwéyòl Usage and Attitudes of Dominican Second-Formers*. Canefield, Dominica: Folk Research Institute, Old Mill Cultural Centre.

Fontaine, Marcel, and Peter A. Roberts. 1992. *Dominica's English-Creole Dictionary*. Cave Hill, Barbados: Learning Resource Center, University of the West Indies.

Friedman, Debra A. 2012. "Language Socialization and Language Revitalization." In *The Handbook of Language Socialization*, eds. Alessandro Duranti, Elinor Ochs, and Bambi B. Schieffelin, 631–647. Malden, MA: Wiley-Blackwell.

Froude, J.A. 1888. *The English in the West Indies or the Bow of Ulysses*. London: Longmans, Green & Co.

Gal, Susan. 1984[1978]. "Peasant Men Can't Get Wives: Language Change and Sex Roles in a Bilingual Community." In *Language in Use*, eds. John Baugh and Joel Sherzer, 292–304. Englewood Cliffs, NJ: Prentice-Hall.

———. 1988. "The Political Economy of Code Choice." In *Codeswitching: Anthropological and Sociolinguistic Perspectives*, ed. Monica Heller, 245–264. Berlin: Mouton de Gruyter.

———. 1989. "Language and Political Economy." *Annual Review of Anthropology* 18: 345–367.

García-Sánchez, Inmaculada. 2010. "Serious Games: Code-Switching and Gendered Identities in Moroccan Immigrant Girls' Pretend Play." *Pragmatics* 20(4): 523–555.

Garrett, Paul B. 2000. "'High' Kwéyòl: The Emergence of a Formal Creole Register in St. Lucia." In *Language Change and Language Contact in Pidgins and Creoles*, ed. John McWhorter, 63–101. Philadelphia: John Benjamins.

———. 2003. "An 'English Creole' that Isn't: On the Sociohistorical Origins and Linguistic Classification of the Vernacular English of St. Lucia." In *Contact Englishes of the Eastern Caribbean*, eds. Michael Aceto and Jeffrey Williams, 155–210. Philadelphia: John Benjamins.

———. 2004. "Language Contact and Contact Languages." In *A Companion to Linguistic Anthropology*, ed. Alessandro Duranti, 46–72. Malden, MA: Blackwell.

———. 2005. "What a Language is Good For: Language Socialization, Language Shift, and the Persistence of Code-specific Genres in St. Lucia." *Language in Society* 34(3): 327–361.

———. 2006. "Contact Languages as 'Endangered' Languages: What is there to Lose?" *Journal of Pidgin and Creole Languages* 21(1): 175–190.

———. 2007. "Language Socialization and the (Re)production of Bilingual Subjectivities." In *Bilingualism: A Social Approach*, ed. Monica Heller, 233–256. New York: Palgrave Macmillan.

———. 2012. "Language Socialization and Language Shift." In *The Handbook of Language Socialization*, eds. Alessandro Duranti, Elinor Ochs, and Bambi B. Schieffelin, 515–535. Malden, MA: Wiley-Blackwell.

Garrett, Paul B., and Patricia Baquedano-López. 2002. "Language Socialization: Reproduction and Continuity, Transformation and Change." *Annual Review of Anthropology* 31: 339–361.

Geertz, Clifford. 1988. *Works and Lives: The Anthropologist as Author*. Cambridge: Polity Press.

Giddens, Anthony. 1979. *Central Problems in Social Theory*. Berkeley: University of California Press.

Gilroy, Paul. 1987. *There Ain't No Black in the Union Jack: The Cultural Politics of Race and Nation*. Chicago: University of Chicago Press.

———. 1993. *The Black Atlantic: Modernity and Double Consciousness*. Cambridge: Harvard University Press.

Gmelch, George. 2003. *Behind the Smile: The Working Lives of Caribbean Tourism*. Bloomington: Indiana University Press.

Goffman, Erving. 1974. *Frame Analysis*. New York: Harper and Row.

———. 1981. *Forms of Talk*. Philadelphia: University of Pennsylvania.

Goldman, Laurence R. 1998. *Child's Play: Myth, Mimesis and Make-believe*. New York: Berg.

Göncü, Artin, Ute Tuermer, Jyoti Jain, and Danielle Johnson. 1999. "Children's Play as Cultural Activity." In *Children's Engagement in the World*, ed. Artin Göncü, 148–172. Cambridge: Cambridge University Press.

Goodridge, Cecil A. 1972. "Dominica: The French Connection." In *Aspects of Dominican History*, ed. Government of Dominica, 151–162. Roseau: Government Printery.

Goodwin, Charles, and Alessandro Duranti. 1992. "Rethinking Context: Introduction." In *Rethinking Context: Language as an Interactive Phenomenon*, eds. Charles Goodwin and Alessandro Duranti, 1–42. New York: Cambridge University Press.

Goodwin, Marjorie Harness. 1990. He-*Said-She-Said: Talk as Social Organization among Black Children*. Bloomington: Indiana University Press.

———. 2006. *The Hidden Life of Girls: Games of Stance, Status, and Exclusion*. Malden, MA: Blackwell.

Goodwin, Marjorie Harness, and Charles Goodwin. 2000. "Emotion within Situated Activity." In *Communication: An Arena of Development*, eds. Nancy Budwig, I. Uzgiris, and James Wertsch, 33–53. Greenwood Publishing.

Goodwin, Marjorie Harness, and Amy Kyratzis. 2007. "Children Socializing Children: Practices for Negotiating the Social Order Among Peers." *Research on Language and Social Interaction* 40(4): 279–289.

———. 2012. "Peer Language Socialization." In *The Handbook of Language Socialization*, eds. Alessandro Duranti, Elinor Ochs, and Bambi B. Schieffelin, 365–390. Malden, MA: Wiley-Blackwell.

Green, Duncan. 1999. *Hidden Lives: Voices of Children in Latin America and the Caribbean*. London: Cassell.

Grenoble, Lenore A., and Lindsay J. Whaley. 2006. *Saving Languages: An Introduction to Language Revitalization*. New York: Cambridge University Press.

Grillo, Ralph D. 1989. *Dominant Languages: Language and Hierarchy in Britain and France*. Cambridge: Cambridge University Press.

Griswold, Olga. 2007. "Achieving Authority: Discursive Practices in Russian Girls' Pretend Play." *Research on Language and Social Interaction* 40(4): 291–319.

Guldal, Tale M. 1997. "Three Children, Two Languages: The Role of Code-selection in Organizing Conversation," Ph.D. dissertation, Trondheim: Norwegian University of Science and Technology at Trondheim.

Gumperz, John J. 1982. *Discourse Strategies*. Cambridge: Cambridge University Press.

Halliday, Michael A.K. 1964. "The Users and Uses of Language." In *The Linguistic Sciences and Language Teaching*, eds. M.A.K. Halliday, A. McIntosh, and P. Strevens, 75–110. London: Longmans.

Halmari, Helena, and Wendy Smith. 1994. "Code-switching and Register Shift: Evidence from Finnish-English Child Bilingual Conversation." *Journal of Pragmatics* 21(4): 427–445.

Hammond, S. A. 1945. "The Reorganisation of Schools, Section 12." *Colonial Development and Welfare Report*. Roseau, Dominica: Education Department.

Handler, Richard. 1988. *Nationalism and the Politics of Culture in Quebec*. Madison: University of Wisconsin Press.

Hanks, William F. 2001. "Indexicality." In *Key Terms in Language and Culture*, ed. Alessandro Duranti, 119–121. Malden, MA: Blackwell.

Heath, Shirley Brice. 1982. "What No Bedtime Story Means." *Language in Society* 11(1): 49-76.

Hecht, Tobias. 2002. "Children and Contemporary Latin America." In *Minor Omissions: Children in Latin American History and Society*, ed. Tobias Hecht, 242–250. Madison: The University of Wisconsin Press.

Heller, Monica. 2003. "Globalization, the New Economy and the Commodification of Language and Identity." *Journal of Sociolinguistics* 7(4): 473–492.

———. 2007. "Bilingualism as Ideology and Practice." In *Bilingualism: A Social Approach*, ed. Monica Heller, 1–22. New York: Palgrave Macmillan.

———. 2010. "The Commodification of Language." *Annual Review of Anthropology* 39: 101–114.

Heller, Monica, and Alexandre Duchêne. 2007. "Discourses of Endangerment: Sociolinguistics, Globalization and Social Order." In *Discourses of Endangerment*, ed. Alexandre Duchêne and Monica Heller, 1–13. New York: Continuum.

Henckell, Sascha-Lena. 2007. "Representing the Carib: An Analysis of Tourism and Development on the Island of Dominica," Ph.D. dissertation, Long Beach: California State University.

Henderson, Felix. 1988. *Palé Kwéyòl Donmnik*. Roseau, Dominica: Tropical Printers.

Herskovits, Melville J. 1971. *Life in a Haitian Valley*. New York: Anchor Books.

Herzfeld, Michael. 1982. *Ours Once More: Folklore, Ideology and the Making of Modern Greece*. Austin: University of Texas Press.

Hewitt, Roger. 1986. *White Talk Black Talk: Inter-racial Friendship and Communication amongst Adolescents*. Cambridge: Cambridge University Press.

Higbie, Janet. 1993. *Eugenia: The Caribbean's Iron Lady*. London: Macmillan.

Hill, Jane H., and Kenneth C. Hill. 1986. *Speaking Mexicano: Dynamics of Syncretic Language in Central Mexico*. Tucson: University of Arizona Press.

Hinton, Leanne. 2001a. "Language Revitalization: An Overview." In *The Green Book of Language Revitalization in Practice*, eds. Leanne Hinton and Ken Hale, 3–18. San Diego, CA: Academic Press.

———. 2001b. "The Master-Apprentice Language Learning Program." In *The Green Book of Language Revitalization in Practice*, eds. Leanne Hinton and Ken Hale, 217–226. San Diego, CA: Academic Press.

Hinton, Leanne, and Ken Hale, eds. 2001. *The Green Book of Language Revitalization in Practice*. San Diego, CA: Academic Press.

Hirschfeld, Lawrence. 2002. "Why Don't Anthropologists Like Children?" *American Anthropologist* 104(2): 611–627.

Holm, John. 1989a. *Pidgins and Creoles: Theory and Structure*, Volume 1. Cambridge: Cambridge University Press.

———. 1989b. *Pidgins and Creoles: Reference Survey*, Volume 2. Cambridge: Cambridge University Press.

Honychurch, Lennox. 1982. *Our Island Culture*. Roseau, Dominica: Tropical Printers.

———. 1993[1991]. *Dominica: Isle of Adventure*. London: Macmillan Press.

———. 1995[1975]. *The Dominica Story: A History of the Island*. Roseau, Dominica: The Dominica Institute.

———. 1997. "Carib to Creole: Contact and Culture Exchange in Dominica," Ph.D. dissertation, Oxford: University of Oxford.

Howard, Kathryn M. 2007. "Kinterm Usage and Hierarchy in Thai Children's Peer Groups." *Journal of Linguistic Anthropology* 17(2): 204–230.

———. 2008. "Language Socialization and Language Shift among School-aged Children." In *Encyclopedia of Language and Education*, Volume 8: Language Socialization, 2nd ed., eds. Patricia Duff and Nancy Hornberger, 187–199. New York: Springer.

———. 2009. "Breaking In and Spinning Out: Repetition and Decalibration in Thai Children's Play Genres." *Language in Society* 38(3): 339–363.

Hoyle, Susan M. 1998. "Register and Footing in Role Play." In *Kids Talk: Strategic Language Use in Later Childhood*, eds. Susan M. Hoyle and Carolyn Temple Adger, 47–67. New York: Oxford University Press.

Hulme, Peter. 2000. *Remnants of the Conquest*. New York: Oxford University Press.

Irvine, Judith T. 1989. "When Talk Isn't Cheap: Language and Political Economy." *American Ethnologist* 16(2): 248–267.

———. 1990. "Registering Affect: Heteroglossia in the Linguistic Expression of Emotion." In *Language and the Politics of Emotion*, eds. Catherine Lutz and Lila Abu-Lughod, 126–161. Cambridge: Cambridge University Press.

Irvine, Judith T., and Susan Gal. 2000. "Language Ideology and Linguistic Differentiation." In *Regimes of Language: Ideologies, Polities, and Identities*, ed. Paul V. Kroskrity, 35–83. Santa Fe, NM: SAR Press.

Jaffe, Alexandra. 1999. *Ideologies in Action: Language Politics on Corsica*. New York: Mouton de Gruyter.

———. 2007a. "Minority Language Movements." In *Bilingualism: A Social Approach*, ed. Monica Heller, 50–70. New York: Palgrave Macmillan.

———. 2007b. "Discourses of Endangerment: Contexts and Consequences of Essentializing Discourses." In *Discourses of Endangerment*, eds. Alexandre Duchêne and Monica Heller, 57–75. New York: Continuum.

James, Allison. 2007. "Giving Voice to Children's Voices: Practices and Problems, Pitfalls and Potentials." *American Anthropologist* 109(2): 261–272.

James, Allison, Chris Jenks, and Alan Prout. 1998. *Theorizing Childhood*. New York: Teachers College Press.

Jefferys, T. 1768. *Map of the Island of Dominica*. London: R. Sayer.

Jørgensen, J.N. 1998. "Children's Acquisition of Code-Switching for Power Wielding." In *Code-Switching in Conversation: Language, Interaction and Identity*, ed. Peter Auer, 237–258. New York: Routledge.

Jourdan, Christine. 1991. "Pidgins and Creoles: The Blurring of Categories." *Annual Review of Anthropology* 20: 187–209.

Kempadoo, Kamala. 2004. *Sexing the Caribbean: Gender, Race, and Sexual Labor*. New York: Routledge.

King, Jeanette. 2001. "Te Kōhanga Reo: Māori Language Revitalization." In *The Green Book of Language Revitalization in Practice*, eds. Leanne Hinton and Ken Hale, 119–128. San Diego, CA: Academic Press.

Konmité pou Étid Kwéyòl. 1997. *Kwéyòl in Education: Experiences and Attitudes of Dominican Teachers*. Canefield, Dominica: Folk Research Institute, Old Mill Cultural Centre.

Kouwenberg, Silvia, and John Victor Singler, eds. 2008. *The Handbook of Pidgin and Creole Studies*. Malden, MA: Wiley-Blackwell.

Koven, Michèle. 2006. "Feeling in Two Languages: A Comparative Analysis of a Bilingual's Affective Displays in French and Portuguese." In *Bilingual Minds: Emotional Experience, Expression and Representation*, ed. Aneta Pavlenko, 84–117. Clevedon, UK: Multilingual Matters.

Krauss, Michael E. 1992. "The World's Languages in Crisis." *Language* 68(1): 4–10.

———. 1998. "The Condition of Native North American Languages: The Need for Realistic Assessment and Action." *International Journal of the Sociology of Language* 132: 9–21.

Kroskrity, Paul V., ed. 2000a. *Regimes of Language: Ideologies, Polities, and Identities*. Santa Fe, NM: SAR Press.

————. 2000b. "Regimenting Languages: Language Ideological Perspectives." In *Regimes of Language: Ideologies, Polities, and Identities*, ed. Paul Kroskrity, 1–34. Santa Fe, NM: SAR Press.

————. 2004. "Language Ideologies." In *A Companion to Linguistic Anthropology*, ed. Alessandro Duranti, 496–517. Malden, MA: Blackwell.

Krumeich, Anja. 1994. *The Blessings of Motherhood: Health, Pregnancy and Child Care in Dominica*. Amsterdam: Het Spinhuis.

Kuipers, Joel. 1998. *Language, Identity and Marginality in Indonesia: The Changing Nature of Ritual Speech on the Island of Sumba*. New York: Cambridge University Press.

Kulick, Don. 1992. *Language Shift and Cultural Reproduction: Socialization, Self, and Syncretism in a Papua New Guinean Village*. Cambridge: Cambridge University Press.

Kulick, Don, and Bambi B. Schieffelin. 2004. "Language Socialization." In *A Companion to Linguistic Anthropology*, ed. Alessandro Duranti, 349–368. Malden, MA: Blackwell.

Kwan-Terry, Anna. 1992. "Code-switching and Code-mixing: The Case of a Child Learning English and Chinese Simultaneously." *Journal of Multilingual and Multicultural Development* 13(3): 243–259.

Kyratzis, Amy. 2000. "Tactical Uses of Narratives in Nursery School Same-Sex Groups." *Discourse Processes* 29(3): 269–299.

————. 2004. "Talk and Interaction among Children and the Co-Construction of Peer Groups and Peer Culture." *Annual Review of Anthropology* 33: 625–649.

Kyratzis, Amy, and Jiansheng Guo. 2001. "Preschool Girls' and Boys' Verbal Conflict Strategies in the United States and China." *Research on Language and Social Interaction* 34(1): 45–74.

Kyratzis, Amy, Traci Marx, and Evelyn Reder Wade. 2001. "Preschoolers' Communicative Competence: Register Shift in the Marking of Power in Different Contexts of Friendship Group Talk." *First Language* 21(63): 387–431.

Ladefoged, Peter. 1992. "Another View of Endangered Languages." *Language* 68(4): 809–811.

Lancy, David F. 1996. *Playing on the Mother-Ground: Cultural Routines for Children's Development*. New York: Guilford Press.

Lave, Jean, and Etienne Wenger. 1991. *Situated Learning: Legitimate Peripheral Participation*. Cambridge: Cambridge University Press.

Le Page, Robert B., and Andrée Tabouret-Keller. 1985. *Acts of Identity: Creole-based Approaches to Language and Ethnicity*. Cambridge: Cambridge University Press.

LeVine, Robert A. 2007. "Ethnographic Studies of Childhood: A Historical Overview." *American Anthropologist* 109(2): 247–260.

Lytra, Vally. 2007. *Play Frames and Social Identities: Contact Encounters in a Greek Primary School.* Philadelphia: John Benjamins.

Maffi, Luisa. 2005. "Linguistic, Cultural, and Biological Diversity." *Annual Review of Anthropology* 29: 599–617.

Maguire, G. 1991. *Our Own Language: An Irish Initiative.* Philadelphia, PA: Multilingual Matters.

Makihara, Miki. 2005. "Rapa Nui Ways of Speaking Spanish: Language Shift and Socialization on Easter Island." *Language in Society* 34(5): 727–762.

Mantz, Jeffrey W. 2007a. "How a Huckster Becomes a Custodian of Market Morality: Traditions of Flexibility in Exchange in Dominica." *Identities* 14(1-2): 19–38.

———. 2007b. "Enchanting Panics and Obeah Anxieties: Concealing and Disclosing Eastern Caribbean Witchcraft." *Anthropology and Humanism* 32(1): 18–29.

Maurice, H. 1949/1950. "Biennial Report for the Years 1949, 1950." Roseau, Dominica: Education Department.

Meek, Barbra A. 2007. "Respecting the Language of Elders: Ideological Shift and Linguistic Discontinuity in a Northern Athapascan Community." *Journal of Linguistic Anthropology* 17(1): 23–43.

———. 2010. *We Are Our Language: An Ethnography of Language Revitalization in a Northern Athabascan Community.* Arizona: University of Arizona Press.

Migge, B., I. Léglise and A. Bartens, eds. 2010. *Creoles in Education: An Appraisal of Current Programs and Projects.* Philadelphia: John Benjamins.

Milroy, Lesley. 1987. *Language and Social Networks.* Baltimore, MD: University Park.

Minks, Amanda. 2006. "Mediated Intertextuality in Pretend Play among Nicaraguan Miskitu Children." Proceedings of SALSA XIII. *Texas Linguistic Forum* 49: 117–127.

———. 2010. "Socializing Heteroglossia among Miskitu Children on the Caribbean coast of Nicaragua." *Pragmatics* 20(4): 495–522.

Montgomery, Heather. 2009. *An Introduction to Childhood: Anthropological Perspectives on Children's Lives.* Malden, MA: Wiley-Blackwell.

Morgan, Marcyliena, ed. 1994. *Language and the Social Construction of Identity in Creole Situations.* Los Angeles: University of California, Center for Afro-American Studies.

Mufwene, Salikoko S. 2004. "Language Birth and Death." *Annual Review of Anthropology* 33: 201–222.

———. 2008. *Language Evolution: Contact, Competition and Change.* New York: Continuum.

Mühleisen, Susanne, and Bettina Migge, eds. 2005. *Politeness and Face in Caribbean Creoles.* Philadelphia, PA: John Benjamins.

Myers, Robert A. 1981. "Post-Emancipation Migrations and Population Change in Dominica: 1834–1950." *Revista/Review Interamericana* 11(1): 87–109.

———. 1987. *A Resource Guide to Dominica, 1493–1986*, 3 Volumes. New Haven, CT: Human Relations Area Files.

Nettle, Daniel, and Suzanne Romaine. 2000. *Vanishing Voices: The Extinction of the World's Languages*. New York: Oxford University Press.

Nonaka, Angela M. 2012. "Language Socialization and Language Endangerment." In *The Handbook of Language Socialization*, eds. Alessandro Duranti, Elinor Ochs, and Bambi B. Schieffelin, 610–630. Malden, MA: Wiley-Blackwell.

Nwenmely, Hubisi. 1996. *Language Reclamation: French Creole Language Teaching in the UK and the Caribbean*. Philadelphia, PA: Multilingual Matters.

Ochs, Elinor. 1988. *Culture and Language Development: Language Acquisition and Language Socialization in a Samoan Village*. Cambridge: Cambridge University Press.

———. 1992. "Indexing Gender." In *Rethinking Context: Language as an Interactive Phenomenon*, eds. Charles Goodwin and Alessandro Duranti, 335–359. Cambridge: Cambridge University Press.

———. 1996. "Linguistic Resources for Socializing Humanity." In *Rethinking Linguistic Relativity*, eds. John Gumperz and Stephen Levinson, 407–437. New York: Cambridge University Press.

Ochs, Elinor, and Bambi B. Schieffelin. 1984. "Language Acquisition and Socialization: Three Developmental Stories and Their Implications." In *Culture Theory: Essays on Mind, Self, and Emotion*, eds. Richard Shweder and Robert LeVine, 276–320. Cambridge: Cambridge University Press.

———. 1989. "Language Has a Heart." *Text* 9(1): 7–25.

———. 1995. "The Impact of Language Socialization on Grammatical Development." In *The Handbook of Child Language*, eds. Paul Fletcher and Brian MacWhinney, 73–93. New York: Blackwell.

———. 2008. "Language Socialization: An Historical Overview." In *Encyclopedia of Language and Education*, Volume 8: Language Socialization, 2nd ed., eds. Patricia A. Duff and Nancy H. Hornberger, 3–15. New York: Springer.

Olwig, Karen Fog. 1993. *Global Culture, Island Identity: Continuity and Change in the Afro-Caribbean Community of Nevis*. Chur, Switzerland: Harwood.

Paravisini-Gebert, Lizabeth. 1996. *Phyllis Shand Allfrey: A Caribbean Life*. New Brunswick, NJ: Rutgers University Press.

Patrick, Peter L. 1997. "Style and Register in Jamaican Patwa." In *Englishes Around the World: Studies in Honour of Manfred Göörlach*, Volume 2, ed. Edgar W. Schneider, 41–55. Philadelphia: John Benjamins.

Paugh, Amy L. 2001. "'Creole Day is Every Day': Language Socialization, Shift, and Ideologies in Dominica, West Indies," Ph.D. dissertation, New York: New York University.

———. 2005a. "Multilingual Play: Children's Code-switching, Role Play, and Agency in Dominica, West Indies." *Language in Society* 34(1): 63–86.

———. 2005b. "Acting Adult: Language Socialization, Shift, and Ideologies in Dominica." In *ISB4: Proceedings of the 4th International Symposium on Bilingualism*, eds. J. Cohen, K. McAlister, K. Rolstad, and J. MacSwan, 1807–1820. Somerville, MA: Cascadilla Press.

———. 2012a. "Local Theories of Child Rearing." In *The Handbook of Language Socialization*, eds. Alessandro Duranti, Elinor Ochs, and Bambi B. Schieffelin, 150–168. Malden, MA: Wiley-Blackwell.

———. 2012b. "Language Learning." In *Oxford Bibliographies Online: Childhood Studies*. Heather Montgomery, ed. New York: Oxford University Press. www.oxfordbibliographies.com

Pavlenko, Aneta. 2005. *Emotions and Multilingualism*. New York: Cambridge University Press.

———., ed. 2006. *Bilingual Minds: Emotional Experience, Expression and Representation*. Clevedon, UK: Multilingual Matters.

Payne, Anthony. 2008. "After Bananas: The IMF and the Politics of Stabilisation and Diversification in Dominica." *Bulletin of Latin American Research* 27(3): 317–332.

Peirce, Charles S. 1960. *Collected Papers*, eds. Charles Hartshorne and Paul Weiss. Cambridge, MA: Harvard University Press.

Philips, Susan U. 2000. "Constructing a Tongan Nation-State through Language Ideology in the Courtroom." In *Regimes of Language: Ideologies, Polities, and Identities*, ed. Paul Kroskrity, 229–257. Santa Fe, NM: SAR Press.

Piaget, Jean. 1962. *Play, Dreams and Imitation in Childhood*. New York: Norton.

Quinlan, Marsha B., and Robert J. Quinlan. 2007. "Modernization and Medicinal Plant Knowledge in a Caribbean Horticultural Village." *Medical Anthropology Quarterly* 21(2): 169–192.

Rampton, Ben. 1995. *Crossing: Language and Ethnicity among Adolescents*. London: Longman.

Reisman, Karl. 1970. "Cultural and Linguistic Ambiguity in a West Indian Village." In *Afro-American Anthropology: Contemporary Perspectives*, eds. Norman Whitten and John Szwed, 129–144. New York: The Free Press.

Reynolds, Jennifer F. 2002. "Maya Children's Practices of the Imagination: (Dis)playing Childhood and Politics in Guatemala," Ph.D. dissertation, California: University of California, Los Angeles.

———. 2007. "'Buenos Días/((*Military Salute*))': The Natural History of a Coined Insult." *Research on Language and Social Interaction* 40(4): 437–465.

———. 2008. "Socializing *Puros Pericos* (Little Parrots): The Negotiation of Respect and Responsibility in Antonero Mayan Sibling and Peer Networks." *Journal of Linguistic Anthropology* 18(1): 82–107.

Riley, Kathleen C. 2012. "Language Socialization and Language Ideologies." In *The Handbook of Language Socialization*, eds. Alessandro Duranti, Elinor Ochs, and Bambi B. Schieffelin, 493–514. Malden, MA: Wiley-Blackwell.

Rindstedt, Camilla. 2001. "Quichua Children and Language Shift in an Andean Community: School, Play and Sibling Caretaking," Ph.D. dissertation, Linköping: Linköping Studies in Arts and Science.

Rindstedt, Camilla, and Karin Aronsson. 2002. "Growing Up Monolingual in a Bilingual Community: The Quichua Revitalization Paradox." *Language in Society* 31(5): 721–742.

Rockefeller, Stuart Alexander. 1999. "'There is a Culture Here': Spectacle and the Inculcation of Folklore in Highland Bolivia." *Journal of Latin American Anthropology* 3(2): 118–149.

Rogoff, Barbara. 1990. *Apprenticeship in Thinking: Cognitive Development in Social Context*. New York: Oxford University Press.

Romaine, Suzanne. 2008. "Linguistic Diversity, Sustainability, and the Future of the Past." In *Sustaining Linguistic Diversity: Endangered and Minority Languages and Language Varieties*, eds. Kendall A. King, Natalie Schilling-Estes, Lyn Fogle, Jia Jackie Lou, and Barbara Soukup, 7–21. Washington, DC: Georgetown University Press.

Safa, Helen. 1987. "Popular Culture, National Identity, and Race in the Caribbean." *New West Indian Guide* 61(3–4): 115–126.

Schieffelin, Bambi B. 1990. *The Give and Take of Everyday Life: Language Socialization of Kaluli Children*. Cambridge: Cambridge University Press.

———. 1994. "Codeswitching and Language Socialization: Some Probable Relationships." In *Pragmatics: From Theory to Practice*, eds. Judith Felson Duchan, Lynne Hewitt, and Rae Sonnenmeier, 20–42. New York: Prentice Hall.

———. 2003. "Language and Place in Children's Worlds." Proceedings of SALSA X. *Texas Linguistic Forum* 45: 152–66.

Schieffelin, Bambi B., and Rachel C. Doucet. 1994. "The 'Real' Haitian Creole: Ideology, Metalinguistics and Orthographic Choice." *American Ethnologist* 21(1): 177–201.

Schieffelin, Bambi B., Kathryn A. Woolard, and Paul V. Kroskrity, eds. 1998. *Language Ideologies: Practice and Theory*. New York: Oxford University Press.

Schnepel, Ellen M. 2004. *In Search of a National Identity: Creole and Politics in Guadeloupe*. Hamburg: Helmut Buske.

Schwartzman, Helen B. 2001. "Children and Anthropology: A Century of Studies." In *Children and Anthropology: Perspectives for the 21ˢᵗ Century*, ed. Helen Schwartzman, 15–37. Westport, CT: Bergin and Garvey.

Sheldon, Amy. 1996. "You Can Be the Baby Brother, But You Aren't Born Yet: Preschool Girls' Negotiation for Power and Access in Pretend Play." *Research on Language and Social Interaction* 29(1): 57–80.

Sheller, Mimi. 2003. *Consuming the Caribbean: From Arawaks to Zombies*. New York: Routledge.

Sidnell, Jack. 1997. "Organizing Social and Spatial Location: Elicitations in Indo-Guyanese Village Talk." *Journal of Linguistic Anthropology* 7(2): 143–165.

———. 2005. *Talk and Practical Epistemology: The Social Life of Knowledge in a Caribbean Community*. Amsterdam: John Benjamins.

Siegel, Jeff. 1995. "How to Get a Laugh in Fijian: Code-switching and Humor." *Language in Society* 24(1): 95–110.

Silverstein, Michael. 1976. "Shifters, Linguistic Categories, and Cultural Description." In *Meaning in Anthropology*, eds. Keith Basso and Henry Selby, 11–55. Albuquerque: University of New Mexico Press.

———. 1998. "Contemporary Transformations of Local Linguistic Communities." *Annual Review of Anthropology* 27: 401–426.

———. 2000. "Whorfianism and the Linguistic Imagination of Nationality." In *Regimes of Language: Ideologies, Polities, and Identities*, ed. Paul Kroskrity, 85–138. Santa Fe, NM: SAR Press.

Smith, Gary R. 1991. "The Dominican Kont: An Analysis of Folktales and Storytelling on a Caribbean Island," Ph.D. dissertation, Texas: The University of Texas at Austin.

Smith, M.G. 1962. *West Indian Family Structure*. Washington, DC: University of Washington Press.

Smith, Raymond T. 1996. *The Matrifocal Family: Power, Pluralism, and Politics*. New York: Routledge.

Snow, Peter. 2004. "What Happen: Language Socialization and Language Persistance in a Panamanian Creole Village," Ph.D. dissertation, California: University of California, Los Angeles.

Spolsky, Bernard. 2003. "Reassessing Māori Regeneration." *Language in Society* 32(4): 553–578.

Strachan, Ian G. 2002. *Paradise and Plantation: Tourism and Culture in the Anglophone Caribbean*. Charlottesville: University of Virginia Press.

Stroud, Christopher. 2007. "Bilingualism: Colonialism and Postcolonialism." In *Bilingualism: A Social Approach*, ed. Monica Heller, 25–49. New York: Palgrave Macmillan.

Stuart, Stephanie. 1993. "Dominican Patwa–Mother Tongue or Cultural Relic?" *International Journal of the Sociology of Language* 102: 57–72.

Sutton, Constance R. 1974. "Cultural Duality in the Caribbean." *Caribbean Studies* 14(2): 96–101.

Taylor, Douglas. 1951. "Structural Outline of Caribbean Creole." *Word* 7(1): 43–59.

———. 1954. "Names on Dominica." *Names* 2(1): 31–37.

———. 1977. *Languages of the West Indies*. Baltimore, MD: John Hopkins University Press.

Thomas, Deborah A. 2004. *Modern Blackness: Nationalism, Globalization, and the Politics of Culture in Jamaica*. Durham, NC: Duke University Press.

Thorne, Barrie. 1993. *Gender Play: Girls and Boys in School*. New Brunswick, NJ: Rutgers University Press.

Tollefson, James, and Amy Tsui, eds. 2004. *Medium of Instruction Policies: Which Agenda? Whose Agenda?* Mahwah, NJ: Lawrence Erlbaum.

Trouillot, Michel-Rolph. 1988. *Peasants and Capital: Dominica in the World Economy*. Baltimore: Johns Hopkins University Press.

———. 1992. "The Caribbean Region: An Open Frontier in Anthropological Theory." *Annual Review of Anthropology* 21: 19–42.

Urciuoli, Bonnie. 1995. "Language and Borders." *Annual Review of Anthropology* 2: 525–546.

Urla, Jacqueline. 1993. "Contesting Modernities: Language Standardization and the Production of an Ancient/Modern Basque Culture." *Critique of Anthropology* 13(2): 101–118.

Vygotsky, Lev S. 1967. "Play and its Role in the Mental Development of the Child." *Soviet Psychology* 5(3): 6–18.

———. 1978. *Mind in Society: The Development of Higher Psychological Processes*. Cambridge, MA: Harvard University Press.

Warner, Sam L. No'eau. 2001. "The Movement to Revitalize Hawaiian Language and Culture." In *The Green Book of Language Revitalization in Practice*, eds. Leanne Hinton and Ken Hale, 133–144. San Diego, CA: Academic Press.

Watson-Gegeo, Karen Ann. 2001. "Fantasy and Reality: The Dialectic of Work and Play in Kwara'ae Children's Lives." *Ethos* 29(2): 138–158.

Wenger, Etienne. 1998. *Communities of Practice: Learning, Meaning, and Identity*. Cambridge: Cambridge University Press.

Williams, Brackette F. 1991. *Stains on My Name, War in My Veins: Guyana and the Politics of Cultural Struggle*. Durham, NC: Duke University Press.

Wilson, Peter J. 1973. *Crab Antics: The Social Anthropology of English-Speaking Societies of the Caribbean*. New Haven, CT: Yale University Press.

Wilson, William H., and Kauanoe Kamana. 2001. "'Mai Loko Mai o Ka 'I'ini: Proceeding from a Dream': The 'Aha Pūnana Leo Connection in Hawaiian Language." In *The Green Book of Language Revitalization in Practice*, eds. Leanne Hinton and Ken Hale, 147–176. San Diego, CA: Academic Press.

Woolard, Kathryn A. 1988. "Codeswitching and Comedy in Catelonia." In *Codeswitching: Anthropological and Sociolinguistic Perspectives*, ed. Monica Heller, 53–76. New York: Mouton de Gruyter.

———. 1989. *Double Talk: Bilingualism and the Politics of Ethnicity in Catalonia*. Stanford: Stanford University Press.

———. 2004. "Codeswitching." In *A Companion to Linguistic Anthropology*, ed. Alessandro Duranti, 73–94. Malden, MA: Blackwell.

Woolard, Kathryn A., and Bambi B. Schieffelin. 1994. "Language Ideology." *Annual Review of Anthropology* 23: 55–82.

Wurm, Stephen A. 1998. "Methods of Language Maintenance and Revival, with Selected Cases of Language Endangerment in the World." In *Studies in Endangered Languages*, ed. Kazuto Matsumura, 191–211. Tokyo: Hituzi Syobo.

Wylie, Jonathan. 1995. "The Origins of Lesser Antillean French Creole: Some Literary and Lexical Evidence." *Journal of Pidgin and Creole Languages* 10(1): 77–126.

Young, Virginia H. 1993. *Becoming West Indian: Culture, Self and Nation in St. Vincent*. Washington, DC: Smithsonian Institution Press.

Youssef, Valerie. 1993. "Children's Linguistic Choices: Audience Design and Societal Norms." *Language in Society* 22(2): 257–274.

———. 1996. "Varilingualism: The Competence Underlying Codemixing in Trinidad and Tobago." *Journal of Pidgin and Creole Languages* 11(1): 1–22.

Zentella, Ana Celia. 1997. *Growing Up Bilingual: Puerto Rican Children in New York City*. Oxford: Blackwell Publishers.

Index

A

Abrahams, Roger, 141n3

adult authority and status vis-à-vis children, 21, 89–90, 115–117, 128–135, 139–140, 143–144, 154, 158, 183–184, 194–195, 203–206, 212–215; and terms of address, 106

affect: children's English emotion vocabulary, 150; in children's role play, 173–174, 175, 192–193, 196, 207; intensified expression of through Patwa, 117–125, 128–135, 140, 149–158, 204–207; and language, 14–19, 27n19, 87, 149-150, 168–169, 196, 204, 210

age-graded communicative practice, 3, 14, 24, 25, 86, 87, 89–90, 117, 136, 197, 205–206, 212–213, 214–216

agency, 13–14; children's, 2, 13, 152–154, 168–169, 196–197, 206–210, 213–215; and language shift, 3, 214–217

Agha, Asif, 17, 27n22, 174

agriculture, 6–7, 26n6, 33–35, 37–39, 58–60; attitudes toward among youth, 77–78, 112–113, 220; banana industry, 6, 37–38, 55n13, 46, 50, 54, 64; coffee, 31–32, 58, 71; limes, 36, 55n11; monocrop strategy in, 6–7, 35, 46; paucity of sugar industry, 6, 33; and selling produce at market, 66, 67, 73, 77–78

Ahearn, Laura, 13

Alleyne, Mervyn, 55n3

Amastae, Jon, 26n11, 26n13

ambivalence toward Patwa, 86–87, 89–90, 165, 208–209

Andersen, Elaine, 174

Anderson, Benedict, 29

Appel, René, 30

Aronsson, Karin, 145, 169n1, 197n3–4, 198n5

Arteaga, Alfred, 54n1

Associated Statehood, 38

autonomy, socialization of, 116–117, 136–140, 197. *See also* boldness

B

babies, and birth, 62, 84n8; and language learning, 99–104, 108–109, 121–123, 139–140; and sleeping, 71; as soft, 100, 136

baby talk, 120–123, 149, 204; in children's role play, 178–179, 196

Bailey, Benjamin, 18, 26n14, 26n18

Baker, Patrick, 6, 26n8, 31, 32, 33, 34, 35, 55n6, 55n9

Bakhtin, Mikhail, 17, 18, 154

Baquedano-López, Patricia, 11

Batibo, Herman, 210

Baud, Michiel, 40

Bebel-Gisler, Dany, 55n3

Ben-Rafael, Eliezer, 54n1
Besnier, Niko, 15, 27n19
Biber, Douglas, 18
Björk-Willén, Polly, 187
Blank, Sharla, 26n8
Blom, Jan-Peter, 27n21
Blommaert, Jan, 29, 54n1
Bluebond-Langner, Myra, 2
Blum-Kulka, Shoshana, 144, 174, 197n2
boldness, 116–117, 119–120, 200, 204–206;
    as being "good for oneself" (*bon pou
    ko'y*), 115–116, 119–120, 136, 139,
    145; praising children's, 115–117, 136,
    138–139, 205; socialization of, 136–140.
    See also hardness, softness
Bolonyai, Agnes, 144
Bonner, Donna, 55n2
Boromé, Joseph, 35
Bourdieu, Pierre, 11, 18, 22, 29, 206
Bretherton, Inge, 197n2
Bucholtz, Mary, 26n18
Bully, Alwin, 50
Burton, Richard, 30, 141n3
Butler, Carly, 169n1
Byres, John, 84n2

C
calling-out routines, 104–106, 113n6,
    134–135
Cameron, Deborah, 211
Carib. *See* Kalinago
Carrington, Lawrence, 27n14
Catholicism. *See* religion
Cavanaugh, Jillian, 113n4, 203
child fostering, 20, 61, 64, 69, 70, 74, 75, 76,
    201
children, acting "mannish" (*two nonm*), 129,
    136, 141n15, 181; acting "womanish"
    (*two fanm*), 129, 136, 138–139, 143–144;
    and childcare, 20, 66, 78, 82, 145, 202,
    206; chores and responsibilities of, 69,
    75, 77, 78, 82, 145–146, 191–192, 206;
    and discipline, 37, 88–89, 91–92, 99,
    100, 115–117, 128–135, 140, 163–165,
    183–184, 194–195, 203–206; and gender,
    120, 145–146, 155, 170n4, 171–172,
    175, 179, 180–181, 187, 191–192, 194,
    196–197; hardening and toughening up
    of, 136–138, 140; local theories about,
    101–102, 129, 139–140, 147–148,
    205, 212; importance of research on, 2,

206–210. *See also* babies; child fostering;
    language learning
children's language ideologies. *See* language
    ideology
Christie, Pauline, 7, 9, 10, 26n10–11, 26n13,
    32, 33, 37, 43, 80, 84n3, 90, 119, 141n5,
    141n8, 219, 221n8
class, socioeconomic, 28, 34–36, 55n6, 83–84;
    and children's play, 169, 172, 196–197,
    207; and family name, 34–35, 36–37,
    71–72, 117; and food, 69, 71, 74–75,
    and language, 9, 32–33, 35–37, 38,
    40–41, 54, 84, 86–87, 89–91, 112–113,
    196–197, 199, 202–203, 211–212; and
    language revitalization, 29–30, 217–218;
    and language socialization, 11–12, 14–15;
    post emancipation, 33–36; and religion,
    64, 66, 91, 79–81, 203; and social
    mobility, 1, 9, 36–37, 113, 201, 220; in
    the village, 57, 63, 64–66, 81, 82–84
Clifford, James, 21
code-switching and code choice, 10–11,
    14–19, 23, 27n21, 174–175, 204, 214,
    219; as "acts of identity," 23, 118; in
    adult speech to children, 108–110, 125,
    128–133, 140; in children's speech,
    66, 105, 144–145, 148-149, 159, 169,
    169n2, 173–175, 192–193, 196, 198n5,
    206; in Penville, 66, 72, 90, 101, 113,
    118–119, 125, 140, 202–204; in public
    performances and speeches, 38, 48, 49,
    51–52, 56n19, 110, 111–112, 118, 180
colonialism, 4–7, 26n8, 28–29, 30–39, 58,
    141n3; independence from, 1, 4–5,
    36–39; and language, 4, 7–8, 29–30,
    38, 41–42, 58; and persistence of French
    creole culture, 32–33, 80; Spain, 4,
    30–31; and tensions between French and
    British during, 4–5, 28–29, 30–38. *See
    also* Kalinago; slaves and slavery
commoditization of language and culture, 28,
    50–53, 54, 87–88, 211, 218
Common Entrance Exam, 89, 113n2; in
    children's play, 177–178; results of among
    Penville children, 78, 89, 91, 111, 112
communicative competence, 14, 105–106,
    119, 203
complementarity of English and Patwa, 117,
    123, 200, 219–220
corrections of children's language: English at
    home, 99–103; English at school, 91–94,

96, 98–99; Patwa at home, 103–104,
143–144, 149; 153–154; 165–168;
194–195, 205, 207–208; Patwa at school,
95–99, 205
Corsaro, William, 145
Craig, Dennis, 30, 37
creole culture, 23, 32–33, 38–40, 42–43;
celebration of, 45–50; marketing of,
50–53
Creole Day. *See* festivals and performances
Creole language of Dominica. *See* Patwa
language
creole languages, 7–8, 29–30; and
endangerment, 9–10, 217–218
Cromdal, Jakob, 145, 169n1, 197, 198n5
Crystal, David, 25n1, 210, 218
Cultural Division, Government of Dominica,
40, 45–50, 53–54, 75
cursing (*jiwé*), 17, 76, 119, 124, 128; in
children's speech, 67, 139, 148, 150–151,
168–169, 192–193; socialization of,
136–138, 139

D
dancing and dances, 22, 43, 45–50, 64; *bélé*,
45, 49. *See also* festivals and performances
da Silva, Emanuel, 52
"decline" of traditional culture, discourses
about, 28, 46–50, 53, 63–64
de León, Lourdes, 12, 141n2, 142n17
Devonish, Hubert, 30, 56n26
directive-response sequences in children's peer
interactions, 158–165
discipline, of children, 100, 115–117, 128–
135, 140, 163–165, 183–184, 194–195,
203–206; in school, 37, 88–89, 91–92,
99, 175–176
division of labor between Patwa and English in
speech to children, 24, 128–129, 136, 204
Dominica, coat of arms, 39, 215; colonial
period, 30–39; demographics, 7, 26n7;
independence from Britain, 1, 4–5,
36–39; linguistic ecology, 1, 7–11;
location and geography, 4–7; name,
4, 28, 31; as "the Nature Island of the
Caribbean," 51. *See also* colonialism
Dominican Republic, 4, 48
Dorian, Nancy, 113, 203
Doucet, Rachel, 29, 55n3
Duchêne, Alexandre, 25n1, 29, 54n1, 211, 217

Duff, Patricia, 11
Duranti, Alessandro, 11, 13, 193
Durbrow, Eric, 133

E
economy, 6–7, 26n6, 35–36, 37–38, 46,
50–54, 211; desire for economic
development, 40, 57, 208; making a living
in the village, 64–65, 67, 71, 73, 77–78,
79. *See also* agriculture; tourism
education. *See* schooling
electricity, 62–64
emancipation, 33–36. *See also* slaves and
slavery
emotion. *See* affect
England. *See* colonialism
English language, 1, 4–5, 10–11; associations
with intelligence, 95, 165, 168, 208–209;
attitudes toward, 33, 36, 42, 53–54,
86–95, 100–101, 112–113, 117–118;
borrowings from Patwa, 10, 117–118,
149; as a child language, 108–110, 139–
140; English-only strategy with children,
1, 10, 88–91, 99–101, 112–13, 199, 212;
and "interference" from Patwa, 1, 23–24,
91–95, 104, 203; as language of colonial
administration, 32–33; for official events
and purposes, 110–112; as official national
language, 1, 4–5, 10, 32–33, 39, 43, 54,
210–212, 215–216; and socialization
of attention to others, 106–108; and
socialization of politeness and respect,
104–106; and social mobility, 112–113;
variations in, 10, 26n13. *See also* baby talk;
corrections of children's language; language
policy; schooling
Errington, J. Joseph, 18, 54n1
Ervin-Tripp, Susan, 197n3
Evaldsson, Ann-Carita, 169n1
Evans, Nicholas, 25n1

F
Fader, Ayala, 12, 17, 25n3, 116
family. *See* kinship and family
farming. *See* agriculture
Farris, Catherine, 135
festivals and performances, 22–23, 39–40,
42–50, 211; Carnival, 47, 80, 118; Creole
Day (*Jounen Kwéyòl*), 23, 43–44, 45,
53, 54, 211, 218; Creole Week (*Simmen*

Kwéyòl), 43, 51, 141n12; Cultural Gala, 45, 54, 211; cultural groups, 22, 45–50, 54, 211; Independence Day, 38, 42–43, 45–50, 52–54, 211; National Day, 38–39; and religion, 80, 85n19; World Creole Music Festival, 22–23, 43, 45, 50–52, 210. *See also* dances and dancing; music

Field, Margaret, 12

fieldwork, 19–23; focal children in, 64–66; importance of ethnographic method in, 204, 215–217; language socialization study in, 2, 11–12, 19–22; and relationships with the children and their families, 21; video/audio recordings and transcription in, 20–22, 147–148. *See also* Penville village; focal children and their families

Fierman, William, 54n1

Finegan, Edward, 18

Fishman, Joshua, 25n1, 200, 210, 213

Flinn, Mark, 26n8

focal children and their families, 64–66; Alisia, 66–70; Jonah, 70–72; Kenrick and Tamika, 73–76; Marissa, 79–82; Reiston, 76–79

folklore, 40, 53; *kont* (folk story), 26n11, 45, 49, 50, 56n23, 62, 63–64; *timtim* (riddles), 63–64

Fontaine, Marcel, xiii, 8, 9, 44, 51–52, 203, 210

food and cooking: bread and bakeries 58, 64, 74–75; and change, 37–38, 40, 53, 58, 69, 74–75, 82–83, 85n13; in children's role play, 146, 171–172, 178, 190–191; cooking as a female chore, 67, 124–125, 171–172, 191; foods sold along the road, 118; and language, 113n1, 121, 149; post emancipation, 34; promoting creole foods, 40, 42–43, 53; and social relationships, 71, 74, 80, 128; and socioeconomic class, 69, 71, 74–75, 90; traditional staples, 62, 74, 75; types of kitchens, 70, 71, 73–74, 77, 84n12

footing, 149

France. *See* colonialism

French language, 5, 7–8, 31, 32–33, 36, 80, 112–113; and learning of Patwa, 141n7; and place names, 32

Friedman, Debra, 12, 25n3, 213

Froude, J.A., 36

G

ga (to look at) in children's speech, 103, 143–144, 152–154, 169

Gal, Susan, 12, 18, 26n17, 29, 30, 54n1, 86

García-Sánchez, Inmaculada, 169n1, 197n3

Garrett, Paul, 9, 10, 11, 12, 13, 17, 25n1, 25n3, 26n12, 30, 55n3, 117, 124, 139, 148, 150, 169n1, 217, 220n4

Geertz, Clifford, 21

gender, 11, 14, 17, 26n8, 66; and boldness, 120; in children's play, 145–146, 171–172, 175, 179, 180–181, 187, 191–192, 194, 196–197; and family land, 59–60; and household compositions, 61; and joking, 123–124; and language choice, 15, 44, 87, 78–79, 175, 180, 196–197, 202–203, 207; and language shift, 202–203; men/ boys and, 19–20, 47, 66, 67, 75, 145–146, 172, 181, 187, 202, 203, 207; men and language revitalization, 203; women/ girls and, 19–20, 26n8, 38, 44, 66, 69, 75, 84n6, 91, 124–125, 141n4, 145–146, 159, 170n4, 181, 191, 202; women's regulation of children's language use, 102–104, 105, 153

generation, and language ideologies, 15, 86–87; and language obsolescence, 2–3, 9–10, 12–13, 213–217; and proficiency in English and Patwa, 9–10, 90–91, 108, 120–121, 140, 200–202

Giddens, Anthony, 26n16

Gilroy, Paul, 55n2

Gmelch, George, 40

godparents, 60, 73, 106, 126–128

Goffman, Erving, 15, 149, 174

Goldman, Laurence, 174, 197n3

Göncü, Artin, 197n2

Goodridge, Cecil, 36

Goodwin, Charles, 150, 193

Goodwin, Marjorie, 3, 25n2, 27n24, 144, 145, 148, 150, 159, 162, 169n1, 172, 173, 197n3, 198n7

gossip (*bèf*), 69, 107–108, 118, 119, 125–128, 138, 140, 141n4, 181

Green, Duncan, 2

greetings, 104–106, 113n6, 117, 124, 134–135

Grenoble, Lenore, 12, 25n1, 200, 205, 210, 213, 221n6

Grillo, Ralph, 18, 29

Griswold, Olga, 144, 198n7
Guadeloupe, 4, 31, 34; and creole identity,
 52; and creole language, 8, 30, 38, 52,
 72, 120, 209; and social connections to
 Penville villagers, 58, 61, 73, 74
Guldal, Tale, 198n5
Gumperz, John, 27n21, 174
Guo, Jiansheng, 169n1

H

Hale, Ken, 25n1, 210, 221n6
Hall, Kira, 26n18
Halliday, Michael, 17
Halmari, Helena, 173
Hammond, S. A., 37, 44, 88
Handler, Richard, 55n2
Hanks, William, 14
hardness, and babies, 136, 140; in language,
 88, 99–101, 130, 140; as a personality
 trait, 119. *See also* softness, boldness
health and illness, 26n8, 141n6; caring for ill
 family members, 70, 71, 108; Penville
 health clinic, 58, 66
Heath, Shirley Brice, 72
Hecht, Tobias, 2
Heller, Monica, 18, 25n1, 29, 52, 54n1, 211,
 217
Henckell, Sascha-Lena, 50
Henderson, Felix, 36, 39, 40, 42, 77, 137,
 142n19, 203
Herskovits, Melville, 141n3
Herzfeld, Michael, 55n2
heteroglossia, 17–19, 148–150, 207, 214, 220,
 214, 219
Hewitt, Roger, 169n1, 170n3
Higbie, Janet, 38
Hill, Jane, 16, 30, 42, 154
Hill, Kenneth, 16, 30, 42, 154
Hinton, Leanne, 25n1, 200, 210, 214, 221n6
Hirschfeld, Lawrence, 25n2
Holm, John, 7, 26n10–11, 26n13, 55n3
Honychurch, Lennox, 5, 25n4, 26n8, 31, 33,
 35, 36, 38, 55n12, 56n20, 58, 84n2,
 84n9
Hornberger, Nancy, 11
household compositions, 60–61, 84n1
houses and homes, 64, 67–69, 70–71, 73,
 74, 76–77, 79, 84n12; and children's
 disruption of, 129, 147–148; and
 koudmen, 34, 62; language use in, 62, 63,
 89–91, 99–110; 113, 139, 140, 143–144,

149, 180, 194–195, 199, 202–203, 205,
 207–208; and leaving the front door
 open, 182; and plumbing, 64, 69, 73,
 74, 141n16; and socioeconomic class, 67,
 80, 83; as unfinished, 67–68; women's
 responsibility for, 69, 202
houseyards, 61, 69, 70, 73, 75, 85n14, 88; and
 children's disruption of, 129, 147–148;
 and gossip, 125; and language use, 89,
 118, 149, 158, 193–195, 204–205, 207
Howard, Kathryn, 12, 25n3, 117, 169n1, 206
Hoyle, Susan, 174
hucksters, 26n8, 67, 73, 77
Hulme, Peter, 26n8

I

identity and language, in children's peer
 interactions and play, 150, 181; and
 code-switching/code choice, 16, 17–19,
 23, 118–119; during the British colonial
 period, 35–36; and the nation, 9–10,
 23–24, 28–30, 38–39, 46–48, 52, 53–54,
 210–213, 215–216, 218–220; in the
 community, 86–87, 90, 113, 117–120,
 200, 219–220; and Patwa revitalization,
 9–10, 38–39, 43, 47–48, 215–216, 218
imaginary play. *See* role play
Independence from Britain, 1, 4–5, 36–39; *See
 also* colonialism; festivals and performances
indexicality, 14–15, 26n18, 86–87; 204–205;
 and affect, 15–17, 18–19; in children's
 peer interactions and play, 25, 145, 149–
 150, 173–175, 206–207
input, 26n14, 91, 138, 148, 204, 214–215
interpreting children's speech, 101–102, 147
Irvine, Judith, 18, 26n17, 30, 52, 54n1, 86, 87

J

Jaffe, Alexandra, 3, 16, 26n17, 29, 42, 54n1,
 211, 212, 220n1
James, Allison, 13, 21, 25n2, 145
Jefferys, T., 58
joking, 48, 62, 81, 111–112, 118–120, 123–
 125, 138, 203. *See also* teasing
Jørgensen, J.N., 169n1–2, 170n3, 197
Jourdan, Christine, 55n3

K

Kalinago, 4–5, 7, 25n4, 26n8, 30–31, 38,
 55n5; demographics of, 7; in Penville, 58

Kalinago language, 7–8, 26n11, 84n3, 210;
    place names, 7
Kempadoo, Kamala, 164
King, Jeanette, 213
kinship and family, 20, 57–61, 70–71; and
    common household compositions, 60–61,
    84n1; and marriage, 60–61; perceived
    breakdown of, 53. *See also* focal children
    and their families; godparents
Kokoy language, 7, 10, 45, 210
Konmité pou Étid Kwéyòl (KEK), xiii, 9,
    22–23, 40–44, 50–52, 101, 210–213. *See
    also* language revitalization
Korbin, Jill, 2
koudmen, 34, 45, 62
Kouwenberg, Silvia, 26n9
Koven, Michèle, 155
Krauss, Michael, 25n1, 200
Kroskrity, Paul, 26n17, 29, 54n1
Krumeich, Anja, 26n8, 136
Kuipers, Joel, 3, 15, 16
Kulick, Don, 11, 12, 13, 16, 25n3, 27n19,
    113–114n6, 116, 141n2, 220n3
Kwan-Terry, Anna, 173
Kwéyòl. *See* Patwa language
Kyratzis, Amy, 25n2, 144, 145, 159, 169n1,
    172, 173, 174, 197n3

L
Ladefoged, Peter, 25n1
Lancy, David, 197n3
land, 58–60; family/inheritance of, 59–60, 73,
    77; in post-emancipation period, 33–34,
    58
language and nation-building, 29–30
language and place, 7, 15, 24, 25, 32, 43–44,
    84n5, 87, 96–99, 106–108, 111–112,
    114n9, 118–120, 139–140, 143–144,
    149, 151–152, 171–172, 173–174, 180–
    196, 202, 205, 207, 209–210
language as commodity. *See* commoditization
    of language and culture
language endangerment, 1–2, 3, 9–10, 25n1,
    41, 51, 46, 200, 213–217; and creole
    languages, 9–10, 217–218; and reversing
    language shift, 210, 213–218
language ideologies, 14–15, 17, 26n17,
    29–30, 87; children's, 13, 14, 78, 90,
    165–168, 196–197, 207–210, 214; and
    language shift and endangerment, 3, 16,
    213–217; and language socialization, 11,

12, 14–15, 20, 26n17, 199–200, 216;
    regarding Patwa and English during the
    colonial period, 33–38; regarding Patwa
    and English since Independence, 10–11,
    18–19, 28–29, 37–44, 66, 80, 86–91,
    139–140, 151, 201, 203–206, 210–213;
    among teachers, 91–95. *See also* language
    learning
language learning, local theories of, 99–104,
    108–109, 121–123, 139–140
language maintenance, 3, 12–13, 23, 199, 205,
    210–213; and affect, 15–16; and children's
    play, 148–149, 168–169, 172–173,
    196–197, 199–200, 206–207, 209–210,
    216, 220
language policy, informal English-only with
    children in the community, 1, 10, 88–91,
    99–101, 112–13, 199, 212; national
    official, 1, 4–5, 10, 32–33, 39, 43, 54,
    210–212, 215–216; Patwa as subversive to
    official, 33, 35, 206; in schools, 4, 10, 37,
    43–44, 62–63, 88–89, 91, 95–99, 201;
    and subtractive bilingualism, 37. *See also*
    Konmité pou Étid Kwéyòl
language revitalization, 1–2, 9–10, 12,
    25n3, 30, 213–218; and children,
    148–149, 168–169, 172–173, 196–197,
    199–200, 209–210, 213–217; and
    male participation in, 203; of Patwa in
    Dominica, 9–10, 40–44, 50–51, 101,
    210–213, 218–219. *See also* Konmité pou
    Étid Kwéyòl
language shift, 2–3, 199, 217; and affect,
    15–17; awareness of, 86–87, 104, 215;
    among the Kalinago, 7; and language
    socialization, 12–13, 25n3, 213–217; from
    Patwa to English, 1, 9–10, 53–54, 62–64,
    87–91, 199–206, 218–220; and play,
    148–149, 197, 197n4, 200, 209–210;
    reversing, 209–210, 213–218. *See also*
    language revitalization
language socialization, 11–14, 116–117, 204;
    and affect, 15–17, 18–19; and language
    ideologies, 14–15, 216; in multilingual
    societies, 12, 117; among peers, 11,
    81, 89, 144–145, 148–149, 151–153,
    159–165, 168–169, 172–173, 184–192,
    196–197, 200, 206–210, 215; and
    language shift, 12–13, 25n3, 213–217;
    in school, 91; study in the fieldwork, 2,
    11–12, 19–22

languages of Dominica. *See* Patwa language;
    English language; Kalinago language;
    Kokoy language
Lave, Jean, 138, 145
League for the Suppression of French-Patois, 37
Leather, Jonathan, 9, 44
Leblanc, Edward, 38, 45
Le Page, Robert, 23, 55n3, 118
LeVine, Robert, 25n2
literacy, in English, 10, 33, 35, 39, 44, 70, 72,
    73, 82, 91, 93, 100–101, 201; and the
    English-Creole dictionary, xiii, 41, 210;
    and imagined communities, 29; in Patwa,
    4, 9, 41–42, 44, 54, 113, 210; 212; and
    negative attitudes toward Patwa, 36, 41
Lytra, Vally, 145, 170n3

M
Maffi, Luisa, 25n1
Maguire, G., 54n1
Makihara, Miki, 12, 140
making a living. *See* economy
Mantz, Jeffrey, 26n8, 79
Marie, Ophelia, 40
marriage. *See* kinship and family
Martinique, 4, 31, 34; and creole identity, 52;
    and creole language, 8, 30, 38, 52, 120;
    and social connections to Penville villagers,
    61
Maurice, H., 37
Meek, Barbra, 12, 14, 25n3, 169n2, 197, 214
Migge, Bettina, 30, 44, 104
migration, 26n7, 38, 61, 63, 84n1, 89, 90,
    114n9; and child-fostering, 20, 61, 64, 69,
    70, 74, 75, 76, 201; and remittances, 61,
    77; to Roseau, 38, 63, 89; for temporary
    work, 70, 71, 73, 74, 79
Milroy, Lesley, 66
Minks, Amanda, 149, 169n1, 197n3, 198n5
"mixture," racial, colonial, 35–36;
    contemporary, 7
Montgomery, Heather, 216
Morgan, Marcyliena, 212
Mufwene, Salikoko, 25n1, 26n9, 217
Mühleisen, Susanne, 104
mulatto elite, 33–37, 55n6, 55n12
music, 45–53, 56n25, 64; Christmas caroling
    (*siwennal*), 80; on Creole Day, 43; folk
    songs, 49–50; *jing ping*, 47, 53; marketing
    of, 28, 50–53, 54, 87–88, 211, 218;
    World Creole Music Festival, 22–23,

43, 45, 50–52, 210. *See also* festivals
    and performances; dances and dancing;
    folklore
Myers, Robert, 28, 55n8–9

N
narrative, children's code-switching in,
    155–158
National Development Corporation (NDC),
    9, 51–53
Nettle, Daniel, 25n1
Nonaka, Angela, 12, 25n3
Nwenmely, Hubisi, 30

O
Obeah (witchcraft), 69, 79, 85n18, 119, 151,
    161
obedience, expectation of from children,
    100, 116–117, 131–133, 136, 139–140,
    203–204
Ochs, Elinor, 11, 12, 13, 14, 15, 18, 26n16,
    26n18, 27n19, 141n2
Olwig, Karen Fog, 55n2

P
Paravisini-Gebert, Lizabeth, 37
Passeron, Jean-Claude, 22
Patois. *See* Patwa language
Patrick, Peter, 18
Patwa language (Kwéyòl, Patois), xiii, 1, 4–5,
    7–10, 26n11; as an adult language, 19, 87,
    125–133, 138–140, 143–144, 163–163,
    175, 205; and affect, intensification of,
    117–125, 128–135, 140, 149–158, 204–
    207; and age-graded use, 3, 14, 24, 25,
    86, 87, 89–90, 117, 136, 197, 205–206,
    212–213, 214–216; ambivalence toward,
    86–87, 89–90, 165, 208–209; and
    arguing, 109–110; attitudes toward, 1, 4,
    23–24, 28, 29–30, 33, 36–37, 39, 41–42,
    47–48, 53–54, 55n6, 86–95, 100–101,
    112–113, 117–120, 123; and boldness,
    136–139; and borrowings from English,
    8, 10; called Kwéyòl, xiii, 1, 41–42, 48;
    children's competence in, 117, 201–202,
    216; children ignoring, 76; as commodity,
    50–53, 87–88; and community identity,
    113, 117–118, 200; as a control strategy,
    128–135; as cultural heritage, 1, 28,
    38–39, 40; and discipline of children, 103,
    128–135; escalation to, 128–133; and

ga (to look at), 143–144, 152-154; for gossip, 125–128; and "interference" with English, 1, 23–24, 91–95, 104, 203; and intimacy, 120–123; for joking and teasing, 110, 119, 123–125; and language shift to English, 1, 9–10, 53–54, 62–64, 87–91, 104, 199–206, 218–220; maintenance, 210–213, 216; as a moral discourse, 103, 128, 133–135, 155–165; origins of, 4–5, 7–8, 26n11, 30–36, 58; orthography, 41; place-related constraints on children's use of, 98–99, 143–144; as a secret language, 33, 120, 128; for supernatural beings, 151–152; variations in, 8. *See also* baby talk; corrections of children's language; Konmité pou Étid Kwéyòl; language planning and revitalization; language policy; literacy

Paugh, Amy, 12, 25n3, 26n15, 84n5, 113n4, 134, 135, 141n2, 169n1, 173, 182, 192, 197n3, 198n6–7

Pavlenko, Aneta, 15, 16, 27n20, 150

Payne, Anthony, 7

peasantry, formation after emancipation, 32, 33–36, 55n9, 86

peer groups, children's, exclusion and inclusion in, 158–165, 191; language use in, 4, 15, 145, 150, 155, 199, 207–210; organization of, 20, 144–149, 172–175, 196–197, 207. *See also* play; role play

peer language socialization, 11, 81, 89, 144–145, 148–149, 151–153, 159–165, 168–169, 172–173, 184–192, 196–197, 200, 206–210, 215; and language maintenance, 168–169, 196–197, 200, 207–210; and "shadowing," 187, 188

Peirce, Charles, 14

Penville Cultural Group, 22, 48–50, 71

Penville village, 19, 57–64, 82–83, 88; attitudes toward, 57, 86–87, 111, 117–118; and cable television, 64; demographics, 57; and electricity, 62–64; geography of, 58, 118; history of, 58, 61–64, 84n2; metaphor of "bringing in" things from the outside, 57, 62, 86, 87, 100, 117. *See also* religion; roads

Philips, Susan, 54n1

Piaget, Jean, 197n2

play, 3–4; children's, 144–149, 172–175; and common childhood activities, 58, 118, 145–146, 173; and reversing language

shift, 200, 207, 215–217; negotiating children's social hierarchies in, 18, 144–145, 149–152, 158–169, 169n2, 172–175, 189, 196–197, 199, 207–208; Patwa as, 206–207; and ring games, 53, 146, 216; and toys, 71, 72, 79, 118, 146–147, 173; unmonitored by adults, 147, 168–169, 184. *See* peer groups; peer language socialization; role play

politeness, 87, 110, 116–117, 120, 136, 139; and gender, 120; praising children for, 105, 138; routines with children, 104–106, 128

Portsmouth, 5, 19, 32, 37, 80; Penville villagers selling produce at market in, 61–62, 66, 67, 73, 78, 90; secondary school in, 79

power, and adult authority over children, 13–14, 89–90, 115–117, 128–135, 139–140, 143–144, 194–195, 203–206, 212–215; English and, 35–36, 39, 113, 165–168, 203–206; and language, 4, 13, 17–18, 29–30, 54, 203–208, 210–213, 217–218; negotiation of in children's peer play, 18, 144–145, 149–152, 158–169, 169n2, 172–175, 196–197, 199, 207–208; Patwa and, 44, 87, 117–120, 128–133, 135, 149–152, 203–206; in the research relationship, 21; and symbolic capital, 17–18, 29–30, 41, 52, 82, 165, 169, 200, 203, 206, 208; and symbolic domination, 18, 29, 217; of schools regarding language, 22, 37, 211–213

pretend play. *See* role play

Q

Quinlan, Marsha, 26n8

Quinlan, Robert, 26n8

R

Rabess, Gregory, 40, 41, 42, 43, 52, 203

race, during colonialism, 4, 28, 30–37, 55n6, 55n10, 55n12; contemporary demographics, 7; and racial "mixture," 7, 35–36. *See also* Kalinago; slaves and slavery

radio, 38, 45; Patwa programming on, 39, 41, 77

Rampton, Ben, 154, 169n1, 170n3, 206

register, 17–19, 27n22, 159, 174–175, 205; English as a child language, 108–110,

139–140; Patwa as an adult language, 19, 87, 125–133, 138–140, 143–144, 163–163, 175, 205; Patwa baby talk, 120–123, 149, 178–179, 204

Reisman, Karl, 141n3

religion, 32, 33, 39, 55n7, 79–82, 151–152; Baptist, 55n7; Catholic, 8, 31, 32, 33, 55n7, 73, 79–81, 84n4, 85n19; Evangelical, 55n7, 79–80, 203; focal families' participation in, 66, 67, 71–72, 73, 75, 78, 79–82, 178, 179–180; and language, 8, 15, 31, 79–80, 200, 202–203, 207; Methodist, 7, 85n19; and participation in cultural groups, 85n19; Pentecostal, 55n7, 79–80, 91; and prayer, 48, 52, 72, 81–82, 110, 176, 179–180; Protestant, 8, 28, 33, 80; Rastafarian, 67, 79; Seventh Day Adventist, 55n7, 79–80; and socioeconomic class, 64, 66, 91, 79–81, 203. *See also* Obeah (witchcraft)

respect, socialization of through English, 104–106, 116–117, 129–130, 136, 139–140, 200, 204

Reynolds, Jennifer, 169n1, 172, 197n3

Riley, Kathleen, 26n17

Rindstedt, Camilla, 197n3–4

ring games, children's, 53, 146, 216

roads, 8, 32, 34, 36, 37–38, 82; fixing of, 45, 63; and food, 38, 74; and gossip, 125; and language use, 81, 90, 105, 118, 125, 180–181, 202, 205; importance of in Penville, 58, 61–63, 84n7, 90; and public standpipes, 73, 74, 75; social functions of, 47, 107, 118, 141n4

Roberts, Peter, xiii, 210

Rockefeller, Stuart Alexander, 55n2

Rogoff, Barbara, 137, 145

role play, children's, 146, 172–175, 196–197, 197n4, 198n5, 207; English-speaking roles in, 172, 173–174, 175–180; as farmers, 192–195; and gender, 146, 171–172, 175, 179, 180–181, 187, 190–191, 196–197; as hunters/animals, 171-172, 185–192; language choice in, 25, 168–169, 173–175, 196–197, 207; and language revitalization, 216–217; negotiation about in English, 150, 173–174, 182–183, 188–189, 191; as parents (playing house), 171–172, 178–179, 190–191; Patwa-speaking roles in, 25, 172–174, 180–195, 207; and place, 181–182; and playing school,

165–166, 171–172, 175–178, 185–189; and "playing transport" (drivers and passengers of vehicles), 181–185; religious and other official roles, 179–180

Romaine, Suzanne, 25n1, 217

Roseau (the capital), 5, 7, 10, 32–34, 37, 58, 62, 66, 80, 90, 112, 212; and cultural events, 43–44, 45; elite, 36–37, 38; and fieldwork, 19; migration to, 38, 63, 89; sale of handicrafts in, 73, 77–78; and the first schools, 36

rural/urban contrast, 1, 7, 22, 24, 28, 33–36, 38–44, 53–54, 83, 210–211, 215; and food, 83; and language, 1, 9, 25, 28, 35–36, 38–44, 54, 117–119, 210–212, 215–216

S

Safa, Helen, 55n2

Schieffelin, Bambi, 11, 12, 13, 14, 15, 18, 26n16–17, 27n19, 29, 55n3, 87, 114n6, 116, 141n1–2, 169n1, 173, 174, 197n3, 198n7

Schnepel, Ellen, 30, 55n2

schooling, and children's language ideologies, 208–209; in children's play, 165–168, 171–172, 175–178, 185–189; colonial education reports about, 37, 88; compulsory, 4, 36; and Creole Day, 42–44; history of in Penville, 62–63, 88–89; and influence on caregivers' language use with children at home, 22, 88–91, 99–104, 141n12, 199, 203–204; language policy in, 1, 4, 10, 22, 37, 43–44, 62–63, 88–89, 91, 95–99, 113n3, 201; and language shift, 200–201, 213–214; language use in, 22, 37, 41, 88–89, 91–99, 112–113, 120, 130; Penville Preschool, 58, 84n4; Penville Primary School, 58, 75, 91, 100, 110–112; school as village community center, 110; secondary, 1, 44, 69, 79, 89, 91, 112, 113n2, 208; and teachers' advice to parents, 76, 99–100; and teachers' language ideologies, 91–95, 130, 149, 203–204; teaching Patwa in, 1, 4, 42, 44, 53–54; 210–213, 216. *See also* Common Entrance Exam; language ideology; language policy; literacy

Schwartzman, Helen, 26n2, 197n3

semi-speakers, 113, 203

shaming, 15, 105, 130, 133–135, 168–169
Sheldon, Amy, 169n1
Sheller, Mimi, 40, 50
sibling caregiving, 20, 66, 82, 145, 206; and
    dada role (elder caregiving female), 159
Sidnell, Jack, 114n6, 202, 220n2
Siegel, Jeff, 16
Silverstein, Michael, 14, 17, 29, 204
Singler, John Victor, 26n9
slaves and slavery, 4–5, 7–8, 31–36, 55n4, 58;
    and emancipation, 33–36; and maroons
    (escaped slaves), 5, 31–32
sociability, importance of, 104–106
Smith, Gary, 26n11, 56n23, 113n3
Smith, M.G., 84n6
Smith, Raymond, 84n6
Smith, Wendy, 173
Snow, Catherine, 144
Snow, Peter, 13
softness, in babies, 100, 136; through illness,
    141n6, in language, 88, 119–120; as a
    personality trait, 119–120, 136, 139. *See
    also* hardness
Spain. *See* colonialism
speech economy, 18, 29, 33, 54, 57, 203, 209–
    211; children's, 18, 168–169, 209–210
Spolsky, Bernard, 213
St. Lucia, 28; and language, 8, 17, 26n12,
    41–42, 148–149, 220n4; and social
    connections to Penville, 61, 69
Strachan, Ian, 40
Stroud, Christopher, 55n1
Stuart, Stephanie, 9, 26n11, 56n18, 141n5,
    141n8
subject/subjectivities, 11, 13–14, 116;
    bilingual, 13–14, 24, 117, 136, 140,
    105–206, 220n4
suck teeth, 109, 114n10, 127–128, 133, 164,
    191, 194
Sutton, Constance, 141n3

T

Tabouret-Keller, Andrée, 23, 55n3, 118
Taylor, Douglas, 7, 26n11, 37, 141n15
teasing, 72, 101–102, 115–116, 119, 123–125,
    136–138, 139, 140, 147, 151, 168–169.
    See also joking
television, impact of, 47, 63–64, 77; BET
    (Black Entertainment Television), 47
Thomas, Deborah, 55n2, 221n5
Thorell, Mia, 197n3
Thorne, Barrie, 197n3

Tollefson, James, 55n1
tourism, 4, 7, 10, 26n6, 28, 40, 50–53, 69,
    77–78, 87, 112–113, 211
Trouillot, Michel-Rolph, 2, 6, 26n8, 28, 30,
    32, 55n9
Tsui, Amy, 55n1

U

Urciuoli, Bonnie, 55n1
Urla, Jacqueline, 55n1

V

verbal play, 4, 123–125, 136–138
Verhoeven, Ludo, 30,
Verschueren, Jef, 29
Vieille Case village, 58, 84n2; and religion, 79;
    and school for Penville children, 62–63,
    78; and social connections to Penville
    villagers, 48, 61, 89–90, 111
"voice," 17–18, 150, 172–173, 181, 196,
    207; children revoicing adult language,
    154–158
Vygotsky, Lev, 13, 145, 197n2

W

Warner, Sam L. No'eau, 213
Watson-Gegeo, Karen Ann, 145, 154, 197n3
Weatherall, Ann, 169n1
Wenger, Etienne, 138, 145
Whaley, Lindsay, 12, 25n1, 200, 205, 210,
    213, 221n6
Williams, Brackette, 55n2
Wilson, Peter, 141n3
Wilson, William, 213
witchcraft. *See* Obeah
Woolard, Kathryn, 11, 16, 18, 26n17, 29,
    55n1, 87, 204
World Creole Music Festival (WCMF). *See*
    festivals and performances
World Trade Organization, 46
Wurm, Stephen, 200
Wylie, Jonathan, 8, 26n10–11

Y

yards. *See* houseyards
Young, Virginia, 55n2
Youssef, Valerie, 26n14, 150
Ypeij, Annelou, 40

Z

Zentella, Ana Celia, 12, 16, 25n3, 142n18,
    149, 169n1, 170n3